𝕷𝖎𝖋𝖊 𝖔𝖋
𝕾𝖙. 𝕵𝖔𝖘𝖆𝖕𝖍𝖆𝖙

MARTYR OF THE UNION

Archbishop of Polotsk
Member, Order of St. Basil, the Great

By THEODOSIA BORESKY

Canonized by the Holy See in Rome, Sept. 12, 1643
Canonized as a Universal Saint, June 29, 1867
Official Feast Day of St. Josaphat, November 12

*"I have other sheep of another fold and these also will I
bring, so that all might be of one fold."*

"Nihil obstat.
Philadelphia, Pa., January 17, 1955.

Rev. Roman Lobodych
Censor Eparchialis

No. 2584/54.0.

I M P R I M A T U R .
Philadelphia, Pa., January 17, 1955.

✠Constantine
Tit. Archbishop of Beroe
Apostolic Exarch."

Library of Congress Catalogue Card Number 55-9797

First Edition

Published by Comet Press Books
11 West 42nd Street, New York 36, N. Y.

Manufactured in the United States of America
65

TABLE OF CONTENTS

iii

iv

PREFACE

The desire of the Divine Saviour, Jesus Christ, before his death, "You shall all be of one fold," was the ideal that burned with an unquenchable fire within the heart of St. Josaphat. This divinely inspired ideal fortified him in the priesthood for which he gave his life to become the martyr and champion of the Holy Union, the union of the Eastern Rite Church with the Apostolic See in Rome.

Zealous Ukrainian Catholics throughout the world, together with fellow Catholics of other rites are working and praying for that great unity of Christendom. Therefore, it is important to acquaint them with the life and work of St. Josaphat so that they may be inspired by his spirit and take to their hearts the ideal for which he and many other martyrs gave their lives so that the prophecy of the Divine Savior might be fulfilled.

It is incumbent upon all good Christians to foster the ideal of Christian unity. All Catholics are called upon to spread the Gospel of Christ, to be missionaries of Christ by their good example and fervor in daily life for the Church founded by Him and which Church shall endure even unto "the consummation of the world." We are members of the Mystical Body of Christ and a living body demands active participation of each member to insure proper functioning of the whole.

Great temples have been built to other saints of various nations, festive celebrations made in their honor, books and pamphlets printed describing their lives and graces, but St. Josaphat, one of the greatest of all martyrs seems to have been neglected and forgotten, thus accounting for the indifference towards him, although he was canonized by the Apostolic See as a universal saint on June 29, 1867 with his official feast day celebrated on November 12.

The sources from which material was obtained for the book are as follows: "The Life and Struggles of the Martyr, St. Josaphat Kuncevich, Archbishop of Polotsk, bishop of Vitebsk and Mstyslav, member of the Basilian Brotherhood," written by Jacob Susha, the bishop of Kholm and Belgia of said Brotherhood in the year 1665 in Rome and reprinted by Rev. Martin in Paris 1865; "The Life of St. Josaphat, the archbishop and martyr of the Ukrainian Brotherhood of St. Basil the Great," written by Nicholas Contieri Eromano of that Order in Rome 1867; "Apostle of the Unity of the Church in the XVII Century, St. Josaphat and Greek-Slav Church in Poland and Russia," by Rev. Alphonse Jepin, Order of Benedicts printed in Paris 1898; "The Story of the Union," written by His Excellency Pelesh, Vienna 1878; "Life of St. Josaphat," by Rev. Eugene Kozanevich.

Since this book is written for those who may know very little of the Ukrainian people and the Eastern Rite Ukrainian Catholic Church, in order to give them the necessary background for a better understanding of the subject of the book, the actual life story of St. Josaphat is preceded by an explanation of what the Union is, what schism means and in what way these influences entered and affected Ukraine and the life of St. Josaphat.

As the Catholic Church is a universal church embracing all nations and several Rites of the Catholic faith, there is no doubt but this little book will be welcomed by both Latin Rite and Uniate Catholics and through a better understanding promote more harmonious relations between them.

THE HOLY UNION

Why is Union with Rome and the Apostolic See called holy? The Union is considered holy by the Ukrainian people because it has brought the Ukrainian nation back to the Catholic Church under the leadership of Christ's Vicar on earth, the Pope of Rome and connected it with the foremost cultural center of the world and with the source of the living spirit which all nations of the world honor. It restored the Ukrainian people to their ancient faith which they accepted during the reign of King Volodimir the Great in Kiev in the year 988, when there were no religious dissensions or schism. Even after the year 1054 when the Greeks out of political ambition separated from the Apostolic See in Rome, the Ukrainians were not very prompt in following their example. Frequent attempts were made afterwards to return to the fold of the Catholic Church.

The Union is holy for the Ukrainian nation in that Rome recognizes its distinction from the Polish and Russian nation and in that way acknowledges its right to its own national religion without forfeiting its connection with the highest authority and dignity of the world. Under the authority of the Apostolic See, religious discipline is maintained which is the foundation of all united public effort and national order.

1

Is it true that Poland persuaded Ukraine to the Union? It is reported that the Poles persuaded Ukrainians to the Union with Rome in order to separate Ukraine from Byzantium. On the contrary, Poland and the Poles were always opposed to the Union with the exception of a few individuals. The Polish priesthood was especially against it. If the Union with Rome did not exist, then the Polish priesthood would have far greater power over the Orthodox Church than one united with Rome and under its efficient management. The Polish bishops wrote on March 25, 1752 to Rome that it should take care not to show too much favor to the Ukrainian churches lest their Rite should outshine the Latin.

The fact is that the Polish Catholics absolutely refused to admit the Uniate bishops to the Diet or Senate despite the influence of Rome. But they readily admitted the Orthodox priesthood and gave it a voice all during the reign of old Poland. There were numerous instances of such discrimination by the Polish Catholics towards all Uniate Ukrainians.

Another important fact is that Moscow was the first to break the Union with Byzantium in the year 1589, while Ukraine rejoined the Union with Rome in 1596.

Byzantium for many centuries was united with Rome and even after separation it from time to time returned to the Union. One fact remains outstanding that as Byzantium separated from Rome out of political ambition, so Moscow separated from Byzantium for the same reason, so that both Byzantium and Moscow tried to influence the Ukrainian people against Rome for their own ends and not the benefit of the Ukrainian people. For this reason the only friend the Ukrainian Union with Rome had was the Apostolic See itself.

The Polish King Casimir who conquered Ukraine in 1370 requested Byzantium to create an Orthodox diocese in Halich. This the Byzantian patriarch did in 1371 and turned over several provinces of Ukraine to the Orthodox faith. Thus Poland held to its insistence on the Orthodox faith for Ukraine.

Before its acceptance of the Union the Ukrainian Church was indeed in a deplorable state. The offices of preaching and teaching with the accompanying duty of holy example were forgotten. Bishops were persons of worldly ambition. Some of them were old and unfamiliar with theology, or they were married persons with wives and children and ambition to gain a "good living." They invariably bought their Sees from others. Sometimes the Sees were sold to two or three contenders and a bloody battle would follow for possession. The Sees were held by kings' chancellors or other wealthy lords and gentlemen. The Metropolitans themselves knew little about religion and cared less for the Church.

The entire East was in the decadent era. The priesthood was entirely unenlightened. There were no seminaries, very few schools so that the priesthood differed very little from the unenlightened masses. The Orthodox Church decayed before the very eyes and the best people, unable to tolerate the circumstances, left for other churches. Such was the state of the Ukrainian Church before the Union with the Apostolic See.

The merchants who traveled about observed other churches of the Latin Rite and voiced their discontent. Only the common villagers living in darkness kept on without finding fault in their way of life because they had nothing with which to make comparison. All this was to the advantage of Poland so that it did not even dream of changing or improving conditions. Why? Because the decay and disharmony in the churches would help to destroy the Ukrainian nation and be thus more easily assimilated into Poland.

Constantine Ostrowsky was a descendant of a powerful noble family and he owned thousands of cities and villages so that the Byzantian patriarchs gave him a free hand in the affairs of the Church and all such appointments had to be approved by him. All the gentry and priesthood in his ownership were subject to him. He had an army of his own and held important posts in the Polish Diet; he made various agreements or alliances with other neighboring owners. The total income from his holdings netted approximately fifteen million gold pieces, which in those times compared with the wealth of Rockefeller or Ford.

The prince was attached to the Eastern Church and its fall also grieved him deeply. He, therefore, set about to change things. However, instead of helping, matters grew worse, which proves the ineffectiveness of persons not called to the service of the Church.

He began at first on a very good plan when he held talks with the Papal Nuncio concerning the Union and change of calendar. Sometime before these talks, Ostrowsky had been seeking teachers for the Academy he founded, stating that he would accept persons of the Latin Rite, but no one would volunteer. Because he was uninformed about such matters, he hired anyone who came such as Calvinists and other heretics and rebels who did not have a broad outlook on life but came merely because he paid well. The Academy became famous because the prince owned it and not because anyone got much of anything out of attending it. The teachers taught mostly polemics which they called "the defense of the Orthodox Church" and which were in reality anything but a defense, since there was no order or system in it as there was no agreement among the teachers. In other words, although the old prince invested large sums of money in his school he did not supply it with the proper instructors so that it soon closed its doors.

Connected with the Churches were the brotherhoods originally organized by the gentry for the purpose of enlightenment of the masses. Their aim was worthy but ineffectual because they were headed by ordinary people who had no training or capacity for making decisions on Church matters.

They began a "reform" of the Church which, as a worldly organization, they were incapable of accomplishing. The first result was that the brotherhood fell under the influence of demagogues from the top rank to the bottom.

In the Grecian East under the rule of the Turks, there were numerous patriarchs with high titles but without means of support, because the Turks robbed them continually. Therefore, these poor patriarchs traveled to all the countries of Europe to beg sustenance from the Latin as well as the Orthodox authorities. Often they traveled to Moscow for charity and on the way stopped to visit Ukraine with the same aim in mind for they had to pay the Turks for permission to retain their places in the Church.

In the year 1586, there came to Ukraine such a beggar patriarch, Joachim from Antioch. He interviewed a committee of the Lwiw Brotherhood made up of the citizens and gave permission in writing to the said brotherhood to oversee the priests and bishops and even granted the right to excommunicate whomever they wanted. By this act the Eastern patriarchs permanently undermined respect for Church authority among the Ukrainian people. From then on the brotherhoods which would have been very useful, if they had remained subject to their bishop, could not be controlled. Why? Because they were given blanket authority over the Church, the bishops, archbishops and even the right to pass on the decisions made at religious assemblies. This power of the brotherhoods was further approved by another Greek patriarch, Jeremiah, this time from Byzantium, who three years later in 1589 also came to visit Ukraine for the purpose of collecting money. What these two Greek patriarches did to the cultural and well-meaning brotherhood was equal to supplying them with poisoned swords to destroy that which was highest and best among men. This

5

was a kind of Bolshevism on the Church plain sowed for the purpose of impoverishing the Ukrainian Church.

The Greeks in their limited point of view had a selfish purpose in mind. They could get much bigger grants of money for the rights they gave to the brotherhoods and on the other hand might receive yet greater revenue from the bishops and priesthood who, pressed by the brotherhoods, would request decisions to be made in their favor now and then and would pay for them.

That the Grecian patriarchs understood what they were about is proved by the fact that they did not place the same powers in the hands of ordinary people in their homeland, but on the contrary defended themselves against such an occurrence. Therefore, they deliberately, for purely material gains ruined every possibility of creating order in the Ukrainian Church. The patriarch Jeremiah fought with three other patriarchs for the same See and all four gave rich gifts to the women of the harem of the Turkish Sultan who would recommend them to be approved for appointment as patriarchs.

Following the Greek patriarchs came groups of abbots and monks and priests all for the same purpose to collect money; failing to receive all that they demanded they incited the people to rebellion against such authorities. In addition, not possessing any great education or knowledge of church matters, they brought about tremendous confusion, for each showed his own system. As a result no one knew when to sit down, when to stand, when and what services to conduct. A chaos was created in which all quarrelled.

The worst result was demagoguery from the rank and file. Politicians set themselves up as judges of what was right and wrong in the Church and began unnecessary lawsuits between the brotherhoods and the bishops for which they

6

collected considerable sums of money from the people and thus made an easy living for themselves. Their defense was that they were protecting the rights of the people.

These Greek renegades who brought dissension to the Ukrainian Church also occupied themselves with spying and sold information to the Turks and Muscovites and Poles at the risk of the lives of those with whom they came in contact.

In the words of St. Basil, "There was no king in Israel. Everyone did that which was right in his own eyes." The greatest damage was in the political dissensions aroused in the masses. This was the chief cause for the material fall of the Ukrainian people. There is no agitation of such great interest as of a religious nature. This took up so much of the time of the business people that they neglected their businesses and lost out to the competitive Poles and Jews and were forced to move to the suburbs. Poland was originally weaker than Ukraine. With the dissensions, Ukraine fell lower.

The invasion of the heretics was like a tornado swooping down to destroy all the churches which it touched. Because of the failure of the gifts of the Holy Spirit in schismatic bodies, the result was total disharmony and lack of respect for Church authority among the people. This was followed by cultural and material chaos that led the Ukrainian nation to its downfall. Ukraine is a veritable land of milk and honey and in its marvelously beautiful and harmonious environment are formed profoundly religious personalities highly sensitive to the disharmony so foreign to their natures.

The cultural activity started by the brotherhood came to naught because ordinary lay people tried to bring about a religious reform. The world generally ignores the important truth that power is of the spirit and only the Catholic

7

priesthood and those especially chosen possess it. All that is left of the publications of these brotherhoods are a few polemic books.

Finally it became apparent to all thinking people that there was no hope for salvation in the East since the East itself was deteriorating and thus could not revive but only destroy the Ukrainian nation. Although Prince Ostrowsky had great influence on the Polish government, he did not try to persuade it to help with the cause of the Union for there was not the slightest inclination towards it. Poland had enough of its own problems. Even though the Polish Church was in a better position than the Ukrainian, it likewise had several sects to contend with.

There was a famous Polish lecturer, Peter Skarha, who when questioned by the Ukrainians as to why there was no system or order in their Church, replied that the Latin Church was under a universal leader of all nations whose authority they respected and no one else had the right to interfere with Church matters.

There was no use even in thinking of receiving any assistance from the Polish King Sigmund III in bringing about Union with Rome, for he had given the Greek patriarch Jeremiah in 1589 full authority over the Ukrainian Church and an iron key of protection. Furthermore, he sent instruction to all the city and state governments to permit the Greek patriarch to do as he pleased with the Ukrainian Churches.

All the bishops and numerous of the priesthood journeyed to meet Jeremiah. The Polish king also met with him and together with the patriarch they appointed Michael Rohoza as the new Metropolitan of the Orthodox Church. Although the Greek patriarch had ordained a new Metropolitan, he appointed one of his bishops as Exarch who had authority in his absence over the Church dignitaries. Thus began the cause for all the contentions between the people and the religious and among the bishops themselves. What was the purpose of making division among them? So that having divided them, it would be all the easier to rule over them. All the bishops were, of course, perfectly aware of this and from the beginning realized that their only salvation was in the Union with the Apostolic See.

It came to the point where men from respectable families were ashamed to enter the Orthodox priesthood so that only the stupid and the very poor became priests.

Bishop Terlecky, named Exarch, was quite pained by the appointment and the deliberate plan of ruination for the Ukrainian Church while the Polish Church grew and flourished under the orderly management of the Apostolic See.

A year after the departure of the patriarch, on June 24, 1590, the bishops gathered in the city of Belza and in writing made a declaration signed by the Exarch Terlecky that henceforth they would consider the Pope of Rome as the titular head of the Church under whose authority they would bind themselves for life and to whom they would bring their disputes for settlement. The reason they gave for making this momentous decision was that they did not want to be further responsible for what was going on in the Ukrainian Churches. The first document was signed by Kirilo Terlecky, Exarch and Bishop, Lentius Pelchitsky, Gideon Balaban, and Dionisius Zbiruysky.

Terlecky waited a whole year until after the second Assembly in Brest before he informed the king of their action. The king replied by letter on March 18, 1592 promising justice and equality for the priesthood with those of the Latin Rite, which he never fulfilled. The first bishops who were faithful to the Uniate Church were real martyrs. "They which live should not henceforth live unto themselves but unto Him which died for them and rose again."

Fortunately for them, a man of strong character, Ipaty Poty was appointed bishop, well-educated, acquainted with the ways of the world, a descendant of an ancient illustrious family which had managed somehow to survive the devastating Mongol invasion and the partitioning of Ukraine among its border enemies.

Two days before a new Assembly at Brest on June 21, 1593, and three months after his appointment as bishop, Ipaty Poty received a long letter from Prince Ostrowsky in which among other things he presumed to dictate to the Pope the conditions for the Union and wished to discuss changing some of the sacraments. This he urged the bishop to bring up on the floor of the Assembly, which the bishop flatly refused.

The story was spread among the people that the bishops had sold the Church into slavery to the Latinists and Rome. Nonetheless, the bishops had decided to accept all their sufferings and proclaimed that they had decided for the good of the Ukrainian Church and people to place themselves under the authority of the Apostolic See. "As true servants of God they would not trust in their good deeds nor expect justification for their works but would place their only hope in the compassion of God."

In the meantime, Prince Ostrowsky, opposed in his ambitions, resented the daring of the bishops to act upon Church matters without his authorization and began an open challenge, calling them traitors, unnatural people, without shame or authority, because the greater number of people considered him as their rightful leader.

Ipaty Poty, bishop from the See of Volodimir in the province of Wolyn, although himself a man of high birth and a senator, noted the dreadful hatred of the Prince, and decided to make friends with him by showing him his own humility. He, therefore, fell at his feet and with tears in his eyes begged him not to oppose the saving of the Church but rather to uphold the bishops in their difficult task. This affected the Prince. He promised then that unity should prevail for the glory of God. But this was only a momentary lapse of the proud magnate. Actually he had already come to an agreement with the Protestants and had sent his personal representative to Toronto for a conference, stating that he would defend their "freedom" with an army of twenty thousand and the Pope of Rome he boldly called "Anti-Christ." In a special communication, he wrote that he was for all evangelists and would protect them. Thereafter he constantly influenced rebellion by the people and priesthood against the Uniate bishops. Such fierce opposition by the proud Prince who had been foiled in his ambition alarmed the Polish king into believing that he might cause an uprising in the whole country. A conference was called of the ministers who also feared the Prince's threats and they voted unanimously that the Ukrainian bishops should not be permitted to go to Rome in the interest of the Union. This order reached two of the bishops, Poty and Terlecky too late as they had already reached the city of Krakow on their way to Rome. Another conference was held by the ministers as they feared that a cavalry division of the Prince's army would overtake them and kill them. But they could come to no agreement. The Apostolic delegate, Malaspini, when asked for his advice, refused to make a decision under the circumstances. In the end a meeting of the bishops was called in which they agreed to go to Rome regardless of consequences as they could no longer bear the chaos in the Church.

On November 25, 1595, Terlecky and Poty came to Rome as delegates. Clementine VIII who was then Pope, had previously been Nuncio in Poland and understood the Ukrainian problem. The Holy Father, therefore, received with great joy the tidings that the delegates from Ukraine had arrived to discuss reunion with the Apostolic See. The Pope agreed to permit the Ukrainian Rite and the old calendar although this was not for the highest good because the opposition couldn't have been any worse to the Union than it was. However, since this wasn't a matter of faith the Apostolic See readily agreed. The Apostolic See did not only allow the Eastern Rite but rather encouraged Ukraine to adhere to it permanently.

The actual signing of the Union was on December 23, 1595 at the Vatican in the Room of Constantine The Great in the presence of the Holy Father, Cardinals and other Church leaders and representatives of various nations. A letter written June 12, 1595 was read, signed by all the Ukrainian bishops petitioning to be accepted into the Union, to renew their ancient tie with Rome, which had originally been drawn up at the Florentine Assembly.

Pope Clement VIII issued a special bull on the occasion of the union of the Ukrainians with the Holy See to solemnize this memorable event. "We permit, we allow, we approve all the Sacred Rites and Ceremonies used by the bishops and clergy in the divine offices, in celebration of Mass, administration of Sacraments and all other religious functions which were introduced by the Greek Fathers." (Magnus Dominus, 1595)

Cardinal Antoniani replied in the name of the Holy Father: "By the grace of God you are returning to the rock on which Christ built His Church. You are returning to the Holy Roman Church after one hundred fifty years of separation for the good of yourself and your people. You have understood that the members of a body separated from it cannot exist of themselves, as a branch cut off from a tree cannot bear fruit and a stream shut off from its source goes dry so no one can have God for a Father who does not have the Church for a Mother."

Whereupon the delegates made their vows of faith. The Pope also spoke to them emphasizing discipline in the Church, which does not seek material advantages but only the Godly life and salvation of souls and promised eternal

12

protection and help of the Apostolic See. Then he gave his blessing. To commemorate the occasion medals were printed in gold and silver. These officially announced to the world that the Ukrainian people had returned to the Holy Union.

The delegates were gladdened by their accomplishment. However, Prince Ostrowsky continued to oppose them. Since he owned the towns and cities and villages and all in them were in his pay and under his rule, they were forced to obey him and he was accustomed to being obeyed on spiritual as well as worldly matters. If only he had backed the Union, the Church would have right then established a firm foundation on which the nation could have withstood.

It is easier to ruin than to build so that ruination spread rapidly. The worst or most rebellious of all was Vilna in Lithuania. The Greek patriarch Jeremiah died in 1594 but in his stead one named Pigas from Alexandria in Africa sent his representatives to Ostrowsky who forced them on the people. This continued while the famous Assembly was to take place in Brest.

The opening of the Assembly took place on October 6, 1596 which was well attended by the bishops and priesthood despite strong agitation against the Union for many realized that the only salvation for the Ukrainian Church was in the Union with Rome.

To the congress came also Papal representatives, Latin priests from neighboring countries and king's messengers. Ostrowsky was also there with his company of soldiers and delegates including Protestant, Calvinists and Lutherans. However, Prince Ostrowsky had made it clear that he would not attend their Assembly but invited them instead to come to his "congress," a "viche" or debate which was to be directed by Nicephorus and Cyril Lucar, the representatives of the Eastern patriarch.

When the Ukrainian bishops, together with the Papal delegates and priesthood were celebrating Mass in the Cathedral of St. Michael at the opening of the Assembly, none of the Prince's company came to attend Mass, for they were then starting their debate in a Protestant hall.

Three of the king's personal representatives who attended the Assembly, Prince Nicholas Radival, Prince Leo Sapiha and Demeter Halensky, called upon Ostrowsky and accused him of breaking his own word by taking an armed force to a religious congress and holding such an Assembly in the company of heathens who did not belong to the Eastern Rite and as a layman presiding over it himself. Even a king would not do this but would rely upon Church authority in such matters as a religious assembly.

He replied that all he wanted to do was to hold a peaceful debate but none of the arguments convinced him that he had been the first to propose the Union. The bishops could not debate with him the truths of the faith and so decided to excommunicate him and his company as there was no other way to deal with him.

On Saturday morning, October 9, 1596, all the Churches rang their bells. All the bishops in Pontifical vestments and in the company of Papal delegates and priesthood marched to the Church of St. Nicholas in Brest where the Metropolitan Rohoza celebrated Pontifical Mass. The archbishop of Polotsk, Hermogen, gave the sermon officially announcing the acceptance of the Ukrainian Catholics into Union with Rome.

The Metropolitan and bishops wrote a pastoral letter informing the people of the reunion with Rome.

All those who took part in the debate were excommunicated. They protested saying that they refused to accept the Union which was signed without their approval.

Ostrowsky's religious debate finished as a great scandal for the Greek delegate Nicephorus who had presented falsified documents indicating himself as a representative of a non-existent patriarch from Byzantium and was appre-

14

hended as a Turkish spy, tried and sentenced. Proofs against
him were so strong that even Ostrowsky could not save him
and he died later in prison.

Ostrowsky hired writers of various sects to publish pamphlets against the bishop, the contents of which were so
abominable, the authors preferred to remain anonymous. He
also hired lecturers to distribute these pamphlets by the
thousands.

The bishops had not the same means of retaliation so that
soon much of the unenlightened masses and priesthood who
had at first been for the Union were won over by the opposition. The hired servants of Ostrowsky claimed the bishops
had been "bribed" or bought out. In the meantime, the
bishops lost their places in the Diet to which they were entitled because the Polish bishops were opposed to their being
placed on an equal footing with themselves and the king was
afraid to further annoy the Prince.

When the Metropolitan Rohoza undertook a journey on
visitation he was met by a hailstorm of stones that would
have killed him if he had not been riding in a strong carriage. The Prince also confiscated a large part of the property of one of the bishops and never returned it to either
the Uniate or the Orthodox Church. But God is just and
finally the Prince was properly punished.

Led by the example of Prince Ostrowsky and other Ukrainian magnates, the Polish and Lithuanian princes began also
to rob the Ukrainian people of church properties so that the
Metropolitan Ipaty Poty barely managed to get by. Great
and small agitators started chaos, robbing and murdering
as they went. The holdings which had accumulated through
the centuries by the gifts of the pious and which, now that
the Church was under better management, could have been
made use of for various much-needed educational projects
were confiscated. They began with lawsuits and ended with
murders. The priesthood, which must have realized what the

agitation was leading to, the prince bluffed by promising that the various sects, such as the Lutherans, Calvinists, Arians, etc., would join the Orthodox Church, if they would continue to oppose the Union, and upon joining forces with the various sects they would gain the majority and have a thus greater voice in the government.

No doubt the prince, influenced by his false advisers, believed this story himself for he went so far as to call a conference of all the heretics. But nothing could possibly come of it as it is a well-known fact that a sect will sooner die out by itself than join forces with another no matter how similar they may be.

But the evil agitation did not stop with the robbery and stoning of the Church leaders. The Union has a whole list of martyrs murdered by its haters. Among the first martyrs to the Union was the great Ipaty Poty whose two fingers of one hand were cut off in broad daylight on the street.

In Kiev they drowned in the River Dnieper the Basilian monk Anton Greekovich. They cut off the head of the Byzantian deacon Matthew as he walked peacefully along the road, just because he was a sincere supporter of the Union.

The Latin Rite Polish authorities gave the Ukrainians no protection whatever. The only real protection the Ukrainian Church had was in the Apostolic See. The Poles gave no protection to the Union as it was to their highest interest that it should cease to exist.

In Kiev, a number of secret agents of the Greek Theophanus awaited an opportunity to murder the famous Metropolitan William Rutsky.

The archbishop of Vitebsk, Josaphat Kunchevich, the subject of this book, was murdered in a horrible manner and his body tortured after death.

The result was that numerous young people of the better class Ukrainian families joined the Polish Latin Rite Church because their parents, brought up in the Orthodox Church, hated the Uniates and the Orthodox policy of hatred did not appeal to them.

The chief agitator against the Holy Union, Constantine Ostrowsky in his old age experienced the pain of seeing his own two sons leave their father's Church and join the Polish Latin Rite. When his second son, John, joined the Catholic Church he commanded his imprisonment and when imprisonment failed to change his mind he would have cut off his head but his son stopped him by saying gently, "It wouldn't do for your sword which has seen so many magnificent battles and conquered so many of your enemies to be stained by the blood of your son. Rather take my sword and use that. I would gladly die a thousand deaths for the sake of the Catholic faith."

Finally a third son also joined the Polish Church and the family was separated. The extensive Ostrowsky estate disintegrated. The properties that had belonged to the Ukrainian Church were donated to the Polish Church by his sons. Before long, the ancient, powerful noble family of Ostrowsky was heard of no more.

This example of the prince's sons proves that the reason the younger generation joined the Polish Church was not because of any material advantages such as better jobs and social contacts to be gained by membership but the contentious hatred and persecutions that were present in the Orthodox Church drove them from it.

When the souls of the youth are empty they easily become filled with love for a foreign Church, as the soul of a human being cannot remain empty; it must be filled either with love or hatred.

Having learned such a difficult lesson from their forefathers, the Ukrainians should be a good example to others not to encourage hatred either in themselves or in their children but instead encourage love and respect for the Ukrainian Catholic Church of the Eastern Rite to which

17

they belong. This love is nothing more than obedience to the commandments of God: to love God above all things and our neighbor as ourselves. No other faith had such power over the Ukrainians as the Catholic. The Orthodox Church existed as long as it was backed by the state authorities. However, the Uniate Church had no backing but rather opposition of foreign authorities who ruled Ukraine. The Orthodox Kozaks opposed it and the Russians persecuted it. Under Polish and Austrian rule many Uniate priests were forced to give up because they couldn't make a living. Many of these priests were shot to death. Russia sent them to Siberia when it conquered Halich.

What good did all these persecutions do? Did they destroy the Union? Indeed they did not! The Union has remained. Where does the Church then get its power, persecuted as it has been for all these centuries? From the true living faith, which as a clear source pours itself forth from the Rock of St. Peter at the Apostolic See. It is the window into a world not befogged by hatred. This is the stone ladder to the high light of culture through the high school of discipline and faith. Byzantium has long ago fallen in misery and faithlessness despite its golden churches and the great church of the Muscovites has turned to dust which had been under the protection of the kings. But the Ukrainian Catholic Church persecuted by all has remained faithful to its Union with Rome and continues to survive despite everything. The storms of centuries blow against it but it continues to grow.

The Church of Ukraine may, it is hoped, someday regain its ancient prestige and influence in Christ's vineyard and help the Ukrainian nation to be restored to its former dignity and importance.

As soon as the iron curtain lifts it will be the Ukrainian priesthood qualified by knowledge of the language and Rite who will go as missionaries to convert the Russian nation to the faith.

18

CHAPTER I

THE FOUNDING OF THE CATHOLIC CHURCH

Jesus Christ came to earth to establish the Kingdom of God which would last until the end of the world.

Because he spent only three years spreading the knowledge of the Kingdom of God and He desired that this work should continue, he chose for himself twelve apostles who would carry on this work under His direction.

Over a period of three years He taught them by words and example. These teachings the Son of God intended to complete and strengthen after His Resurrection by sending them the Holy Ghost which coming upon them filled them with the power to teach the truths of the Holy Faith, the power to speak in all languages and finally that people might believe that they are His apostles or emissaries of Christ, the Saviour gave them power to perform miracles.

While the Son of God lived, the apostles had no need of a leader to be the head of their company for He was Himself the visible head or master. As Christ did not have an opportunity to remain with them for long as their chief, it was necessary for Him to choose a successor and to accustom him to this position. This is done by all practical men and Jesus was God as well as man, with a complete understanding of

19

human nature and the need of an organized body. Every organization regardless of its nature or size must have a responsible head for the orderly management of its business, either appointed or elected to his office.

The Church of Christ on earth is not any different from an organization in the respect that it must also have a titular head to conduct its affairs efficiently and to which all peoples of all nations and races are obedient with regard to matters of religion.

If Christ had been but an ordinary intelligent and ambitious man he would have chosen a successor if He expected that His work would last for some time. Let any ruler leave his country over a period of time, giving everyone the power to do as he pleases, then upon his return, he would find not even a trace of his kingdom. At His first meeting with St. Peter he informed him of the place awaiting him: (St. John 1-42)

"And he brought him to Jesus. And when Jesus beheld him, he said, Thou art Simon, the son of Jona; thou shalt be called Cephas, which is by interpretation a stone."

He had not yet become an apostle of the Lord and he had already called him the foundation stone upon which he was to build the Catholic Church. Time progresses and does not stand still. Jesus was not to remain long among his beloved apostles, strengthening them in their faith in Him as their Messiah and in return for Simon Peter's faith in Him, he promised him the place of honor as head of His Church, constituting Peter after Himself Shepherd of the Church.

(Matthew 16-18)

"And I say also unto thee, that thou art Peter, and upon this rock I will build my Church; and the gates of hell shall not prevail against it."

Whenever God has chosen someone for leadership, he prepares him for it with the necessary gifts and graces. It was noteworthy that St. Peter accompanied Jesus everywhere, to

Mt. Tabor and the Mount of Olives (to Gethsemene) and that Jesus turned to him and questioned him. To Peter he revealed His greatness and His coming trial. He was more firm with him and left in his care the group of apostles. He favored him over the other apostles who perceived this immediately and though some were tougher, more learned, more faithful to Him, none among them objected or were jealous or discontented or even annoyed for they considered it entirely natural that only one among them must be the head of all. While Christ still walked the earth he appointed St. Peter as his successor, but he did not give him this position before His death as He saw with the eyes of His Spirit Peter's coming downfall, therefore, He wanted the other apostles to see him first in his fall and in his repentance. Not until a few days before His ascension did He grant him this position. It was to the penitent and sorrowful Peter, renewed and strengthened in faith and burning with love for the Saviour that Jesus turned and said: (St. John 21—15, 17)

"So when they had dined, Jesus saith to Simon Peter, son of Jonas, lovest thou me more than these? He saith unto him, yea, Lord, thou knowest that I love thee. He saith unto him, Feed my lambs. He saith to him again the second time, Simon, son of Jonas lovest thou me? He saith unto him, yea Lord; thou knowest that I love thee. He saith unto him, Feed my lambs. He saith unto him the third time, Simon, son of Jonas, lovest thou me? Peter was grieved because he said unto him the third time, lovest thou me? And he said unto him, Lord thou knowest all things; thou knowest that I love thee. Jesus saith unto him, feed my sheep."

The apostles understood perfectly what these words meant for from that moment they all brought their problems to Peter. They did nothing without his counsel and obeyed him in all things.

For instance, at their first meeting at Jerusalem, while they discussed the matter of admitting the heathen into the

Church, it was Peter who arose as the shepherd of his flock and head of the Church to make known the desires of their Lord: (Chapter XI Acts of the Apostles 2-18)

"I was in the city of Joppa praying: and in a dream I saw a vision, a certain vessel descend as it had been a great sheet, let down from heaven by four corners; and it came even to me:

"Upon which when I had fastened my eyes, I considered and saw four-footed beasts of the earth and wild beasts and creeping things and fowls of the air.

"And I heard a voice saying unto me, Arise, Peter; slay and eat. But I said, "Not so, Lord, for nothing common or unclean hath at any time entered into my mouth. But the voice answered me again from heaven, what God hath cleansed, that call not thou common. And this was done three times; and all were drawn up again into heaven. And behold, immediately there were three men already come into the house where I was, sent from Caesarea unto me.

"And the Spirit bade me go with them, nothing doubting. Moreover, these six brethren accompanied me and we entered into the man's house: And he showed us how he had seen an angel in his house which stood and said to him, Send men to Joppa and call for Simon whose surname is Peter; Who shall tell thee words whereby thou and all thy house shall be saved.

"And as I began to speak, the Holy Ghost fell on them, as on us at the beginning. Then remembered I the word of the Lord, how that He said, John indeed baptized with water; but ye shall be baptized with the Holy Ghost. Forasmuch then as God gave them the like gift as he did unto us, who believed on the Lord Jesus Christ, what was I that I could withstand God?

"When they heard these things they held their peace and glorified God, saying, Then hath God also to the Gentiles granted repentance unto life."

In what way was Peter better than John or Bartholomew or Mark? They all said nothing for they recognized that it was the spirit of their Lord speaking through Peter and they accepted him as their rightful leader and head of the Catholic Church.

As all of the apostles, including St. Peter, soon were called upon to bear witness to the Godhead of Christ, by the shedding of their blood in martyrdom, therefore, it was necessary to have others take their places as their emissaries to carry on the work of spreading knowledge of the Kingdom of God. Although during their lifetime they held the general supervision of the Church in their own hands, they appointed bishops to whom they gave power to ordain other bishops as their successors, so that the office might never fail. They also appointed a second order of the ministry or priests upon whom "when they had prayed, laid their hands."

Every living body must have a head. Immediately upon the death of St. Peter, the Bishop of Rome was chosen as his successor, although there were still living apostles. The Bishop of Rome is the natural successor to St. Peter. Why is this? In Rome, not only did St. Peter set up his altar but in this throne he ruled the Catholic world for over twenty-five years until his death. At Rome he gave his life for Christ. He chose Rome as his last resting place. It is a notable fact that all respect the will of St. Peter for, ever since all the apostles, the bishops and other dignitaries of the Church recognize the Bishop of Rome as the undisputed successor to St. Peter.

If we examine the history of the Church we will find that the language of the civilized world at the time of our Saviour's coming was Greek. Though the lands became politically Roman they remained intellectually and socially Greek. From the East the Gospel was brought into the West; the Church of Rome is a Greek Church, "a colony of Greek Christians and Hellenized Jews." The original language of the Church, not only in the East but also in the West, was Greek.

The earliest principal writers of Ecclesiastical history were Greeks, Eusebius, Socrates, Suzomen, Theodoret, Evagrius.

All the Oecumenical councils were held in the East and their decrees and canons and the Nicene Creed were written in Greek. A Synod of the Greek Church, that of Laodicea A.D. 367, determined the canon of Scriptures and so "made the Bible." Thus Greek Christianity is the parent of Latin Christianity.

To the Greek Church the Armenians, Transylvanians, Slavs, including Bulgarians, Russians and Ukrainians and many other once heathen nations owe their conversion. Uninterrupted successions of Metropolitans and bishops of the Greek Church can be traced back to Apostolic times.

The same Eucharist is offered now, the same hymns are chanted by the Eastern Christians of today as those of the Churches of St. Athanasius, Basil and Chrysostom.

It was not until the Pontificate of Pope Damasus 366-384 and the translation, at his bidding, of the Vulgate edition of the Bible by St. Jerome that the Roman Church became completely Latinized and turned from a Greek into a Latin Church.

However, we will note that for the first ten centuries after the death of St. Peter, all bishops, archbishops, and patriarchs some of whom may have had greater learning, were more holy, more faithful and ardent propagators of the Kingdom of God, nonetheless, they sought advice from Rome in all their needs and respected its authority on matters pertaining to faith and morals. All religious conferences took place at Rome or under the direction of the Pope or his delegate. All the bishops of the Eastern Church and the Byzantine patriarchs turned to Rome for counsel and to it brought all their disputes for settlement and their requests for approval of appointments to their Sees.

St. Basil the Great is known to have sought the help of Pope Damasus in the year 372 in the management of the Eastern Church likewise the patriarchs of Byzantium, St. John Chrysostom sought the help of Pope Innocent, St. Flavian of Pope Leo in 490; and Nikiforus of Pope Leo XII; St. Ignatius of St. Nicholas, Pope in 867. These great lights of the Eastern Church sought counsel, aid and inspiration in the Popes of Rome as well as affirmation of the teachings of Christ in dealing with heresies. Not only the holy and Catholic bishops turned to Rome but also the heretics in order to justify themselves or exonerate themselves. Even Photius, the head of the opposition, twice appealed to Rome, falsely renouncing his teachings and seeking affirmation of a fraudulently obtained position as patriarch. Why did they all turn to Rome? Why was there no conference held over ten centuries unless first approved by the Bishop of Rome? Why was not any religious truth accepted until it was first ratified by Rome? Everyone recognizes that the Pope of Rome is the true successor of Christ. From this center of obedience to authority in all things pertaining to religion flows the living Spirit that animates the Church.

CHAPTER II

THE SEPARATION OR SCHISM OF
THE GRECIAN CHURCH

Until the fourth century and the foundation of Constantinople, Christianity continued to be, both in the East and West, a Greek religion. But after Constantine settled his capital in the old Greek city of Byzantium, Greek Christianity continued to be the religion of the East and Latin by degrees supplanted it at Rome.

For nearly ten centuries, with only a few minor exceptions, the desire of our Saviour, "You shall all be of one fold" was fulfilled. There was harmony between the Eastern and Western Church although the liturgy was in different languages and Rites. Of course some of the Byzantine bishops, especially after the transferring of worldly power to Byzantium or New Rome were blinded by pride and arrogance, backed by the flatteries of Grecian kings, with an inordinate desire to place themselves on an equal basis with the Pope of Rome.

The two Sees were placed by the Oecumenical Councils on an equality so that conflicts for supremacy soon arose between the patriarchs of Old and New Rome but the contest was an unequal one as the place of power over the East fell into foreign hands and was not under the rule of the Greek kings. Not one from among them, however, had the courage to call himself a successor to St. Peter. Fortunately there were not many of these and they were soon followed by Catholics who sought approval from Rome.

Rome, freed from restraint, was able to become, beginning with the middle ages, a firm barrier against the wickedness and injustice of Emperors and kings, so that the Christian world owes to the Church of Rome the deepest debt of gratitude for its championship.

However, eventually, through the pride of the patriarchs and the political schemes of Grecian kings and because of heresy among the Greeks, a breach began to form between the Eastern and Western Church. The Greeks, jealous of the superiority of the Romans, burned with secret hatred and awaited only the proper opportunity to denounce the Roman Church and to use that as an excuse to separate themselves from it. The devil, father of all controversy, confusion and the enemy of unity found himself a helper in Photius who was the first to tear the seamless garment of Christ. It began as follows:

St. Ignatius, the patriarch of Byzantium, basing himself upon the writings of St. John, denounced Bardasa, the prime minister of the Greek Emperor, for living with a relative outside of wedlock and refused him permission to receive Holy Communion on Advent Sunday, A.D. 857, a day on which it was customary for high officials to receive Holy Communion from the patriarch. Ignatius excommunicated Gregory, the bishop of Syracuse, for his notoriously immoral life, which laid him open to the censures of the Church. The angry Bardasa thereupon prosecuted Ignatius for defamation of character.

Since Bardasa had gained complete ascendency over the mind of the Emperor Michael the Drunkard, he determined to employ it to the ruin of both the patriarch and his patroness Theodora. Therefore, he prevailed upon the Emperor to consign her and her daughters to a monastery and when Ignatius opposed the scheme, he also was sent into banishment to the island of Terebinthus.

Ignatius was born of an illustrious and noble family. His mother was Procopia, a daughter of Emperor Nicephorus and his father, Michael Rhangabe. Bardasa realized that the people would resent the deposition of so holy and beloved a patriarch as Ignatius. By way of appeasing their indignation, he obtained the appointment of Photius, the Emperor's secretary, popular among the crowd, but a married man of irascible temper, to the patriarchate (857-867) and again (877-886).

Ignatius was kept imprisoned and every possible method of torture was used to force him to accede his position to Photius. Finally, rendered unconscious by his long sufferings and starvation, he traced the sign of the cross relinquishing his dignity to Photius.

Photius thereupon announced his election to Pope Nicholas stating that the Emperor, bishop and clergy had forced on him the appointment against his own will, the unwelcome burden from which Ignatius had resigned on account of old age.

Since Gregory had been bishop of a diocese which had been taken from Rome and conferred on Constantinople by Leo the Isaurian and he was also under the ban of Rome, his consecration of Photius was regarded by the Pope as an insult to the Papal See. He resented the deposition of Ignatius without being consulted and wrote to Photius that his legates would inquire into the report to him as to the validiy of his hurried ordination.

The Emperor also wrote to the Pope requesting him to send legates to Constantinople to assist him in the task of restoring union and discipline.

Therefore, to the deposition of Ignatius and consecration

in his place of Photius is to be ascribed the penultimate stage in the schism between East and West.

Four important Synods between 862-879 were held at Constantinople. The first was summoned by the Emperor and Ignatius was advised by the Pope to attend. Nicholas was represented by his two legates Rodvald, bishop of Porto and Zacharius, Bishop of Anagni. The council was attended by three hundred eighteen bishops, the same number which was present at the First Council of Nice. It was afterwards said at Rome that the legates, partly from fear and partly from bribery, presented the matter falsely so that the Synod confirmed the deposition of Ignatius.

An earthquake lasting for forty days after the council meeting devastated Constantinople and alarmed the Emperor and Bardasa while the terrified citizens accounted it as a just retribution for the persecution of Ignatius. Ignatius, rightful head of the Church, suffering unjustly, naturally sought the help of the head of the Western Church. A petition was drawn up and sent to the Pope, which after it was signed by ten metropolitans, fifteen bishops and a large number of priests and monks, was brought to Rome by Theognostes, an archimandrite of Constantinople.

Two parties arose in Constantinople, the followers of Ignatius, the patriarch of the people, who excommunicated Photius as a usurper and those of Photius, the patriarch of Bardasa.

The Pope declared that he had given no instructions for the deposition of Ignatius and the appointment of Photius. In a Synod at Rome (862) he ordered Photius deposed, declaring his appointment as uncanonical, annulling his Orders and threatening him with excommunication and indicating Ignatius to be the rightful patriarch of Constantinople.

In a second council at Rome, in the following year he declared the judgment of Rome to be the "voice of God."

Nicholas excommunicated his own legates for their part in

the matter and pronounced anathemas against Photius and his consecrator Gregory and restored Ignatius.

The Emperor ignored the anathemas while Photius continued to hold the See.

Michael, the Emperor, wrote a vehement letter to the Pope, expressing his resentment with the interference in the affairs of the Eastern Church. He further accused the Pope of ignorance of the Greek language and spoke of Latin as "a barbarous jargon." The Pope replied by the same messenger in 866 accusing the debauched Emperor of disrespect to God's Church and to himself who derived his authority from St. Peter. He took advantage of the Photian schism to impose his authority on the See of Constantinople.

He advised him to cease calling himself Emperor of the Romans and warned him of the fate of former Emperors Nero, Diocletian and Constantine who had persecuted the Church.

The Emperor, at the instigation of Caesar Bardasa was assassinated in 866 on the charge of conspiring against the throne.

The angry Photius called a Synod at Constantinople in 866, denounced Pope Nicholas I, accusing the Western Church of heresy for:
1. Observing Saturday as a fast day.
2. Using milk and cheese during lent.
3. The enforced celibacy of the priesthood.
4. Restriction of Chrism to Bishops.
5. The Double Procession of the Holy Ghost.
6. Promotion of deacons to the Episcopate.
7. Consecration of a Lamb according to the Jewish system.
8. Shaving the beards of the clergy.

The excommunication of the Pope was signed by the Caesar, Basil the Macedonian, three Eastern patriarchs and about a thousand bishops and archimandrites. Thus came about the first open break or schism between the Eastern and Western Church.

This schism did not last long, for Basil I made Emperor in 867-886 desired to gain the good will of the people who loved the saintly Ignatius by confirming his restoration as patriarch which position he continued to hold without further disturbance until his death on October 23, 877.

The ordination of the irascible Photius was annulled, his excommunication being written in sacramental wine.

However, upon the death of Ignatius, since most of the Eastern bishops were schismatic and had chafed under Ignatius they favored the restoration of Photius so that he was again nominated to the patriarchate by Basil in order to promote unity in the Eastern Church. As Photius had previously instructed Basil's son, this added to his favor.

The unabashed Photius again wrote a very humble letter of obeisance to Pope John VIII requesting approval of his position, while at the same time he instigated new persecutions at home against Rome.

A fourth Synod was called in 879, attended by three hundred eighteen bishops, representatives of the other patriarchs and two legates sent by Pope John.

Photius defended his position successfully so that the Papal legates ratified his restoration to the patriarchate.

However, Photius did not retain his dignity for long. The Pope soon learned of his falsity and ordered his excommunication through his legates, together with all his adherents.

Basil was succeeded by his son Leo VI (886-912), who held the dignified title of Philosopher and who desired above all things the unity of the Eastern and Western Church. It was he who ejected Photius from his See and imprisoned him in a Roumanian monastery where he died in 891. By his death the schism of more than thirty years apparently came to an end.

There followed seventeen patriarchs who occupied the Sees of Byzantium who were loyal to Rome and recognized the Pope of Rome as head of the Church throughout the world. Between them and thirty-seven Popes of Rome uninterrupted communication continued until the year 1043.

At that time arose a proud and ambitious man, Michael Cerularius who renewed the schism. Jointly, with the Metropolitan of Bulgaria, Leo of Achrida, he wrote a long letter replete with invective against the Latin Church to John, the bishop of Trani in Apulia, in which he not only renewed all the old controversies brought up by Photius but added to them.

A copy of the letter fell into the hands of Cardinal Humbert who was then resident at Trani and who had it translated and sent to Pope Leo IX. Although the letter caused both indignation and astonishment at Rome, the Pope answered all the controversial points brought up by Cerularius and sent his Papal legates to Byzantium. He sent Cardinal Humbert himself, the archbishop of Amalfi, Frederic of Lorraine and Cardinal archdeacon of Rome who became Pope as Stephen IX (1057-1058).

However, Cerularius refused to see them and closed the Latin Churches and monasteries, whereupon they excommunicated him and all those with him who refused to obey the Apostolic See to which the "special care of all the churches belong." On July 16, 1054, the legates left their writ of anathema on the altar of St. Sophia and obtaining the protection of the king's guards, they returned by way of Ukraine to Rome. Although later on in the reign of King Isaac Kommena, Cerularius was deposed and ordered exiled, the controversy he had renewed remained as a poison after him. It is true that for sometime the Church returned to its former unity after the Assembly convened at Lugden, but it did not last long. Greece returned once more to schism under which it has remained until now. This is the history of Greek schism.

Driven from Constantinople by the Ottomans, who put an end to the Eastern Empire, a large number of Greek refugees fled into foreign lands where they founded Uniate Greek churches acknowledging the Pope of Rome as the head of their Church. But the great mass of the Greek people have remained Orthodox.

From the above facts we can understand what schism means. Schism is a Greek word and means disunity, separation. In the Church it means separation from obedience to the lawful successor to Christ as head of the Church. A schismatic is one who does not recognize the Pope of Rome as head of the Catholic Church. Separation is not the only error of the schismatics. After a time they also become heretics.

A heretic is one who disagrees with the teachings of his Church as inspired by the Holy Spirit. Therefore, the present schismatics not only do not recognize the Pope of Rome as the natural successor to Christ and St. Peter, but often disagree with the following truths of the Church:

1. That the Holy Father is infallible in matters of faith and laws of the Church.
2. That the Holy Spirit comes from the Father and Son.
3. That the Blessed Virgin was conceived without sin.
4. That there is a special place where souls go after death called Purgatory where they are given opportunity to atone for their unconfessed minor sins.

In these four truths the schismatics do not always believe although everyone else accepts them without question.

CHAPTER III

SCHISM IN UKRAINE

Let us now consider how the schismatic disease crept into the Ukrainian Church and what havoc it wrought there.

After the deposition of the Patriarch Photius in the year 867 and the return of St. Ignatius to his rightful patriarchal See from which he had been unjustly deposed, the two Ukrainian kings Askold and Dyr, sent couriers to Byzantium requesting that preachers and priests be sent back with them. St. Ignatius was an ardent Catholic himself and sent other priests of the same order as himself to Ukraine. They sowed the first seeds of Christianity in Ukraine. A church was built in Kiev to which the patriarch Ignatius sent a bishop and although Christianity did not at that time take deep root in the country, it was kept alive through the merchants in their commercial relations with Byzantium.

Igor conquered Askold and Dyr in 882. He married a Viking beauty named Olga who ruled Ukraine in her son's infancy 945-972. In the year 955, she made a pilgrimage to Byzantium for the purpose of obtaining knowledge of the true God. She was baptized by the Patriarch Polyeuktes, together with her retinue. The patriarch, well pleased by her earnestness, dismissed her with the blessing, "Blessed art thou amongst Ukrainian women, from generation to generation, the Ukrainian people will call you blessed." In turn she promised to exert her influence in spreading the faith throughout Ukraine. She took back with her several missionary priests and from then on the Catholic religion spread rapidly throughout Ukraine.

In his adventurous and stormy career, Volodimir, the grandson of Olga had forgotten the principles of the Catholic faith Olga had instilled in him, therefore, he dispatched messengers from Kiev all over the world to examine the various religious systems. When these messengers arrived at Byzantium and heard the patriarch himself celebrating the Eucharist in the Church of St. Sophia, with all the magnificence of the Greek ritual, they were so impressed with the splendor of the ceremony and so persuaded with the truth of the faith that they said, "We did not know if we were in heaven; for there is nothing like it on earth. There in truth God has his dealing with men and we can never forget the beauty we saw there nor can we any longer abide in heathenism."

After his conquest of Cherson, to cement his alliance with the Byzantine court, Volodimir married Princess Anna, the Christian sister of the Emperor Basil II.

On August 1, 988, the marriage and Baptism of Volodimir took place in the Church of Panagia, the Most Holy Mother of God. At the same time he ordered the Baptism of all the people of Ukraine by the priests and bishops of Byzantium who had arrived with his bride Anna for the occasion.

Thus Ukraine accepted Christianity at about the same time as the Catholic patriarchs ascended their thrones in Byzantium.

Under the influence of his Christian wife, Anna, Volodimir established schools and imported teachers from Byzantium to teach the principles of the Christian faith. He built churches and accompanied bishops on their missionary work throughout the country, so that civilization advanced rapidly and the spread of the Catholic faith was widely diffused.

The piety of Volodimir and his son Yaroslav, who succeeded him, penetrated the national life and to them much of the piety and learning is attributed, which until all learning and knowledge was swept away by the Mongol invasion, combined to characterize Ukraine.

The system carried out by Volodimir of parcelling his hereditary fiefs amongst his many sons, created independent appanages having absolute sovereignty within their own dominions with only a nominal subjection to the Grand Prince from whose control they sometimes revolted and assumed the title to themselves. Ukraine was thrown into discord through their conflicts.

In 1221 Genghis Khan took advantage of the dissensions of its princes to fall upon Ukraine. If the country had been united, it might have succeeded in repelling the invasion. As it was, in the absence of all means of political concentration, it rendered it an easy prey to its border enemies who did not scruple to fan the feuds of the princes by promising to join them as allies against those of the same flesh and blood as themselves, which led to the dismemberment of Ukraine.

However, the Ukrainian Church was not only the mediator in the quarrels of the princes but to its Metropolitan and bishops it is indebted for its preservation and coherence all during its stormy history.

Harassed from every side, oppressed by schism from within and cruel persecutions from without, for ages past the existence of the Ukrainian Uniate Church has been one continuing martyrdom under the grinding oppression of its successive conquerors.

Yaroslav was a theologian as well as a legislator. He continued the work begun by his father, Volodimir, building churches and monasteries. He founded the famous Pechersky monastery as a training school for the clergy which also became the birthplace of Ukrainian literature. Through him the nomo-canon was translated from the Greek and the first code of laws written in the Ukrainian language. He supplied the Pechersky monastery with works of the Greek Church and had them translated into the Ukrainian language and circulated throughout his kingdom. The Bible, as translated by Cyril and Methodius, says Nestor the Chronicler, was an important feature in the teachings of the schools of Volodimir and Yaroslav. If the early promise of intellectual life and literary development had not been hampered by the terrible Mongol invasion that devastated Ukraine, that nation instead of being retarded would have been among the foremost European nations in culture and civilization.

Therefore, from the very outset Ukraine had been Catholic and united with the Roman Church and this union with Rome lasted longer than that of the Greek Church. Although Cerularius became a schismatic, Ukraine did not accept the schism.

At the same time that Cerularius separated from the Catholic Church, the Greek Metropolitan Theopemptus sent to Ukraine, died. King Yaroslav Mudry, having learned that the Greek Church had separated from the Roman, did not send to Byzantium for a new Metropolitan to take Theopemptus' place as had been the custom in the past after the death of a Metropolitan but instead called a Synod of Ukrainian bishops and instructed them to select a Metropolitan from amongst themselves. At the Assembly of the bishops a very holy priest, Ilarion, a native Ukrainian, was chosen. It was Ilarion with the consent and approval of Yaroslav Mudry (The Wise) who welcomed ceremoniously and respectfully the Papal legates who had been rejected by the proud Cerularius on their return to Rome through Ukraine. It is to be regretted that the bishops did not continue to carry out King Mudry's advice for Ukraine would not have known schism to this day. After the death of Ilarion they did not select a Metropolitan from amongst themselves but as in former times sent to Byzantium for one.

It is true that at first the Greeks at Byzantium recognized the fact that Ukraine would not accept schismatic but only Catholic men and sent those to Ukraine, but after a period of time through various contacts by way of trade and political intercourse, the Ukrainians became accustomed to Greek schism so that by the year 1104, we find in the Metropolitan See for the first time a schismatic, the Greek Nikiphorus. Having a schismatic Metropolitan, it was not long before Ukraine became drawn into the Greek schism. Nonetheless, Ukraine was not entirely overcome by schism. Several times it broke with Byzantium and selected its own Catholic Metropolitans. Even during that period it raised several saints who were accepted and acknowledged by the Apostolic Church.

Beginning with the middle of the twelfth century and lasting throughout the thirteenth century, Ukraine was schismatic until Isidor Bulharin was nominated Metropolitan of Ukraine. The Greeks at that time thought of establishing closer unity with the Roman Church for they feared the Turks and expected to receive help in these battles from the Pope and other Western powers.

The Eastern Emperor, John Palaeologus (1425-1448) entered into communication with the Papal See, presumably with the object of the reunion of the churches, but principally with the hope of obtaining help against the Turks. He expressed an honest desire on the part of both Emperor and patriarch for reunion, their willingness to embrace the faith and obey the Church of Rome and their wish for a general council. Although the Church of Constantinople differed from the Western Church in the procession of the Holy Ghost, it nevertheless wished for union with it and the Greeks desired the decision of the Roman See on this question. The Emperor realized that without aid from the West, there was little prospect of defending his position, considering the inadequate defense of the capital, the diminution of its population and reduced revenues.

Pope Eugenius IV wrote to him, rejoicing that God had put into the heart of such a great Prince the desire to lead the Greek Church into reunion with the Church of Rome. The Pope promised to send his legates to confer with them concerning an arrangement of terms for reunion, so that as soon as it was completed, and the Eastern Church returned to the bosom of the Roman Catholic Church, the Greeks might rely on Western support and assistance.

Pope Eugenius IV opened the Council of Ferrara. The Muscovite Metropolitan Isidore who was a friend of the Pope in favor of the union of the Eastern and Western Church, tried more than the rest of the Greek and Ukrainian representatives to bring about a closer unity of the two Churches. His efforts were not entirely without success as both the Pope and Emperor were determined to effect a reunion.

In the year 1439 in Florence, where the Assembly had moved from Ferrara, all the representatives of the Greek and Ukrainian Churches finally agreed upon a compromise. The chief speaker for the Latins was Julian Caesarini and for the Greeks Bessarion, Mark of Ephesus and Isidore, the Muscovite Metropolitan. The four principal points of discussion which had already been raised at Ferrara were:

1. The procession of the Holy Ghost.
2. The use of leavened or unleavened bread.
3. The nature of Purgatory which had been fully debated at Ferrara.
4. The Pope's supremacy.

The chief and longest debate was on the Procession of the Holy Ghost. Bessarion contended that the difference between the two Churches was not one of doctrine but of expression; whilst Mark of Ephesus declared all holders of the Double Procession to be heretics and schismatics.

The compromise effected permitted each Church to use either leavened or unleavened bread. The addition of the Filioque Clause to the Creed and the other points were conceded by the Greeks; the supremacy of the Pope as successor to St. Peter and Vicar of Christ was acknowledged and the treaty of union was subscribed in which the Pope guaranteed the aid requested.

Isidore was rewarded by Pope Eugenius for his important role with the title of Cardinal Legate for Poland, Lithuania, Ukraine and Muscovy. Isidore did not remain long in Rome but returned in triumph, sailing on the River Buda, everywhere announcing the Union of the Eastern Church with Rome.

Nowhere was the supposed reunion of Christendom more thankfully and joyfully received than in Ukraine. Letters conveying words of encouragement and welcome were delivered by envoys to the patriarch and Emperor. The Ukrainian king ordered public thanksgiving with processions, litanies and prayers in all parts of Ukraine as the Ukrainian people had become tired of the yoke the Grecian patriarchs had placed upon them.

It seemed that after the period of chaos, one of peace would reign, but the devil did not sleep in his work of disharmony. In a short while through the persuasion of Bishop Mark of Ephesus, the unbelieving Greeks rejected the Union with Rome.

On December 12, 1452, Isidore celebrated Pontifical Mass in the presence of the Emperor and Eastern patriarchs according to the Latin Rite in the Cathedral of St. Sophia and there the Union of the Churches was proclaimed.

The Emperor and all who had signed the Union were received with a storm of indignation. Everywhere the Unionists were branded as traitors, sacrificing their Church

40

for material gain in preference to the good of their souls and slighting God to serve the Pope. Eventually it came about as one of them had said, that he would rather see in the streets of Byzantium a Sultan's turban than a Cardinal's hat.

In a few years all signs of the Union were obliterated. Thus ended the last united effort of a council to heal the schism between the Eastern and Western Churches.

The Turks came to rule their homeland and their proud patriarchs not content with obedience to the Roman Pope had to bow low in the dust before the heathen Turkish sultans and beg their quarter. This is the reward of Heaven for the pride and rebellion of the Greeks who as it was commonly said, preferred to see the Crescent of the Turks than the Tiara of the Pope in the Churches of Constantinople.

In the words of St. Basil, "God gave them over unto a reprobate mind because they received not the love of the truth, he sendeth them strong delusion that they should believe a lie."

One of the most lamentable facts which center around the fall of Constantinople is that it was mainly effected by Greeks, the corps of Janissaries (soldiers of the Turks formed from the kidnapped children of Christian parents) who fought against Christians of their own blood and the indifference of the Greeks who had little spirit in fighting under disunited schismatic leaders.

Constantinople fell on May 29, 1453. The Emperor, having asked the forgiveness of all whom he might have offended, received the Holy Eucharist in Communion at St. Sophia. His body was later found amidst a heap of slain with his sword still in his hand, so that he died a hero. As a sign of victory, his head was cut off and sent to the Sultan.

Isidore of Moscow in terror and despair was barely able to make his escape from the city in disguise.

The victorious Sultan Mahomet allowed the Greeks to choose their own patriarchs. However, the patriarchal palace was occupied by the Sultan while the patriarch had to take residence in the monastery of the Apostles.

The Cathedral of St. Sophia, the Metropolitan Church of the East, the noblest Christian Temple in the world, built to commemorate the Wisdom of God was converted into a Mohammedan Mosque, the crescent taking the place of the cross on the summit of its dome. About forty other churches were converted into Mosques, Mahomet allowing the Greek Church to celebrate its services in the remainder.

Moscow did not welcome Isidore in the same manner as he had been received in Ukraine. Despite the fact that he brought friendly letters from the Pope to the Grand Prince, Basil received him with the greatest indignation and rebuked him as a traitor to the Orthodox Church. He easily foresaw that through union with Rome his power over the Metropolitans and consequently the Church would be broken. The Muscovite Tsars, taking example from the Greeks were anxious to retain their power to select the Metropolitan and thus to keep the Church in submission.

When upon arrival at Moscow Isidore appeared before the bishops and priests to instruct them to announce the proclamation of the act of Union at Florence, Basil publicly denounced him as a traitor and apostate and ordered him imprisoned in a monastery from which he escaped and fled to Kiev. Not feeling secure there, he journeyed to Rome where because of his service to the Church in bringing about a union, he was sent to Constantinople, where, as stated above, the Union also met with violent opposition. There he was safe as long as the Palaeologi were Emperors, but after the fall of the Eastern Empire, he escaped to Rome with difficulty. For sometime after Isidore's exile as Metropolitan of Ukraine, Poland, Lithuania and Russia, there were Catholic Metropolitans in Ukraine sent by either the Pope of Rome or by the Byzantine patriarchs who had continued their union with Rome.

Between 1453-1599 no less than thirteen of the patriarchs of Byzantium continued to acknowledge the union with Rome and were subject to its authority. Driven away from Constantinople by the Turks, some uniate Greek citizens fled into foreign lands and there established their own Uniate Greek Churches. The Pope of Rome whose supremacy they acknowledged permitted them to retain the doctrines of the Greek Church, its liturgy and all the essentials of their faith. However, the greater mass of Greek people have continued in the Orthodox faith since the fall of Constantinople.

The council of Florence had failed to bring the Muscovites into obedience to the Roman Church, therefore, Pope Paul II, acting upon the advice of Cardinal Bessarion arranged a marriage between Ivan III and Sophia, daughter of Thomas, brother of the last two Palaeologi and heiress of the Greek Emperors. However, no sooner had Sophia arrived in Russia than she was converted by Ivan the Terrible to Orthodoxy so that Moscow succeeded to Constantinople as the second Rome and became the champion of Orthodoxy.

After a time, under the influence of Basil III of Moscow upon Alexander of Poland, a tyrannical Metropolitan, Jonah, 1448-1462, consecrated in a Synod of Russian bishops and who was the confessor to Helen the wife of the Polish king, was soon able with the backing of the Muscovite king to destroy all semblance of the hated Union and to bring about the return of schism to Ukraine. All trace of the Union was destroyed and Ukraine plunged into schismatic darkness. In Ukraine the words of the Divine Saviour were fulfilled: (Matthew 12-45)

"Then goeth he and taketh with himself seven other spirits more wicked than himself and they enter in and dwell there; and the last state of that man is worse than the first. Even so shall it be unto this wicked generation."

The Byzantine inertia and contentiousness finally overpowered Ukraine.

As it was the custom for the existing ruler to appoint the patriarch of Constantinople, which under the reign of Turkey was Mahomet and his successors, this dignity became a source of great profit to the Sultan. He invariably chose the most unfit of the candidates rather than one who merited this high ecclesiastical office and gave it to the highest bidder among them. The greater the trouble and scandal to the Church the more it was to the Sultan's benefit as upon his deposition at the request of the Greeks, the appointment of another patriarch in his place would bring more money into his pocket.

Hence, in order to retain their patriarchal Sees, the patriarchs of Constantinople became the servile instruments of the Sultan and his viziers.

The Greek patriarchs didn't care about the welfare of the Ukrainian Church but only in exacting the most money from it, as they had to pay tremendous sums of money to the Sultans and viziers who had given them their positions. Of necessity, therefore, those became Metropolitans who were of the greatest help and benefit financially to the patriarchs and the bishops, on their part found methods for extorting money from the simple priests. As to the priests they bent all their powers to accumulate benefices, enrich themselves through the treasury of the Church and secure inheritances for their families. The buying of a living and thus making religion a business was the natural result of the schism from its inception. Consequently, another evil manifested itself, Church offices were taken over by the ambitious, avaricious and luxury loving men who wanted an easy, untroubled life, thus bringing the Church into disrepute.

It can be understood from the above that the bishops were held in very low esteem and whatever authority still remained to their office was further undermined by the patriarchs who organized brotherhoods all over the land which had power over the management of the Church. These brotherhoods were not only independent of the bishops but had the right of censorship. They had the power to audit the Church books, to fire and hire priests and when necessary they could appeal directly to Byzantium. Naturally, the brotherhoods made the most of the opportunity of independence to the detriment of the Ukrainian Church. Having such wide powers it was not surprising that they clung faithfully to the patriarchs and did their best to promote their interests, which were schismatic.

Schism fed on darkness. The community selected one from among themselves and paid the bishop to ordain him as a priest. Some of them did not even know how to read and write or sometimes the priesthood was passed on from father to son. The father taught the son the Mass, prayers and office from memory, then collected money from the people to have him ordained as a priest. No one thought of seminaries for priests, neither the Polish government nor the Ukrainian bishops. The main purpose was to keep the priesthood in a degraded state of illiteracy and ineffectiveness. The fate of the priest was doleful. He was under the thumb of a politically appointed bishop and unconscionable gentry of the village. The priest eked out a livelihood for his family as a common serf for the wealthy landowner. He was actually in a more despicable position than a common peasant in his parish. The black-robed priesthood or monks lived under no better circumstances. They had to tolerate much abuse from their benefactors. But the most tragic consequences of the politically motivated schism was that the Order of Monks lost its asceticism and holiness which had distinguished it in the times of St. Basil the Great and Anthony and Theodosius Pechersky. The rules and precepts of the saints and monastic life were forgotten. It is true that outwardly a few penances were practiced but internally there reigned spiritual darkness and a looseness of morals. In other words, there came to pass a great disintegration of the spiritual and edu-

45

cational life in Ukraine which had flourished so powerfully upon its acceptance of Christianity, which at that time enjoyed the blessing of communion with the Roman Church.

How did the Ukrainian people fare under this lack of leadership? The people received no instruction on spiritual matters for there was no one to teach them. There were no sermons or catechising. They read no spiritually enlightening books as there were none, and they did not know how to read. They learned their prayers by word of mouth; they fasted and revered the holy pictures. This constituted all of their knowledge of religion. That they remained Christian was due entirely to the influence and diligence of their predecessors who had been brought up under better circumstances in the times of a united Church. The most unfortunate result of the schism was the prevalence of superstition among the populace. This is the fatal result of schism in any nation that permits it to enter its borders.

"When the unclean spirit is gone out of a man, he walketh through dry places seeking rest and findeth none. Then he saith, I will return into my house from whence I came out and when he is come he findeth it empty, swept and garnished" . . . . . .

CHAPTER IV

THE UNION OF THE UKRAINIAN CHURCH WITH ROME

Finally Almighty God in His divine compassion heard the prayers of the unfortunate but deeply religious Ukrainian people who had for centuries, despite many adversities and calamities retained a powerful living faith in God. As a reward for their sincere devotion to God there soon was to appear the light of truth which would snatch Ukraine from the enfolding darkness of Byzantium.

For His divine purposes God sometimes uses channels which do not seem at all capable. Such was the case in the person of the patriarch Jeremiah who came apparently to visit the Ukrainian Church and to strengthen it in its schism but actually to demand more money from its shepherds. However, observing the unfortunate state of affairs in Ukraine, he organized a reform, wrote pastoral letters and deposed the Metropolitan Onesiphorus Diwochko for his unexemplary life and in his place ordained Michael Rohoza, chosen by the middle and military class and also appointed as bishop Cyril Terlecky, a wise and learned man, also chosen by the people as exarch with authority over bishops and the Metropolitan. According to common reasoning, the

47

Ukrainian Church should have, after this reform, risen from its low estate and strengthened itself in its schism, but God had other plans. The work of the Patriarch Jeremiah was only a preparation of the field for Union. Not long afterwards, while staying in Roumania, the patriarch wrote Rohoza that he should send him fourteen thousand gold pieces for his ordination. There is no doubt but that the "good" shepherd wanted to denude his sheep. Finally, the eyes of the Ukrainian church hierarchy were opened to the true condition of their Church and the reason for the anxiety of the Greek patriarchs. The weak-willed Rohoza might have paid this stupendous sum if it had not been for Terlecky, who having understood the Greek aim towards the Ukrainian Church, tried with all his might to free it from the domination of Byzantium. He came to the conclusion that the salvation of the Ukrainian Church lay in its union with Rome.

Through his efforts there gathered in conference in the year 1594, at the Lithuanian city of Brest, the bishops Ignatius, Poty of Volodimir, Gregory Zahorsky, archbishop elect of Polotsk, bishops Leontin Pelchitsky of Pinsk, Dionisius Zbirsky of Kholm and John Gogol, together with Metropolitan Rohoza. At that conference they bound themselves to a life of implicit obedience to the Pope of Rome and the Court of St. Peter.

"Before the throne of God we solemnly promise, in so far as we are able, to enlighten our brethren and our people and with the help of God to bring all into Holy Union. All schisms arise because men have revolted against the one great, true and only King, our Lord Jesus Christ. The good order and agreement of the people can continue only as long as the rulers of the Churches themselves obey in common the one head. Why should the Church be united in one body? That discipline and order might be maintained in her of whom it was said, "Ye are the body of Christ and members in particular for that the one and only Head who is Christ Jesus, governs and unites each to each." The Lord constituted Peter after Himself, Shepherd of the Church, saying to him, 'Feed my sheep.'"

The next year they met again at Brest and agreed to send Poty and Terlecky to Rome requesting acceptance.

Pope Clementine VIII welcomed the representatives from Ukraine eagerly and agreed to everything the Bishops demanded and on December 23, 1595 officially accepted them into the Union. He issued a special bull on the occasion of the union of the Ukrainians with the Holy See to solemnize this memorable event:

"We permit, we allow, we approve all the Sacred Rites and Ceremonies used by the bishops and clergy in the divine offices, in the celebration of Mass, administration of Sacraments and all the other religious functions which were introduced by the Greek Fathers." (Magnus Dominus, issued 1595)

Upon return of the bishops to Ukraine, the Metropolitan called a Synod according to the instruction of the Holy Father to be held at Brest where on October 8, 1595, they were officially sworn into obedience to the visible head and Vicar of Christ, the Pope of Rome and were joined with the One, Holy Catholic and Apostolic Church. From that time on, the Ukrainian Church remained in Union with Rome, which, with the grace of God, it has largely preserved to this day despite many obstacles, difficulties and annoyances.

It would be difficult to place the guilt of disobedience to the care of the unity of the Church by mentioning for instance, the methods used by the powerful Prince Ostrowsky, who at first seemed to be inclined towards the Union but when the bishops, without asking his leave, completed the agreement of Union, became its greatest enemy in destroying the work, also the Catholic middle class instead of promoting the good work protested against it and stifled its organization. What was most terrible is that the rulers of the Church themselves took part in the dissensions. No doubt in the confusion and separation which reigned supreme throughout the whole East it was forgotten that those separated from the Church no longer had the grace of the Holy Spirit, the communication failing as the Apostolic succession had been cut off. Those who first separated received ordination from the Apostolic Fathers, but they who were cut off had neither power to baptize nor ordain, nor could communicate to others the grace of the Holy Spirit from which they themselves had fallen. In the words of St. Basil, "they who will not accept the ordinances of the Church elect of God, resist the command of God."

Suffice it to say that the work of the Union had first to go through the crucible of fire and water, to suffer many wrongs, and persecutions even to be drenched with the blood of its martyrs in order to effect a regeneration. Whenever dramatic presentations, lectures, preaching and exemplary lives are of no avail, then the blood of martyrs must be the soil for the new growth. The truth of the words of Tertulian will live forever, "The blood of martyrs is the seed of new Christians."

The time had come when God permitted the blood of his beloved to be shed for His sake that falling upon barren soil, it might produce strong soldiers to fight the battle of truth and light. Ukraine, devastated by the Mongols, whereupon it was easily parcelled by her border enemies, Poland, Lithuania and Russia and then overrun by the quarrelsome, contentious schism of the Greeks, was barren soil. There were few men left in that period who could understand the ideal of the son of God, "You will all be of one fold," who would not only defend this ideal, be willing to give their lives for it, but were also capable of implanting it into the hearts of their fellowmen.

The Union of the Ukrainian Church was no easy accomplishment. It suffered enmity on every side from the Polish middle class politicians, from the ill-tempered fanatical Muscovite schismatics, and even from the mediocrity and imprudence of some of its faithful. Therefore, the Union had to be cemented by the brutal shedding of blood.

As in the first centuries of Christianity, after each period of persecution, the Catholic Church not only did not suffer loss of its prestige, but, on the contrary, gained an increase in membership after each such trial, thus it seems God in this period desired for a similar purpose the powerful seed of bloodshed, this time not for the conversion of the heathen souls, but what is much more difficult the snatching of thousands of souls from the bottomless pit of schism.

It is fitting in the eyes of Divine Providence, that persons of very humble esteem in the eyes of the world should be chosen for the accomplishments of God's greatest work, the more strikingly to manifest his omnipotence in functioning through these chosen channels. As in the beginning in the work of Apostleship, in spreading the knowledge of the kingdom of God, very humble, unlearned fishermen were chosen. Thus, later when it became necessary to stir up the ashes of a dying faith of the Christians and to reform the Catholic Church, He chose persons of humble rank, unknown to the world, and through them carried out His purpose. Therefore, to fulfill the prediction of His beloved Son before His death, He chose for Himself a man who in the eyes of the world was not illustrious by birth nor great in learning nor even great in wealth, but one who distinguished himself throughout his life before God through his living faith and sincere, warm love. This was St. Josaphat. He became a true Apostle to the Ukrainian Church, the protector and pillar of the Holy Union. He was the nurturer throughout Ukraine of the ideal of the Saviour, "You shall all be of one fold."

CHAPTER V

THE CHILDHOOD AND YOUTH OF ST. JOSAPHAT

Ukraine, the promised land of milk and honey, wonderfully productive, with rich stores of treasures so attractive to her jealous and covetous neighbors, who were very happy to have partitioned it off when the opportunity presented itself after devastation by the Mongolian invasion, that they claimed it was theirs from the beginning of time. For instance, in the Kiev and Podolia districts one plowing and sowing suffices and where bees and wild fowl are to be found in such abundance that boys could scoop up eggs into canoes, where even dogs are fed with meat and fish; where the atmosphere, in a charming setting of smiling skies is marvelously magnetic, producing personalities of a constructive, creative, robust and obliging nature; and where it has been said by foreign writers that a person who has once visited it cannot depart except in great reluctance and will never forget it for it will continue to draw him like a magnet. Here in the town of Volodimir, principality of Wolyn, the future St. Josaphat was born to a pious and humble family. His father, Gabriel Kuncevich, was a middle-class gentleman, but because of poverty, he was forced to follow a trade, which was that of a grain merchant. Moreover, he was highly esteemed by his fellow citizens for his integrity of character and on that account they elected him as a councillor of their town. His wife, Marianna came of a modest noble family in Volodimir. In the year 1580 when a son was born, they Christened him John, in the Church of St. Parasceve (Paraskevia). As they were earnest and genuine Christians, they did their best to instill the same faith into the heart of their child from the cradle. As soon as he could utter a word or join his hands he was taught to pray. His mother, Marianna, sang to him the song, "O Mary, Mother of God, pray for us," as a lullaby.

Public schooling was out of the question for a land occupied by foreign invaders. Although a gentleman's daughter, Marianna scarcely knew how to read and write. Nevertheless, she had a prodigious memory for she could relate many parables from the Bible and the life of the Holy Family. Possessed of a fertile imagination, she was never at a loss for good stories. Instead of Mother Goose or some other fables, Ukrainian babies are taught the life of the Holy Family, especially the life of the child Jesus. Deprived of schools, this was one way to preserve intact their native tongue and their own faith.

From his earliest years, St. Josaphat showed an uncommon religious interest. He was a serious boy with marvelous presence of mind, reflective, but sparing of words, thinking a great deal more than he said, full of admiration for his mother's piety. "Virtue passes easily from the hearts of mothers into the hearts of children."

In the Ukrainian home God is always served first. In the early morning the whole family, including servants, say their prayers in common for His blessing for the day, at table His blessing for the meal and at night the blessing on their rest. Despite the schismatic disease which hit Ukraine after its invasion, the faith of the people was strong and enduring and they held to it firmly.

St. Josaphat can be said to have been raised on the supernatural plane of divine grace. The reason for this, as St. Josaphat revealed later to his friend, Hennedy Khmelnitsky, was due to the following incident:

At one time when his parents took him to the Church of St. Parasceve in which he had been Christened, he was attracted to an ikon of our Lord Jesus on the Cross and immediately began to question his mother as to its meaning. The mother tried as best she could to explain in language understandable to the child about the Saviour of mankind who for love of humanity descended to earth from heaven and permitted himself to be nailed to the cross to save mankind from hell and to open to it the gates of heaven.

The child gazed in wonderment and within him something ardent and mysterious stirred to life, filling him with a great love for the Crucified Lord. "At that moment," said Josaphat to his friend, "I saw a spark of fire leave the side of our Lord and enter my heart. I was suddenly overwhelmed by such an abundance of sweetness and love that I stood very still, seeing and hearing nothing, and from that moment on such a great love was born in me for the Saviour of mankind and my Rite that for thirty years I never once neglected the Church rule and could only think of imitating Him in His life of poverty and suffering."

As a result of the above incident, there was a notable change in the behavior of the child. Astonishing to himself, his life had found direction. He had received the seed of his future apostolate. There spoke and acted through him the future monk. He shunned the childish playthings, avoided bad companions and devoted his whole time to decorating and reverencing holy pictures. As much as he could he ran off to be by himself in some quiet spot or to a Church and if he found the door locked, then he would fall upon his knees before the door on the porch and with folded hands prayed earnestly whence, after a long search, his parents had to take him home. (At the entrance of the Byzantine style Church, there is usually a porch extending along the whole Western Width.)

Thus the existence of God as the Father in heaven and of the pure and humiliated Jesus, His Son, became a living reality to him. His chief concern thereafter was how to please God. This he did by diligent application in all his undertakings and in obedience, love for others, the cheerful acceptance of his duties, disappointments, hardships and misfortunes. He dedicated the remainder of his life to the service of Christ for the salvation of souls.

The unusual earnestness and angelic piety of the small boy aroused the attention of the whole town. They all admired the extraordinary child and asked themselves what would become of this boy? It was only natural that his parents should name him "John," which means "the grace of God." Strangers stared at John and pointed him out as an example to their children. And what was still more wonderful is that his elders aware of his earnestness at Mass began likewise to imitate him and to become better Christians. And so John grew in the grace of God and in His wisdom.

Whenever he did wrong, his mother corrected him with the utmost gentleness, so that her decisive word, "God sees all that you do," was sufficient.

In winter he was invited around to the houses of neighboring farmers to read aloud to them by firelight or candle light after the recitation of the rosary for which several families gathered in various houses each week.

Early in life he learned that it was by gentleness and charity that he could make the best kind of friends. The secret of his magnificent charity which burned in his heart and inflamed his brethren was the grace of the Holy Spirit issuing from the Heart of Jesus as a spark of divine fire, inspiring and purifying his being in order to bring about the miracle of leading his people back to the true faith. Saints

55

are invariably born in troubled times when faith or the independence of the homeland is in danger and there is need of revival of faith and courage in the human heart.

When he had grown up to boyhood, his parents sent him away to the city to school where he learned the Slavonic and Polish languages. The great natural intelligence with which John was endowed helped him to quickly finish school with honors. However, the Holy Spirit in him did greater things, for he had hardly learned the language when he committed to memory the entire service of the Mass. He was only ten years old when he knew by heart all the monastic rules of the Basilian Brotherhood, the various morning and evening services, the offices, which he recited daily from memory and never neglected once over a period of thirty years until his lips were closed by death.

His pious parents, however, did not know the destiny of their son. Since there were other little ones growing up, they wanted to secure his future. They sent him to the big city to a magistrate serving on the city council and a wealthy cloth merchant, Yakinta Popovich, in the city of Vilno, the capital of Lithuania. This city was the center of all kinds of sects and heresies which flowed into it in an unceasing stream from Germany and it was the most morally corrupt of cities.

St. Josephat, having more personal freedom here than at home with his parents was open to all kinds of temptations. Since he was employed in a store, he came in touch with the flowing tide of human life and affairs, as retailed by all kinds of customers and his ears were often filled with distressing anti-religious comments. He had to listen to insults directed against the Catholic Church and especially had to endure the humiliation of deprecating remarks about the Eastern Ukrainian rite from both Roman rite Catholics and Heretics.

The city had many trials for a young Christian as undoubtedly it had valuable lessons to teach. Added to that was the evil example of rank immorality of the younger generation in the Lithuanian Babylon, so that we can understand the many dangers the unworldly young man faced and can readily appreciate the supernatural power necessary to keep him on the path of truth and purity. But God will not permit His beloved chosen for the accomplishment of great things to be corrupted by the worldly disease. Ever preserving lofty and unfettered the thoughts of his soul, he was insensible to the pleasures and attractions of the capital. Although the unworldly youth did not have a guide, God himself protected and counselled him for his heart remained pure and undefiled. He lived through those years untainted with the worldliness about him. His greatest pleasure and diversion was to get away for a while from the store in order to get to Church to pray and adore the Blessed Sacrament. Whenever he had any free time from his duties, he occupied himself by poring over books of Church literature and the lives of the saints.

Throughout the day his spirit and his lips were occupied in earnest prayer and meditation. It sometimes happened that although the merchant Popovich was very fond of John, he scolded him and even punished him for his absorption in prayers. But John was not dissuaded from continuing his prayers, on the contrary, he grew stronger in piety and holiness. Although by nature very strict, Popovich admired John's piety and grew to love him as dearly as if he were his own son. There was nothing unusual in that. Only those people who are corrupt to the core of their being detest holiness and purity.

During John's stay in Vilno, when he was about fourteen years old, a great religious storm broke out in Ukraine. The cause for it was the Union of the Ukrainian Church with Rome. The Metropolitan together with six bishops had sworn allegiance to the Pope of Rome and signed the agreement of Union with the Church of Rome at Brest in the year 1596.

In all the arrogance of his immense power, Prince Ostrowsky struck with all his forces at the Metropolitan and his uniate bishops who had dared to accept the Union without his approval or permission. He sent his agents throughout Ukraine to incite the people into a frenzied passion for religious freedom at all costs, which as a consequence resulted in rebellion against all established authority, especially the Church of Rome and this they did in the name of liberty and patriotism.

Taking advantage of the disturbed state of men's minds, the sects also did all in their power to corrupt and terrorize the people, so healthfully bound in all its fibres to the religion of its ancestors.

The brotherhoods, supposedly organized by the Church through the charity of Prince Ostrowsky for educational purposes, sprang up suddenly all over Ukraine to promote the cause of schism. Under pretext of religious piety, they flooded the cities, towns and villages with contentious pamphlets which attacked in God's name the most ancient and efficacious practices of the Catholic Church, fasting, abstinence, confessions, extreme unction, holy water and candles, prayers for the dead, pilgrimages and declaring that bishops and priests should be married and the convents closed. Once started on the road of negation how could an ignorant peasant stop? If people were to throw all their other religious traditions overboard, God would go overboard too. There was no clear distinction between what was allowable and what was forbidden.

The priesthood, the uneducated middle-class, the unenlightened townsfolk and the rank and file, at the bidding of the Schismatic Prince Ostrowsky, rose up in a body against the Union with Rome and the bishops who had joined the Union.

The Churches and Church properties of those who had joined the Union were forcibly taken from them and given to the schismatics. The Byzantine patriarch Jeremiah and the Muscovite Metropolitan Jonah excommunicated all who had joined the Union. Vilno, the capital of Lithuania, was most concerned with this struggle as it was the center of the schismatics of the middle-class swayed by the literature of the powerful Ostrowsky. All the largest and wealthiest churches were taken away from the Uniates and only the poor little church of the Holy Trinity was left to the Metropolitan with but a few faithful followers of the Union and it seemed then as if this were all that remained of the newly effected Union.

Thus John grew up in the midst of religious controversies. It needed strength and prudence to keep peace within his soul and to preserve the right balance of kindness and justice in his daily contacts.

He did not have a counsellor who could have guided him to the truth in that period of chaos and having little education began to have some doubts. On the one hand he noticed the small number of Uniates with their poor and neglected little Church and he heard nothing but criticism of their church and bishop. On the other hand he noticed the power of the schismatics, their worldly influence and he feared to fall in with the persecuted group excommunicated by the patriarch. To which church should he belong? In which was the truth to be found? He sought the higher truth to which he longed to dedicate himself. What could an unenlightened youth do under the circumstances? Saints invariably follow the straight and narrow path. Guarding and guiding the vast intelligence to know and understand and reduce to order the issues involved, was a powerful will for good.

In all earnestness he got down on his knees before the favorite ikon of the Crucified Lord in Church and asked God the unfailing guide for enlightenment in the direction he should take; "O send out thy light and thy truth, let them lead me, let them bring me into Thy holy hill and thy tabernacles." And God did not forsake His chosen one but revealed to him His divine will. Almost instantly he became aware of the newly revealed truth and at the same time felt in his heart such doubt and skepticism for the Schismatic Church that he unconsciously repeated with the psalmist: (Psalm 24, 4-5)

"Show me Thy ways, O Lord; teach me Thy paths. Lead me in Thy truth and teach me: for Thou art the God of my salvation: on Thee I wait all the day." All his doubts vanished. Thus with a renewed spirit and determination and with a great inward joy he joined the ranks of the Uniates.

From then on there was another change in the life of the young saint. Having once understood the truth, he held to it and in accordance with it planned his life. He went to the church of the Holy Trinity every day, sang in the choir with his high soprano voice. He decorated the altars, rang the bells when necessary and prayed to Almighty God that those who had lost the path might return to Union with the One, Holy Apostolic and Catholic Church.

The multitude had its faith and hope so deeply undermined in the name of liberty that a new kind of apostolate was demanded to bring back the scattered sheep, the poor and ignorant peasant serfs as well as the unenlightened city masses. It was clearly the kind of disease that demanded a desperate remedy. What would become of them if they went on in ignorance of the elemental truth on which their salvation depended? He had come to the awareness of his vocation. It seemed to him that that was the one thing he had to do on earth.

The prophecy of the Saviour upon the cross, "You shall all be of one fold" had sunk deeply into his heart. His holy life attracted the attention of the educated Greek, Peter Arkudia, whom Metropolitan Poty had brought from Rome to help spread the work of the Union. Through his acquaintance with Arkudia, the young Kuncevich gained much that was to be of value in his life and became very attached to the Metropolitan. At this time also he became acquainted with William Rutsky under whose leadership he was later to work for the salvation of Ukraine, and with Hennedy Khmelnitsky, who later became his confessor and the most intimate confidant of his soul. He also met two famous teachers of the Academy of Vilno, Valentine Fabrician and Gregory Grushevsky who were of great help to him later on in his work. Good souls quickly and unexpectedly get to know each other. The Holy Spirit unites them so that they might work together helping one another on the path of Christian progress.

The purpose of John's worldly life had been accomplished. He had reached the height of Christian piety, therefore, God called him to a higher order of sanctity, that of the monastic brotherhood.

He had for some time past turned his eyes within, not so much to avoid seeing the evil of the city, crawling with obscene life, as to see good more clearly. His eyes looked out beyond the regular daily toil and material progress towards the Supreme Good on which everything depends. He loved work and play but he had discovered something better. Not timorous, but very great of soul, he denied himself to possess all. Worldly treasures had lost for him their value. His heart was possessed by a powerful desire to follow Christ who said: (Matthew 19-21)

"Jesus said unto him, if thou will be perfect, go and sell all that thou hast and give to the poor and thou shalt have treasure in heaven; and come and follow me."

Whoever has once heard the call of the Saviour in his heart nothing can deter him from the path, not any promises or obstacles. Thus John gave up the life of a merchant in worldly goods in order to become a merchant of heavenly treasures.

The old merchant Popovich had loved the good young man and having learned of his plans did all he could to keep him by his side. He offered him the hand of his only daughter in marriage, together with all his possessions, but he declined. The voice of God is stronger than that of humanity. Nothing helped, neither threats, nor harsh treatment, nor even the influence of tears could shake his determination to leave the world and henceforth live with God. The decisions of saints are incontrovertible. He had made up his mind to become a monk and by this decision was forced to bring anguish to dear hearts bound to him by ties that the most insensitive respect, but he did not alter it, as he remembered the words of the Saviour, "What profit a man to gain the whole world, if he lose his own soul?"

CHAPTER VI

JOSAPHAT BECOMES A MONK

Who can fail to recognize the vast importance to the Church of the monastic brotherhood when it properly fulfills the duties to which it has been called. The Church which possesses a well-organized, progressive order of monks will always be outstanding. A monastic brotherhood represents the flower of Christian life and is at the same time its guardian, inspiration and salvation. The more of the Holy Spirit such an organization possesses, the greater number will it attract to its ranks of those who will devote themselves to the service of God and strive at all times to attain those graces through which they gain power to draw others to their company. For this purpose the Church organizes monastic orders of a purely contemplative nature, whose members devote themselves chiefly to the salvation of their souls through constant prayer, the mortification of the flesh and complete retirement from the world and who interest themselves in the salvation of other souls solely through the medium of prayer. Another organization of monks of active workers and preachers are those who in addition to the salvation of their own souls occupy themselves directly with the salvation of the masses of humanity. This type of brotherhood is of special assistance to the bishops and the secular priesthood. They give retreats for the spiritual direction and inspiration of spiritual leaders and give missions for the benefit of the masses of the faithful. They preach sermons, write books and publish Catholic newspapers. They teach and guide the youth. They concern themselves with deeds of mercy on a material plane. In other words, they are an Army of Light always ready and willing to lend a hand wherever there is greatest need of help in the battle with the forces of darkness on the spiritual plane. Whenever the brotherhood functions in the fulfillment of the highest ideal of its duties, not only does it spread the glory of God and improve the Church, but is a credit to the Rite and the nation whom it serves.

A monk who comes of a certain race cannot escape the inborn, natural and noble love for his own people. He has, however, to uplift this love and train it to be subservient to his love for God. This love will then be expressed in all his work which directly concerns itself with the salvation of the souls of his people and their spiritual and material improvement.

A progressive monastic order in addition to observing all its regulations and rules, carefully guards the service of the Mass; cares for the beautifying and cleanliness of the Churches; preserves the Church customs; upholds the Church's material interests; develops the Church music, songs and hymns; in other words, it guards the Rite. The enemies of the Church are fully aware of the significance, efficacy and influence of the monastic order. That is why whenever there is a conflict with the Church the monks are the first to enter the struggle. Whenever they fall in the battle, it is lessened. This is the reason why rulers of nations who oppose the Church try first of all to break up or disorganize the monastic brotherhoods and disband the monks. Many such examples can be taken from the history of the Church. This also happened in the history of Ukraine for as soon as schismatic Moscow wanted to destroy the Union with Rome in the conquered nations, the first thing it did was to close all the Basilian monasteries and disperse the monks throughout the Empire.

Since monastic orders as a whole are considered of such vast importance, it can readily be understood how the great Basilian Order exercised such a powerful influence over Ukraine.

Upon the acceptance of Christianity by Ukraine in 988, the day of Grand Prince Volodimir's marriage to Anna, the Christian sister of the Emperor Basil II of Byzantium, monasteries were founded by Volodimir throughout Ukraine. Some of them served as training schools for the clergy while others devoted themselves to composing literature in the native Ukrainian language and to translations from the Greek of works from the Greek Church which he had brought from Byzantium and stored in the original Pechersky monastery. Since that time the monasteries have been the one unfailing source of enlightenment for the Ukrainain nation. They gathered the historical facts and were the first writers or composers of the nation's literature. They organized the educational institutions and spread tirelessly educational propaganda by pen, word and example. All of the spiritual leadership came from the monasteries.

As long as the monastic Order of St. Basil held to its rule and precepts to draw men upwards so that a spiritual posterity might grow up to continue to take their places, the nation remained on a high spiritual level. When the zeal of the monastic orders diminished, then the cultural level of the priesthood and multitude decreased. When people know with full certitude that they are loved by those who pray they likewise turn to prayer. And it is not difficult to love one's brethren and show them that love when the heart is full of the love of God.

Since, according to the custom of the Eastern Church, only

monks could become bishops and if a man were a good monk, lived in complete detachment from self, a life well-filled with virtue and zeal and had a heart responsive to the needs of the people, a soul elevated to God, then he would be eligible as a worthy candidate for bishop in the Church.

It was a bitter fate for Ukraine when the Order fell into schism. With the acceptance of schism, the spirit of St. Basil left the Order. The fervor and zeal established by Anthony and Theodosius Pechersky vanished and the work of salvation of souls was neglected.

The true sanctity of union with God which enables a monk to see clearly and break through the crust that so often overgrows souls who have lost touch with God and restore that grace which nourishes the life of God in the depths of the soul, had fallen away; for that power must be borrowed from God and is linked up intimately with suffering in his own person. To share men's burdens and pardon their sins he must share the suffering of Christ upon the cross which belonged to those who confessed to Him in the sanctifying unity of the Church.

There were no more workers in the vineyard of the Lord in the monasteries who were willing to give themselves wholly and entirely with no reservations whatever, all their time and strength and experience and knowledge, and who by personal example and earnest effort upheld the faith of the people, enlightened their ignorance, catechised the children and continued the work of educating the masses; through public missions planting the seed of faith where the soil was good or where the seed already lying dormant might revive and grow; applying the balsam of compassion to soften hard hearts and bring them to repentence.

It was while Josaphat considered entering the service of God that the Basilian Order found itself in such a fallen state. The majority of the monasteries had accepted schism. It was true that a few still held to the Union because they were under the direct protection of Uniate bishops but strict obedience to the monastic vows and precepts had long been abandoned.

For the strengthening of the Union and to assure its survival in Ukraine, it was necessary to revive the Basilian monastic brotherhood. That is why God sent John to the monastery who was to renew its former power and glory. Invariably great saints appear in troubled times when the faith is at a low ebb and everyone feels the need of a renewal of religious zeal. In Vilno he saw progressive and powerful Latin Orders such as the Jesuits and the bare-footed Carmaelites. He also noted the degraded state of the brotherhood into which he was to enter, but his immense compassion and ardent love for his own Rite and his own people would not permit him even to think of entering an Order other than the Ukrainian Order of St. Basil. From his earliest days he had loved solitude and God. He wanted to serve God with all his heart as a monk, in the life of prayer, work, suffering and self-denial, not ever dreaming of the important mission God had chosen him to accomplish, that he was to give men a new measure of what a man of God can do when grace impels and penance supports him. His one thought was to give back to God all that he had received, his strength, ability and the radiance of his personality as well as his mind and heart.

In the year 1604, John requested the Metropolitan, Ipaty Poty, for acceptance and was gladly accepted which shows the profound impression made by his conduct and character upon his contemporaries. The natural distinction of his personality was the Ukrainian dignity with its at the same time quickness and charm.

He was twenty-four years of age when he put on the black habit of the monk and according to custom changed his Christian name of John to the monastic Josaphat.

Although it is against the rules of the Order of St. Basil

for a novice to take the vows immediately upon entry, nonetheless, Josaphat made his vows at entry with the permission of the Metropolitan Poty.

Although he had not undergone the initial training of the novitiate, a great joy filled Josaphat's heart at having succeeded in surrendering himself wholly to the service of God. His immediate ideal was a healthy, holy life. Only he who has himself experienced it can comprehend and evaluate his unbounded joy. But to this deep joy there was soon to be added a great sorrow. St. Josephat became aware of the corruption of the Vilno monastery. It had degenerated into mere living quarters. Idle or debauched monks who were servants of Christ in name only occupied it, some of them had built their homes beside the monastery. It required sincerity and enthusiasm to put up with it. All the property belonging to the monastery was assigned by Prince Stephen Batory to the management of men from the outside world. This management not only cared nothing for the welfare of the monastery but was miserly with supplies to the archimandrite. And what was still worse, St. Josephat did not find anyone within it capable of guiding him along the path of self-mastery. He did not have a friend whom he could trust and with whom he could discuss his problems.

Since every student needs a teacher, it can be understood how necessary and important it is to have a guide in pursuing the highest study of all, that of self-mastery. There was nothing left for St. Josaphat to do but to depend wholly upon the guidance of the Holy Spirit. The Holy Ghost which had kept him to this time in innocence and purity did not forsake him in this need: He was shown the straight and surest path to holiness which quickly led him to the attainment of self-mastery so that he himself could become a guide to others. No one had shown him the way. In his simplicity, having only one object in view, he walked the path of holiness with a sure step for God Himself guided him along.

Filled with new courage, he could think only of imitating Christ in His life of poverty and suffering. A being overwhelmed by burning love for Christ, he became as gentle as he was pure. Enlightened by the Divine Teacher, he expressed his ideas in terms that all could understand necessary for the life of the soul. Preserved from error by natural good sense and humility, he became a master of interior liberation for others. All who came under his influence could find reasons to love the monastic life and believe in divine goodness. His teachings had so much serenity in them that many were attracted by his genuine goodness and nobility.

The life of the Basilian monk consists of three phases: prayer, study and self-mortification. Prayer is the wordless food of the monk; without it no one has ever become a real monk, and if he is already a monk and neglects prayer, he stops being a monk. To effective prayer must be added attunement with the Holy Spirit, through giving up the world and its passing interests which enables man to see clear through the veil of the flesh to the deepest mysteries of the soul. In the mystical state the soul withdraws into itself and there no longer deafened by the clamor of the world, it turns towards God and in Him sees the secrets of men's souls. From the moment men come into his presence, a saint knows more of the mysteries of their souls than a philosopher can deduce in years of patient study. St. Josaphat learned this through the Holy Spirit. He chose for himself the poorest, most isolated room in the monastery but one closest to the ideal of the Church. He never left his cell even to go into the courtyard of the monastery except to go to Church for Mass and to the refectory.

Famous personalities frequently came to visit the monastery such as the senators with their retinues, but the door of St. Josaphat's cell did not open out of unnecessary curiosity. His cell became another substitute for the Church. Here he learned to pray as the ancient monks prayed. Every day he would make a thousand obeisances, repeating the following prayer after each obeisance: "Lord, Jesus Christ, Son of God, have mercy upon us." Often during his sleep, his lips would repeat the prayer common in the Ukrainian Rite, "God have mercy upon us," as testified by the Rev. Simeon Yatskovich, OSBM. This was not merely lip service to the Eastern Rite but proof of an earnest, sincere and practical love. He spent entire days in prayer. But to the chosen even the whole day is too short for prayer. This was true of Josaphat. There was not sufficient time for him in daily prayer so he got up at midnight and spent more time in prayer either in his cell or in a nearby cemetery in the cold and the wind, often standing with bare feet in the snow to continue his prayers.

Whenever he was not occupied with prayer, he consecrated his time to the study of the Sacred Books which he loved. From them he strengthened his knowledge of the truths of the Catholic Faith and his belief in the unity of the Church. From the Scriptures he gathered facts with which to answer the arguments of the schismatics and made notes from which he later wrote a book entitled "The Protection of the Faith," to confound the subtle and manifold assaults of heresies of sects, half-political, half-religious, which had sprung up on every side, and another "The Christening of St. Volodimir" in which he brought out the incontrovertible fact that Ukraine from the beginning of its acceptance of Christianity had been in Union with Rome and always had acknowledged the Pope of Rome as the undisputed head of the Catholic Church.

The facts which he brought out to confirm his teachings carried more weight because they were taken from the books of Scripture which were used also by the schismatics in their services. In addition to this Josaphat read the lives of the saints carefully whence he extracted all that was exemplary or noble in conduct and pure in thought and from whose example he drew lessons in holiness and virtue. Through his

70

work, reading and austerities he contacted the source of power which unfolded St. Josaphat's spiritual nature and gave momentum to the rest of his life in the work of apostleship. He lived in the presence of saints, first in thought and then in reality.

True holiness is always closely allied with penance and self-mortification. No one can attain to the highest degree of spiritual development until he has gained mastery over his material and physical desires. This truth was recognized by St. Josaphat. Therefore, all his life he treated his body as if it were his greatest enemy, never condescending to spend any anxiety upon it but living as though the flesh were not his own. In the use of food not only was he very moderate, but often fasted several days at a time. He ate only the plainest of foods and never ate meat from the time he entered the monastery. He seldom ate fish. Over a period of five years he drank only water and he would have continued this all his life, if the abbot of the monastery, noticing his weakness had not ordered him sometimes to drink wine. Josaphat intended to make a vow for life to live only on bread and water, but the advice of his confessor kept him from carrying this out. Instead of a linen, he wore a hair shirt that bit into his skin. He never took this off day or night. His bed was so poor a beggar would not want to sleep on it and even this he seldom used but slept on the bare ground, covered only by the hair shirt. His loins he girded with a wire belt whose sharp ends many times dug deep wounds into the flesh.

Whenever a feast day approached or he was to receive Christ in Holy Communion, then it was he bound his loins most closely. In addition to this he used scourges to chastise himself until drops of blood like dew scattered the floor of his cell.

Not only in the cell did he mortify his flesh but he frequently went out into the bitter cold with bare feet and uncovered head into the silence of the cemetery behind the

Church. There he stood upon a stone to which his feet often froze while he flogged himself unmercifully, the blood spattering the snow and after each strike of the scourges (knotted cord fastened with a few spikes and leaden balls) he implored with tears in his eyes, "Lord, Jesus Christ, give us the Holy Union so that we may all be of one fold."

In the protocol of the Apostolic Commission, the Rev. Hennedy Khmelnitsky testified that they found St. Josaphat one night in the cemetery so frozen and blood stained that he was unable under his own power to return to the monastery.

Divine Providence blessed St. Josaphat with a great love for the ascetic life that he might have all the greater power to influence the return to the Union of the schismatics who venerated and esteemed self-mortification as the most meritorious virtue.

Although Josaphat was pure and chaste despite all the pollutions of the world in his time, he grew more fond of these angelic virtues in his life as a monk. He loved purity so much that according to one of his biographers no one ever heard him speak a coarse word. He feared losing even for an instant, by look or touch, the Baptismal innocence which he preserved in soul and body so that he never in his life offended purity in word or deed. All admired and honored St. Josaphat for his purity.

The jealous demon possessed one shameless woman who, jeering at St. Josaphat's ascetic life, determined like Poliphar's wife, to lure the chaste St. Josaphat into sin. The Godless woman came to the door of St. Josaphat's cell in an attempt to persuade him to accede to her wicked plot. But she found another, stricter Joseph. When his rebukes had no effect, St. Josaphat grabbed a stick and beat her into a shameful retreat from the monastery. He preserved his chastity as the greatest of treasures and realizing that the most effective guardian of purity is the Blessed Virgin Mary he prayed to her fervently and was especially devoted to her and to Archangel Michael all his life.

The fame of his sanctity and ascetic earnestness, his long prayers, austerities, continence and saintly monkish straightforwardness soon spread and kindled the admiration of the other monks as well as the outside world. Many famous personages came to the monastery just to see the holy young man and to speak with him. He avoided slighting anyone and received all visitors in a courteous manner but these signs of esteem did not please the humble Josaphat. He preferred seclusion to the visits from uninvited, curious admirers. Therefore, he left the cell in the monastery and sought the refuge of the more secluded chapel of St. Luke. There was silence, solitude, leisure, the nourishing food of the soul. Having placed his table here, he devoted himself once more to his beloved occupations, the pursuit of learning and the cultivation of the mystic and emotional aspect of his nature and complete detachment from self. He prayed, read, studied by day and at night he retired to the seclusion of the cemetery and there chastised his mortal flesh, until he became broken to the life of prayer and suffering and self-denial. He trained and disciplined himself to the exclusion of all that was not immediately necessary for his soul's redemption, in order to attain that unity with God which would make the doing of great things for his fellow man possible. He strove always to choose that which was most difficult, clearing the soul of all that might hinder its capacity to receive the Holy Spirit in all its fullness of divine grace. His natural intelligence was enriched by and gained direction from the supernatural.

"Seek ye first the Kingdom of God and His righteousness and all these things shall be added unto you."

He never thought of the renunciations he made as privations but as conditions necessary to insure the success of his apostleship in bringing about the unity of the Church for which he yearned most passionately. To secure this was the object most prominent in his mind.

He read in the Gospel that demons like those which brought about schism were not to be cast out by anything but prayer and fasting. As it worked out, his task was nothing less than to root out of his land ignorance, apathy and lack of conscience as well as schismatic heresy and to replace them by modesty, temperance, honesty and love for the things of God. One thing he saw quite clearly, the devil was installed in Ukraine and must be driven out. Here in secret and in silence commenced the preparation for his campaign.

Josaphat was pleased with the arrival of the newly appointed archimandrite, Samuel Sinchilo, thinking that in him he might find a competent counselor and guide, but he was mistaken as Samuel turned out to be a very ordinary, uneducated man only outwardly pretending to be an adherent to Union but in his heart a fanatic schismatic.

Josaphat realized perfectly well that he could not accomplish anything by himself in his aims for reform of the Order. With the old monks, although they remained in the Catholic Church, it was impossible to start anything new, as they were set in their ways. That is why he planned on a new generation of monks to help him carry out his plan. Therefore, he urged the young men of his acquaintance who were interested in his monastic life to follow his example by entering the monastery. Gradually several young men were persuaded to enter willing to be the companions of St. Josaphat in seeking after God to do His will so that in their union with Him, they might receive all that he willed to bestow upon them of the grace of charity to serve their people. By the year 1607 there were four novices awaiting the black robes.

With the entry of the new companions into the monastery a new responsibility was laid upon the shoulders of St. Josaphat. He realized that he could not handle the task of teaching these young men how to become good monks and strong

74

fighters for the Union, all by himself. It is not sufficient for the training and practice of the ascetic life to lead others by personal example, but there must be a thorough education, knowledge of theology and training in the understanding of human nature.

Feeling himself unequal to the task, he prayed fervently to Almighty God for help. The Holy Ghost, which had taught him and guided him unfailingly on the path of self-mastery, heard his prayer and sent him a real helper in the person of John Rutsky, whom the Pope, Urban VIII, was later to call "The pillar of the Union, the Ukrainian Athanasius." Along what wondrous paths the wisdom of God guides his chosen people to their appointed work, can best be understood from the life of William Joseph Rutsky, who also lived the life of great severity and attracted all by his nobility, and goodness. He was gifted with a genius for organization but never thought of the honors to be gained from his position. He was always stripped for the conflict, never thinking of the morrow. What money he had he used to found theological schools for the clergy and to renew the Order which would enlighten the faithful by preaching.

CHAPTER VII

JOSEPH RUTSKY AND THE FIRST REFORM
OF THE ORDER

Doleful indeed is the fate of the Church that has separated itself from the true church of Christ. As a limb torn from the tree loses the source of its life, so the church separated from the tree of St. Peter loses its life.

The prophecy of the Son of God was and continues to be fulfilled in the Schismatic churches, "Abide in me and I in you. As the branch cannot bear fruit of itself, except it abide in the vine, no more can ye except ye abide in me." (St. John 15-4).

Since the time it separated itself from the true Church of Christ and His Successor, it not only fails to bring forth fruit but continues to wither and rot. It is enough to consider the numerous stupid, sinful, Godless, sometimes even unnatural sects and heresies that have arisen from the schismatic Church. Not having life within itself, it cannot share it with its faithful. Schismatic bodies through the guilt of disobedience in separation after the first generation no longer possess the grace of the Holy Spirit, the communication failing as the Apostolic succession had been cut off. They have not the power to baptize or ordain nor can communicate to others the grace of the Holy Spirit from which they have themselves fallen.

Many of the faithful, finding in schism neither mental nor spiritual satisfaction, seek it in all kinds of sects, for they have left the fountain of living water found only in the true Church. Many of the better families, missing the true life in the schismatic Church, joined various Protestant sects or whenever they chanced to return to the Catholic Church, they abandoned their ancestral Rite. Among this group of people was the father of Rutsky.

The late William and his wife who came from Kosakiw, were from Moscow, and were both fanatic Calvinists. They held property in Ruta, from which village they took their surname of Rutsky. In the year 1573, there was born to them a son, whom a Ukrainian pastor christened, for as it happened, the Calvinist minister was away and he was given the Christian name of John. This was also to be for the Ukrainian Church "the grace of God."

When the infant grew into boyhood, his father asked him one day what he would like to be and little John replied boldly at once, "I want to be a servant of God." And so he became one. His father wanted to bring him up in the Calvinist heresy and so he sent him to the Calvinist schools and later to the Calvinist Academy in Vilno. Endowed with the highest gifts of mind and body he made great advances in eloquence and literature displaying attainments greater than his years.

Although immorality was especially great among the Calvinist youth of his time, John just as Josaphat preserved the purity of his heart and his chastity. From his earliest years he was drawn to a life of solitude, prayer and penance. Despite this, he invariably made such a profound impression by his conduct and character upon his contemporaries that his very presence precluded any immoral jokes and obscene speech.

He honored the least of his fellows wtih respect and spoke to all with gentleness and courtesy. Handsome, courageous, robust, eloquent, this exceptional young man possessed great intellectual vigor, a grip on reality and spirit of genius in enterprise, an unbreakable will, energy without rival and superb good humor above all.

During his stay in Vilno he often went to the Church of the Jesuits and listening to their sermons he was stirred by the grace of God with the desire to join the Catholic Church. His father who was a fanatic Calvinist, having discovered his liking for the Catholic Church transferred him from Vilno to the care and training of one of his friends who was a country squire on one of the estates of Prince Ostrowsky, amid splendid surroundings and crowds of courtiers. Having placed him on the estate at the court which seethed with the hatred of all that was Catholic, he thought that his son too would learn to hate Catholicism but the reverse happened.

Madame Ostrowsky often arranged discussions between the Catholics and Schismatics. Attending at one time such a debate, led by the schismatics and answered by the Jesuits, Rutsky was all the more convinced that the truth is found on the side of the Catholics.

After the death of his father his mother also an enthusiastic Calvinist sent him to Prague to finish his studies and according to her expectations to affirm himself in Calvinism.

Here his powers were still more brilliantly developed. His features and bearing, his keen eyes and grave demeanor marked him as a person of distinction. His princely character invariably overawed his enemies and charmed his friends.

It was while in Prague that he actually became a Catholic. Here he found himself among fanatic Hussites and having convinced himself of their mistaken faith once more turned to the Jesuits. He attended one of their retreats for several days, made profession of the Catholic faith and requested acceptance into their Order but some strange obstacle prevented him from carrying out this intention. He was not the man to do anything by halves. When he gave himself to God he did so wholly. He yearned most passionately to enter into the study of the doctrine of holiness in the Catholic Church.

When his mother learned of it, in spite of all his efforts to win her over, she denied him further support at the university.

At this time Rev. Boksa returned from Rome to Vilno and becoming acquainted with Rutsky, persuaded him to go to Rome and enter the Brotherhood of Athanasius. Possessing an ambitious and energetic personality, Rutsky set out for Rome on foot after obtaining papers of introduction. He could, of course, have undertaken the journey in comparative comfort, having still at his disposal about a hundred Hungarian ducats, but he divided the money between himself and a penniless friend who was also on his way to Rome.

At Rome he was accepted without any difficulty by the Brotherhood of St. Athanasius. It was the custom of the Brotherhood to demand of all who entered to make their vow in and adhere to the Eastern Rite.

John noted the great disrespect into which the Eastern Rite had fallen in Vilno and not feeling himself called to it, refused to make the vow. For a time he was permitted to stay without making the vow. In the meantime, John with his insatiable thirst for learning applied himself to his studies with great earnestness and when he was finishing the course, Rev. Boksa, his sponsor, returned to Rome. He tried to persuade John to take the vows of the Eastern Rite. When he failed in this, he appealed directly to Pope Clementine VIII and having convinced him of what great value John could be to the Union through his studies, asked him to speak to John about it personally.

Clementine VIII in a few days called Rev. Boksa and John for an audience.

"John," said the Holy Father, "we want you to accept the

Eastern Rite and take your vows in it." These words struck John like a thunderbolt and falling upon his knees before the Pope, he exclaimed in tears, "But, Holy Father! I can't accept the Eastern Rite!"

"John," interrupted the Pope, without letting him finish, "Wc want you to make the vow to accept the Eastern Rite!" For the reason that he judged him correctly, that Rutsky was endowed with a fine understanding, the Holy Father evidently concluded that he would have the power to withstand the work since he hesitated so long in giving his word.

Rutsky pleaded further, "Holy Father! I was born a heretic. I attended the schools of heretics. Since the grace of God led me to the Catholic Church, I have lived according to the Latin Rite. In this Rite I want to continue until I die. I don't even know the Ukrainian alphabet."

But the Pope replied shortly, "John, in the name of Holy Obedience, I order you to give up the Latin Rite and accept the Eastern Rite."

The audience was at an end and Rutsky, overcome by tears fled from the audience chamber. However, in a few days, he made the vow ordered by the Holy Father. After his first sense of disappointment wore off, he determined to give up all for the glory of God and not another murmur was heard from him at an event which shaped and gave efficacy to the main work of his life.

When Rutsky returned to Vilno from Rome in 1593 and introduced himself to the Metropolitan Ipaty Poty, he accepted Rutsky very coolly and did not feel at all inclined to ordain him though educated clergy were very scarce. As Rutsky himself wrote later, the Ukrainian people feared those educated in Rome more than the Latins themselves. The Metropolitan, prejudiced by false suspicions, feared that since Rutsky had to be persuaded by the Holy Father in Rome to take his vows in the Ukrainian Church he would not serve it faithfully until the end.

The bitterness of this personal enmity he met with perfect humility though with an aching heart, since he had made a great sacrifice for the sake of the Ukrainian Church. He always acted with dignity and courtesy in keeping with his noble birth and training.

But he suffered in his soul, still more deeply distressed, repelled by the neglected and forsaken churches and the chaos which reigned among the Ukrainian people, rent by internal dissensions.

It seemed men of the least instructed class became instigators of schism and heresies. The members of the brotherhoods were lawless, devoid of all discipline and responsibility. Heretical writings issued by these brotherhoods were in the hands of the multitude and there was immeasurable wickedness. Some had devised a pretended defense of the schism as a weapon by which they concealed their personal enmities. They pretended to hate each other only on behalf of piety.

Bishops ordained priests for money and unworthy pastors trafficked with the word of God and were hated by the multitude for their greed and rapacity. Many were so poor that being compelled to work for their own bread they had no time to teach the people. Bishops bought consecration only that they might escape the burden of military training. Worldly, avaricious and proud, they looked down with disdain upon men superior to themselves. Ignorance had spread itself over men's souls. Violent, quarrelsome, contentious, their corrupt morals rendered any serious reform among the people impossible. The Monastic Order was hardly more reputable. Having lost their sanctity the religious houses of the Order were filled with idle and debauched monks and fell into decadence. Priests warred on the bishops and those who favored the Union led martyrs' lives.

It required sincerity and enthusiasm to put up with the hardships of these disturbing elements.

"Whenever, I wanted to have a good cry over the bitterness of my fate," he said later, recalling those times, "I hurried to one of our Churches for the services and I invariably came out with tears in my eyes. Thus had schism robbed our Church of its princely robes."

His only comfort during those first years was his friendship with Josaphat who was then still in the service of the cloth merchant. He marvelled at Josaphat's sanctity, his immense compassion and ardent love for the Ukrainian Church and attachment to the Ukrainian Rite, while Josaphat gained much from Rutsky's great learning and worldly wisdom.

Shortly afterwards Rutsky went to Moscow on a mission for the Polish king Vladislav with the idea in mind of persuading the inactive Church there to join the Union. But here also he found discouragement. It seemed that at every step he encountered much heartbreak and disappointment. As silver is tried in the furnace seven times before it is purified, so God tries a human soul until it is purified of all temporary ties through suffering, passing through fire and water before it is accepted for His work. Rutsky also underwent that process of cleansing.

When Rutsky returned to Vilno from Moscow, he found Josaphat in the monastery of the Holy Trinity. St. Josaphat's affection, serenity and genial conversation comforted him in his trials, while his learning and sympathetic understanding completed a congenial friendship with the holy youth. At the beginning he visited Josaphat almost daily and later to be closer to his friend and pupil, he rented a place near the monastery. This association had a most beneficent effect on both men in finding their salvation. Their most cherished occupation was discourses on God, the faith and the Church, moral speculation which has to do with human conduct and the dialectical which trains for argumentation. In this latter

Josaphat became so skilled that there was no escaping from the force of his logic.

As testified to by Rutsky, in all these discussions Josaphat was never known to utter a sinful or an unnecessary word. Often he asked for explanations of the more difficult parts of the Church dogmas or enlightenment on the more obscure parts of the Scripture. Josaphat behaved towards Rutsky who was his elder, with due respect. Rutsky on the other hand loved and venerated St. Josaphat's holiness and his religious ascetic earnestness. There was perfect accord in the tiny book-littered room between the two modest but very great men.

Through the great love and sympathy existing between them, Josaphat benefitted not only personally but planned to aid the Basilian Order. However, Rutsky never even gave the Order a thought. As a matter of fact, he no longer desired to remain in the Eastern Rite and found ways and means to be relieved of his vow. But Josaphat did not lose hope. He realized that prayer will open heaven, that is why he prayed more fervently than ever. Rutsky was then considering which of the Orders he would enter, the Jesuits or the barefooted Carmaelites. He liked both Orders. But this was not the will of God. While thus considering which he would join, he suddenly made a decision that surprised all by accepting the plain black robes of the Basilian Order in 1607. What caused this sudden change in Rutsky?

The historian Susha says: "While Rutsky considered which one of the Latin Orders he would enter, he was attending Mass one Sunday in the Church of the Jesuit Fathers. The sermon was preached that day by the Rev. Fabrician. When he had finished speaking and was about to come down from the pulpit, he suddenly turned to the assembled and added: 'Dear Brethren, I invite you all to an important ceremony a week from today. John William Rutsky, well-known to you all will enter into the Basilian Order at the monastery of the Holy Trinity.' "

Rutsky upon hearing these words rushed to the provincial of the Jesuits to make the complaint that the Rev. Fabrician had publicly insulted him.

In the meantime Rev. Fabrician was trying to exonerate himself by stating that he did not remember having said any such thing after the sermon. Nonetheless, they all insisted that they had heard the invitation. It ended by Rutsky recognizing in it God's intervention and bowed to the will of God so that actually within a week, on the 29th of September 1607, together with five other novitiates, he accepted the black robes of the Order of St. Basil in the Church of the Holy Trinity and four months later made his vows, changing his Baptismal name to that of Joseph. He remained thereafter the obedient son of the Ukrainian Church. What arguments, pleadings and influence of others could not accomplish, St. Josaphat's prayers did. Who could then measure Josaphat's joy in having obtained for his beloved Basilian Order such an enlightened man as a guide for himself and his companions.

Together they began the work of reforming the Order upon the solid and enduring basis of sacrifice, suffering and self-abnegation, each monk to be a living channel by which grace might flow to the souls of men so that drawn by the wounds suffered for the sake of divine love in the servants of the Crucified Lord the multitudes might be converted and return to the true Church. Rutsky's tact, kindness, penetrating knowledge of men, love of souls, fitted him admirably to teach and instruct them in a science of being which taught a loving knowledge of God. He enlightened and enkindled their souls with love, leading them step by step until there was no other thought or desire than to conform to the mind and will of God in service to humanity.

Rutsky brought to the Order a deeply educated mind,

knowledge of the world, its aims and ways, acquaintance with the ascetic life of the Western monks and in addition, he possessed a genius for organization and a powerful, unbreakable will which admitted of no obstacles. Josaphat reflected the mystic asceticism of the East, devotion to his own rite, self-mortification, angelic purity and the many other graces which are the glory of every monastic order. Being of one mind and one aim, they joined forces for the accomplishment of their purpose, pooling the same ardors, troubles, hopes, in the face of a same future, the training of novices.

Rutsky taught them the fundamentals of the faith, the path to mastery of the inner, spiritual life, Latin and Ukrainian, while Josaphat taught them to love the services, the rite and the divine virtue of which he was himself a living example. Thus their time was divided to best advantage between prayer, study and work, yet contact was made and kept with the outside world, for the Order of St. Basil is an active one.

The monastery of the Holy Trinity was practically in ruins. There was not room for many monks. Thereupon Rutsky sacrificed his personal fortune for the rebuilding of the monastery. The Latin Bishop Woyna also gave his valuable assistance to the work. Before long, eight monks could live comfortably in the monastery.

Joseph Rutsky was an extraordinary personality, a phenomenon. His fine breadth of shoulders and powerful voice marked him out as one destined to command, a personality strikingly contrasted with St. Josaphat's. They admired and imitated one another, each finding in the other something of value to complement his own personality.

It seemed as if life in the monastery could go on now without disturbance while they trained a crack regiment of soldiers which would shake the parish clergy from their torpor, wage war against schism and root out the middle-class mentality which was responsible for the spiritual lethargy of the people, but Hell in the meantime also prepared new snares to impede the work of God.

CHAPTER VIII

THE BEGINNING OF THE PUBLIC MINISTRATIONS AND PERSECUTIONS OF ST. JOSAPHAT

Josaphat remained by himself a long time, for he realized that only in being by himself can a monk acquire the strength and power for the spiritual battle with himself and the enemies of salvation. During his first years as a monk, he seldom left his cell, giving himself up entirely to study and self-perfection in virtue and the mastery of the inner life, although he had already gained a reputation for holiness and could have performed a useful service to the Church.

Having now a guide and teacher he felt himself strengthened and worked more and more for the salvation of others. Especially, since he had become deacon it was his duty to preach the word of God and to help the priests with the ministration to souls. These were the first steps taken by the future champion of the Union. He learned first how to handle the weapons with which, when the proper opportunity presented itself, he would wage the battle in behalf of St. Peter's See. Henceforth, he went into town more frequently and met with common people. He mingled with them, asked questions, instructed them in the essential truths of the faith, speaking simply, like Jesus in the Gospel, to make himself understood. His discourses, coming from a heart that spoke to the soul softened their hard hearts and brought them to repentance. Having led them to the Church of the Holy Trinity, he thereupon asked the priests to hear their confessions.

With the schismatics he carried on discussions and disputations about the Church and St. Peter's successor and the Union of the Ukrainian Church with Rome from the beginning of the acceptance of the Catholic Faith, always backing his statements by quotations from the Sacred Books of Scripture which were used in their own churches. His speech was ardent and penetrating, dissolving all doubts so that often he brought them to the point of renouncing schism and returning to the true Catholic Church. No one could resist his charm and kindliness. His teachings in his sermons were so fresh and serene that all could find reasons to believe in divine goodness and the Union. The small group of Uniates slowly grew in number, protected under the wings of the Church of the Holy Trinity which became the center of influence for the Union.

The Schismatics were disconcerted by the increasing popularity of the Union. Their anger was all the greater because the Church of the Holy Trinity was formerly under the thumb of a brotherhood which had been in enmity with the Uniates; now it seemed as if in vengeance, it had become a center for the Uniates. The former owners tried, with the complicity of the civil authorities to take the Church away from the Uniates, but did not succeed. There were other reasons why the Schismatics were so anxious to regain ownership of the Church of the Holy Trinity.

Note:

The Church of the Holy Trinity was first built of wood. Then the father of Constantine Ostrowsky, Constantine, Sr., had the wooden structure replaced by brick. It contained the relics of several saints and martyrs such as Anthony, John and Eustasius (1345). It also had another precious treasure in its possession, a miraculous image of the Blessed Virgin Mary, which St. Luke the apostle is reputed to have painted.

They wanted to rid themselves of the new generation of Basilian monks being prepared by Josaphat and Rutsky. They sensed that these would be future warriors for the Union. That is why they were so anxious to destroy this successfully organized vanguard of the reborn Church.

When they were unable to succeed legally, they determined to do it by subterfuge. The best-loved form of warfare by the Schismatics is trickery. (John 3-20-21)

"For everyone that doeth evil hateth the light, neither cometh to the light, lest his deeds should be reproved. But he that doeth truth cometh to the light that his deeds may be made manifest, that they are wrought in God."

The opposition was headed by the archimandrite Sinchilo and the choriepiscopate of Vilno, Bartholomew Zaschinsky. These were picked, capable men. The first was a former monk and the latter a priest from the diocese of Peremysl who because of a bad reputation had to flee the authorities. Deprived of their means of making a living, they threw themselves at the mercy of the Metropolitan Poty, pretending repentance and begged for quarter.

Because there was a shortage of priests the Metropolitan was willing to accept their promise of good behavior. At the beginning they showed sincerity in promoting the work of the Union so that he appointed the first as archimandrite and the second as choriepiscopate of Vilno.

Since a change of fortune had made schism more popular they obtained first place in the ranks of its leadership. This was how they repaid the Metropolitan for his kindness.

At a conference held with the Church brotherhood they agreed to get rid of Rutsky at any cost, to disperse the monks and Josaphat, who because of his reputation for holiness was held in esteem by all the religious as well as the laity. They made attempts to entice Josaphat into joining forces with them.

Samuel having found in Josaphat beside his holiness, gentleness and obedience, took upon himself the task of inducing him to join their ranks.

In order for this plan to succeed it would be necessary to first part the two friends, to remove Rutsky who through his great learning had a powerful influence on Josaphat and the other young monks.

In May 1608, the archimandrite sent Rutsky on a supposedly important mission some twenty miles distant from Vilno. Hardly had Rutsky left town when Samuel sent for Josaphat. Present also were the choriepiscopate and the president of the brotherhood.

Being fully aware of his love for the Ukrainian Church, they decided to approach him on that basis. "Come to us," said they, "for the sake of our Ukrainian Church, the Rite and language of which the Metropolitan disapproves, desiring to convert us all to the Latin Rite. Consider our sorrowing Mother Church. Come to her aid! The Ancient Slavonic is in danger of being displaced. If you join forces with us, we will be able to defend it."

To which Josaphat answered briefly and modestly, "My assistance to you will be of little value. Father Rutsky will oppose you and spoil your plans."

"There's nothing to be afraid of," replied the schismatics. "If you are with us we will find ways and means of getting rid of Rutsky once and for all and banish him from Vilno." But their promises, pleas and flattery were of no avail, Josaphat remained resolute. Sinchilo, infuriated that his plan had failed, slapped Josaphat in the face. Josaphat suffered this insult quietly and departed sadly deploring their stupidity and their rage and to avoid being praised, said nothing of his experience to anyone. Not until three years later did Rutsky learn of it. (Note: "Life of St. Josaphat" by Korsak, Chapter XX.)

The archimandrite had another plan, before Rutsky returned to get rid of his pupils. He took advantage of the fact that St. Josaphat was very obedient to the rules of the monastery and planned in that way to carry out his nefarious scheme. The demon is not lacking in ideas to ensnare the human soul.

While Rutsky was away Josaphat was in charge of the novitiate. One day the archimandrite rode out into the courtyard of the monastery and commanded Josaphat to send all the monks out to meet Rutsky, their teacher.

He thought that without his companions it would be easier to persuade Josaphat to join the schism and besides he had other schismatic candidates who were to take the place of Rutsky's novices as soon as they left. Josaphat divined at once the reason for the archimandrite's command, while he felt at the same time that as a monk he was obliged to obey this command since it did not interfere either with the will of God or the rules of the Order. Not knowing what to do under the circumstances, Josaphat appealed to Rev. Fabrician of the Jesuit Order for advice, who suspected immediately what it signified and urged Josaphat to send a messenger at once with a letter to Rutsky requesting his prompt return for every delay could cause great harm to the Union. He also wrote a letter to Rutsky from himself.

Rutsky was ill with malaria when the messenger arrived, but as soon as he read the letter he rose with difficulty from his sick bed and made haste in his return journey to Vilno. While travelling, he was again seized with an attack of the illness, but he continued the journey despite his suffering. When he came in sight of the city of Vilno, he began to sing in a weak voice, "We praise the Father, Son and Holy Ghost." He had not yet arrived at the gates of the city when the illness left him by the grace of God. Thus Rutsky's sudden return frustrated the archimandrite's plans.

In the evening Sinchilo returned to the monastery certain that Josaphat had obeyed his command. He was beside himself with rage when he noticed the monks busy with their usual occupations. He accused Josaphat bitterly of disobedience. But Josaphat answered quietly, "It was not necessary to send the youths away because Father Rutsky has returned."

His news silenced Sinchilo at once as he feared to make a stand against Rutsky openly realizing that such a man of wide experience and great knowledge had powerful friends to back him in the city.

Rutsky and Josaphat were fully convinced of Sinchilo's leaning to Schism and complained through letters to the Metropolitan who was then staying in Warsaw. The Metropolitan unable to return at once and at the same time without power to remove Sinchilo and Bartholomew without proper legal sanction, appointed Rutsky as his assistant or Vicar general for the Ukrainians in Lithuania, with the command to have the leaders of the Schismatics closely watched. In addition, he put the management of the property of the monastery into Rutsky's hands, so he stayed on, more firmly established than before the effort to dislodge him and his novices.

For a while both leaders were inactive but soon Sinchilo displayed his hostility publicly. It was at the beginning of winter 1608. Sinchilo was celebrating a feast day Liturgy with the assistance of some of the young Basilian Fathers. When at the Great Entrance the deacon sang, "Wsich was prawoslawnich Kristian da pomanit Hospod Boh wo carstwi swoim," Sinchilo should have then mentioned the name of the Metropolitan Ipaty Poty in a prayer out loud, but he failed to do so. Everyone wondered at this but they thought at first it was just a mistake.

After the blessing of the Holy Gifts, Sinchilo was again

supposed to sing, "First of all God bless His Excellency Metropolitan Ipaty Poty," but here he again omitted the commemoration. At this transgression of the ritual, there was of a sudden an ominous silence; it was clear to all that the archimandrite had broken off with the Metropolitan. It was his way of announcing publicly that he had renounced the Union. At once, all the clerical assistants at the Liturgy left the altar, removed their vestments as a sign of disapproval of the archimandrite's rebellion against the Metropolitan.

This incident plainly demonstrated to all the machinations of Sinchilo and at the same time was indicative of a showdown battle in the near future.

How highly St. Josaphat was regarded by the circle of Schismatics and how distressing was their failure to win him over can best be measured by the fact that although their plans to shake his loyalty to the Union had already failed twice, they planned yet a third scheme, through the townspeople themselves to win over Josaphat.

Three of the townsmen took upon themselves this task. Under the pretense of an important matter of business, one of them invited Josaphat to his house.

Josaphat not suspecting anything foul, set out with a companion to the townsman's home. However, as soon as Josaphat was in the house, they pushed his companion out the door and locked it. Then they fell at Josaphat's feet and pleaded humbly: "We know that you love God and honor Him and that you love your people and their Rite. The time has come for the Ukrainian Church to be restored to its former power. You are the corner stone and keystone and this will come to pass at your command. All of the Ukrainian priesthood esteems you and has put all its faith and trust in you. Don't be the cause of its disunity. Return to the Ukrainian faith and you will assure the salvation of the gentry as well as the common people."

They fell at his feet again and kissed them, repeating their request. Josaphat was unprepared for the event and at first did not know what to say. But having composed himself, he answered them fearlessly, that such matters should be discussed with the Reverend Rutsky and the Metropolitan.

When the townsmen saw that their humble pleas were of no avail in shaking his decision, they determined to use the force of threats to attain their ends. One of them stood by the door while the other drawing closer to Josaphat, threatened to kill him if he would not agree to their plans. The moment was dangerous, Josaphat not expecting a martyr's end so soon delayed his decision by answering them cautiously that such an important matter needed at least some forethought and inspiration from God and promised to give them his answer the next day.

The townsmen agreed to it with the understanding that if he did not concede to their plans he must leave town within a week or risk certain death.

In the meantime, word had reached the seminary of the attempt on Josaphat's life. Fearful for Josaphat's safety, Rutsky and his companions were planning what action they should take when Josaphat returned and his first words were, "I return from hell where I heard the speech of Satan who is trying to persuade me to leave my faith."

The next day when he did not answer them, they wrote him another more urgent letter inviting him to their side, which he answered, "I promised to first consult God for guidance and this I did. And God answered me: (Psalm 20:12-13)

" 'For they intended evil against thee; they imagined a mischievous device which they are unable to perform:'

"And he assured me of safety with these words:

" 'Therefore, shalt thou make them turn their back, when thou shalt make ready thine arrows upon thy strings against them.'

94

"Therefore, you had better let me alone."

Whereupon they sent him another, more threatening letter, if he failed to come to an agreement with them, but Josaphat made no further reply.

He then went to Church and falling upon his face, according to his habit, before God, he pleaded for guidance and the return to the right path for his tempters and while thus in prayer, he heard a voice from heaven: (Psalm 1-1)

"Blessed is the man that walketh not in the council of the ungodly nor standeth in the way of sinners, nor sitteth in the seat of the scornful."

When the Schismatics realized the futility of subverting or undermining Josaphat in his faith or taking over the Church of the Holy Trinity by subterfuge, they decided to use force in accomplishing the deed.

In December 1608, the workers of iniquity gathered at the house of one of their most prominent members and under the direction of Sinchilo and Bartholomew, they voted to break off all relations with the Metropolitan and to place themselves under the authority of the Byzantine patriarch.

Also on the following Sunday, during Matins, when the monks come out into the center of the Church at the Great Offering, ranged in long array on each side, when the "Gloria in Excelsis" is sung, to fall upon them and throw them out of the Church and thereafter to take possession of the Church and the monastery.

The plan was decided upon well in advance. In the meantime a Catholic Uniate city official was informed of the plot by one of his employees and he at once reported to Demeter Karpo, the assistant "voyevod," who brought the matter to the attention of his superior, Radzival. Karpo was thereupon ordered to surround the monastery with his soldiers and to notify Rutsky. He also addressed a threatening letter to Sinchilo and Bartholomew, stating that they would have to answer to the "Voyevod" for any disturbance occurring in the city and in addition ordered the arrest of the townsmen who had threatened Josaphat with death.

After the collapse of their intrigue, the Schismatics became more violent in their hatred. While there was still a chance to win him over to their side, they praised Josaphat to the heavens. They praised his holiness, piety, humility, purity, chastity, his conspicuous faith in the Holy Scriptures and his loving use of it in their Rite. They said that they would kiss his footprints, if only he would join them, but now having lost hope of ever being able to break his steadfast adherence to the Catholic faith, they insulted and assaulted him. Whenever he appeared in town they threw stones, mud and a hail of curses after him and called him "Stupid," "traitor," "renegade" and "imposter." But Josaphat knew how to bear it for his soul's profit. He realized that sanctity thrives under stress of opposition. He recalled the words of the Master Jesus (Matthew 5-11)

"Blessed are ye when men shall revile you and persecute you and shall say all manner of evil against you falsely for my sake." That is why he did not despair but was glad, that he was able for the sake of Christ and unity of the Church, to bear these small sufferings.

His face was covered with tears when he learned that Sinchilo and Bartholomew had found ready credence for their Schism and had goaded the priests of one of the largest Ukrainian churches in Vilno into publicly renouncing the Union, declaring themselves free of any further allegiance to the Metropolitan Ipaty Poty and placing themselves under the authority of the Byzantine Orthodox patriarch. This transaction they requested to be placed on the city records, which showed plainly that they cared nothing for the faith of the Fathers. Thus, gradually all the churches, except that of the Holy Trinity, passed into the hands of the Schismatics, legally, or by fraudulent means.

Those who will not accept the ordinances of the Church elected by God, He gives over unto a reprobate mind and because they resist the command of God, they receive not the love of the truth. God sends them strong delusion that they should believe a lie and have not the sense of guilt of disobedience in Schism. All Schism arises because men have revolted against the authority of the See of St. Peter, whom the Lord constituted after Himself Shepherd of the Church and guardian of the faith and morals.

The intestine dissensions of the Schismatics made them an object of ridicule and sorrow to good Christians. For the years the contest against heresy lasted, it has been declared that more evils happened than were recorded to have taken place since the foundation of the Christian Church in Ukraine.

Who must answer to God for these souls already soiled so hopelessly? What effort had ever been made to save them? What would become of them if they went on ignorant of the elemental truth that their salvation was in the Catholic faith. It seemed to Josaphat this was the task God had assigned to him. If religion still lived in the hearts of the people, the elite had defected in a body. It was a great day for charlatans. Sects, half-political, half-religious, mushroomed everywhere. Then as now souls, overcome with a thirst for God, were being led astray.

Putting this tragic incident aside, he flung himself into his work with greater vigor and effort. He strove for greater perfection in holiness and in study, in the rule and direction of the great monastic and mission work already set in motion and thus prepared himself for the arduous task. Naturally highly gifted, he was quick in understanding and sound in his judgment. Writings left by him verify this. The life spent in constant study and austere mortification of the senses, so conditioned his retentive powers that once he had read or heard something, it became a part of him as if chiseled on stone so that he never forgot or lost track of it.

Instead of isolating him from enjoyment and interest in his fellow man, it aided him in the pursuit of both. He felt a deficiency in not having a higher education. He did not know Latin, which was the language in which the most valuable books of that period were printed, but even such a difficulty was bridged over by persons truly devoted to the work of God, such as Rev. Valentine Fabrician and Rev. Grushevsky, who explained everything to him in the vernacular. Josaphat progressed quickly in his studies so that he was easily able to expound even the most obscure and difficult passages of dogma.

By his devotion and self-control, fortified by grace and prayer, he became a classical example of what God can do with men. During all this troubled time, amid the calamities which came over the Ukrainian Church, he did not neglect his duties as a deacon. He preached and wrote, regulated the services of his own church and improved its appearance as befits the House of God.

The Congregation for the Spread of the Faith, reinforced by facts taken from the reports of his teachers, gave the following account of St. Josaphat's studies: "His course of studies had been brilliant. He spoke well and possessed a remarkable intelligence. He was an authority on the knowledge of the Holy Trinity and enjoyed a peculiar insight into the profound truths of faith which astounded many of his teachers who were at a loss to explain them. This phenomenal faculty of apprehension of abstruse truths was a special gift of the Holy Spirit."

The love that burned in St. Josaphat for his people, Church and rite was so deeply rooted in him and so powerfully active as to save and transmit grace to others because he drew from the eternal goodness of God the assistance of a plenitude of gifts through his divine love of Jesus Christ which possesses all those who are purged of stain and whereby they become sons of God through sanctifying grace. "He that raised up

Christ from the dead shall also quicken your mortal bodies by His Spirit that dwelleth in you." The spirit of love diffused itself over the audience by his mere approach consoling every heart with divine peace.

It was amazing the sureness with which he could unravel the most delicate and obscure cases of conscience, a gift implanted by the Holy Ghost of which thousands of confessors could take advantage for the salvation of their souls. However, the power that he borrowed from God was also linked up intimately with suffering in his own person.

Simple was Josaphat in person and appearance as well as gentle. His one soutane was worn threadbare and as for his great peasant boots he patched them endlessly as long as the patches would hold together. Nonetheless, he walked with a firm gait and erect carriage. Although he was ever a gentleman in manner and appearance, he preferred to give an example of evangelical poverty, as befitted a representative of Christ. He was tall, very slim, with a mass of curly hair and penetrating but very gentle gaze from wonderfully brilliant gray eyes. His heart was filled with the unspeakable joy that one experiences in belonging to God and this he tried to communicate to all.

He recited quotations from the Gospel with such humility, charm and assurance to back his arguments for Union that it left no room for discussion or dispute. A marvelous renewal of religion followed all his sermons which revealed the secret way of happiness, giving back hope to men of peace in their homes and hearts by the reception of the Holy Spirit in the Holy Eucharist as transmitted by priests ordained by the Apostolic See.

CHAPTER IX

THE DISPUTE BETWEEN THE SCHISMATICS AND UNIATES

The Schismatics now flung themselves into an open battle with the Uniates. Sinchilo, together with his friend Bartholomew, after publicly announcing their separation from the Catholic Church, sent their accomplices throughout the entire diocese to convince and induce the priesthood and their congregations to rebel against the Metropolitan and the Union.

Upon unstable souls vacillating like waves of the sea, the winds of Schismatic dispute beat with terrible force. It was not surprising that recently converted masses and the priesthood not yet firmly established in the Catholic faith, lived in ignorance of the elemental truths on which their salvation depended and readily joined the schism, surrendering their Churches into its hands. The Brotherhood of Vilno, one of the wealthiest in Ukraine, printed pious pamphlets written in a peevish tone by ignorant and rash Heretics attacking in God's name the most devout practices of the Catholic Church, which it distributed throughout the land in protest against the Metropolitan and the Union. In addition to this, the Brotherhood collected funds with which to finance fresh recruits for the Schismatic Church.

When the Metropolitan was informed of the spread of the rebellion, he ordered the suspension of Sinchilo, but thinking in the kindness of his heart that Sinchilo might repent, he refrained from having the order carried out and requested him instead to appear before him in person to justify his actions. Sinchilo answered with new threats.

Thus rebuffed and reviled, the Metropolitan suspended him from his position as archimandrite and ordered his excommunication. Then he sent an order to the city magistrates to restore the churches which were illegally obtained by the Schismatics. But they would not heed this order. All awaited the outcome of the new session of the Assembly, after which many predicted the return to Schism. And they were not mistaken.

King Sigmund was one of the kings who was most friendly to the Union. He recognized in it not a political but purely religious matter. He had clear and well deliberated convictions of his own on the importance of Catholic truths as well as being influenced by the Pope of Rome. For this reason he backed those who were adherents to the Union whenever he could. At that time, however, finding himself in difficult straits, in order to get the backing of the hostile Polish gentry for the war, whose opposition had to be surmounted, he had to proceed cautiously. The Schismatics profited by the extremity in which the king found himself and having on their side influential friends and money for bribery of officials and gentry, they obtained what they wanted. The result was that the Assembly passed a decree conferring the same right to the Uniates and the schismatics to keep the churches they held, together with all properties connected with them in their possession at the time of the decree, regardless of whether they were obtained legally or not before the time of the Assembly, with a clause to the effect that if either side failed to abide by the decision peacefully, it was to pay a fine of ten thousand silver marks for any disturbance. The king was forced to sign this decree.

The schismatics received the news with exultation. They secured the advantage by this decision for practically all of the Ukrainian Churches in Lithuania were in their hands.

Of the senators and representatives who were Catholics, only the Ukrainian Metropolitan Ipaty Poty raised his voice in protest to demand justice. "A judgment has been passed against us," he exclaimed, "without due process of law or defense of our rights, which is the right even of criminals and evil doers! We suffer humiliation because we struggle for unity and peace, while our adversaries profit by their chaos and rebellion. They are permitted to join with the Protestants against us Catholics but we are not permitted to join forces with other Catholics in order to live in peace.

"Gentlemen and senators, we don't ask for favors, we do not even shield ourselves behind Canonical Law, the right to which you cannot deny us; we are even prepared to pay the fine, but we beg you in the name of justice to discover the truth before passing such a damaging sentence upon us.

"We requested the king and the hearing committee to hear our side and that of our adversaries for reconciliation of differences but we were not given this opportunity. Twice we came to answer accusations and twice we were insulted and repelled but there was no examination of the facts in this case which would form the basis of a successful mediation."

This speech of the champion for the rights of the Union stirred the hearts of a few of the gentry.

The Latin bishop Woyna, having been an eye-witness to all the injustices which had been brought about by Schism against the Union lamented the flagrant perversion of justice.

It was after his appeal to the king and the Assembly that the clause was added to the effect that if either side, after the year 1507 should find itself deprived of justice, it could appeal to the Ecclesiastical Tribunal. Despite this added clause, the Uniates were defrauded for they were forced to resort to the courts of law to win back their losses. Endless litigations, opposition and infinite contradictions and disappointments were encountered, meanwhile the Schismatics were free to seize the revenues of the properties and churches taken from the Uniates.

Under this decree, the excommunicated Sinchilo could also return to his post as archimandrite until he was removed by court order after due process of the law. Opposition and calumny had not hindered Poty from a strenuous administration of his diocese. He at once informed King Sigmund of it, requesting him to appoint Rutsky in Sinchilo's place.

The Metropolitan thereupon called Rutsky to Warsaw and gave him his appointment together with the documents from the king confirming his appointment and commanding the city officials to turn over the management of the Uniate Churches and all their properties, according to the decree of the Assembly, into his hands. The threat of new persecutions caused Rutsky to return to Vilno without delay. But upon the reading of the king's proclamation, the city arose in rebellion. The officials who were Schismatic and friendly to Sinchilo not only refused to obey the command but backed the insurrection.

Also the excommunicated Sinchilo came to the rebellious town, celebrated the Feast Day Mass and announced publicly in Church, that the decree of the Assembly had given him the right to return as the archimandrite and stated that he would forcibly take over the Church of the Holy Trinity. And on the 9th of March 1609, on the Feast Day of the Forty Martrys, Sinchilo, with an armed troop behind him hastened to the Church of the Holy Trinity. When the choir had stopped singing Rutsky came out of the Church, followed by Josaphat and the other monks. They were about to demand of Sinchilo the meaning of the attack when all at once the troop disbanded as if faced by an army.

All were at a loss as to the cause of the sudden retreat. The historian Korsak claims that the holy and gifted Basilian nun, Basilicia Sapizanka, engrossed in prayer during the period of the attack, was in spirit taken to the front of the Church of the Holy Trinity and saw St. Basil, together with his Forty Martyrs in full armour confronting the Schismatics. When the Schismatics saw this miracle they fled in terror. Subsequently this became the subject for a painting hung over the door of the Church to commemorate the occasion.

Sinchilo took the matter to court. In the court, out of forty members of the jury, there were only twelve Catholics, therefore, it was not surprising that Sinchilo won the case. He was given the right to be archimandrite and the Metropolitan was relieved of his jurisdiction and Rutsky was removed from his position as archimandrite. When the Metropolitan was informed of the treachery, he brought the entire matter before the Ecclesiastical Tribunal as matters pertaining to the Church were involved on which the civil court had no right to make a decision.

The king appointed as his proxy for the hearing the Prime Minister, Leo Sapiha, a man highly esteemed for his wisdom and scrupulous justice. He had the entire matter investigated and wrote out an order to the magistrates to return all the Churches to the Metropolitan and reaffirmed Rutsky in his position as archimandrite. In addition, he punished the Schismatics with a fine of ten thousand marks for breach of the peace.

Samuel Sinchilo and Bartholomew were sentenced to be exiled for insurrection against the king and the rightful

Metropolitan. Thereupon, all the Churches were restored to the Metropolitan. To the Schismatics only one Church remained, that of the Holy Ghost, which they had built at their own expense.

The Schismatics determined to take vengeance on the Metropolitan. The whole city was in an uproar against the rightful shepherd. It happened at the time that the king was staying in the city with a number of senators. Nevertheless, the Schismatics persuaded a hireling, John Tupeka, to make an attempt on the life of the Metropolitan. For this loathsome deed the Schismatic priests gave him their blessings even holding a prayer service for the success of their evil plot. The day the Metropolitan was returning from a conference with the Papal Nuncio in the company of friends and attendants, in the center of town, the would-be murderer fell upon him. The Metropolitan shielded himself from the blow with the staff he held in his left hand but the attacker broke the staff with his sword and cut off three fingers from the hand with its bishop's ring and also the double golden chain on which was suspended the Metropolitan's cross, slashing his clothing to the skin.

The force of the blow caused the Metropolitan to fall to the ground in a faint. At first it was thought that he was dead. After an anxious moment strength returned to the old man. He came to himself and thanked God that he could shed a little blood for the sake of God's work as a true servant of God, putting no trust in his good deeds, nor expecting justification for his works, but placing his only hope in the compassion of God, who stayed him even in this emergency.

By the will of God the assailant was apprehended although, in the ensuing chaos he could easily have gotten away. He readily admitted that he wanted to kill the Metropolitan out of religious zeal, convinced that he was doing a good deed and according to the practice he was tortured but would not divulge any further facts in connection with the attempted murder.

A man of firm principle, pitiless to himself, he was unwearied in his love of souls. Full of gentleness, he pleaded for mercy for his would-be assassin but he was ignored and the guilty one was sentenced to death by being torn apart in four sections.

As soon as the news had spread of the attempt on his life, the Metropolitan received many messages and visits of solicitude. Although no name had been more hated among the people at that time, no ingratitude drove him to relax his efforts.

Josaphat and Rutsky who had been in his company, took the fingers that were cut off and brought them to the Church of the Holy Trinity, placing them on the altar, as an initial offering of the blood of martyrdom for the attainment of Union, singing the hymn while they did so, "We Praise the Holy Trinity of God."

Josaphat, recently ordained a priest, hurried to the prison when he had learned of the sentence of the assailant. Obtaining permission from the authorities, he found Tupeka in despair awaiting his horrible death. Full of Apostolic zeal for the salvation of souls of the condemned, he spoke to him with such persuasive gentleness and sweetness that the grace with which the words were spoken brought the guilty one to his knees and almost without knowing it, he made the sign of the cross for the first time in years and not only confessed his guilt but with great sorrow made confession of all of his sins and prepared for his death. Josaphat's sense of the kinship of all human beings would not permit him to leave the man until death. Just before his execution Josaphat comforted him by urging him to accept his death as atonement for his evil deed and to expect a better life after death.

Thus ended the strife between the Uniates and Schismatics led by Sinchilo and his companions in Vilno. Sinchilo and

Bartholomew were exiled and the Schismatics defeated and angry held sullenly aloof for a while after their final evil venture. Even the proud Brotherhood calmed down, not daring to raise its voice in defense of the schism. But Ukraine had yet to pass through much tribulation before the Union took deep root among the people.

CHAPTER X

ST. JOSAPHAT AS A PRIEST

At the age of thirty, and five years after his entry into the Basilian Order, Josaphat was ordained a priest by the Metropolitan Ipaty Poty.

"Seek ye first the Kingdom of God and His righteousness and all things else shall be added unto you."

St. Josaphat had trained and disciplined himself in secret by prayer and penance to the exclusion of all desires, so that fortified against all which could impede his union with God he might receive the sublime gift of contemplation and thus become a living channel by which grace would flow to the souls of his people. Imbued with the Holy Spirit he became immersed in his Apostolic labors in the fulfillment of his life's work and the desire of the Blessed Saviour: (John 17-11)

"And now I am no more in the world, but these are in the world and I come to Thee. Holy Father, keep through Thine own name those whom Thou hast given me, that they may be one as we are."

Up to this time, as a deacon, his work had been restricted in the capacity of assisting at liturgical functions. Now as a priest his special and peculiar care was that those entrusted to him would enjoy the spiritual guidance of a tried and learned master.

He was above petty hatred towards anyone. He was prepared to love his enemies and to lay down life itself, if occasion should demand it. He began publicly, through his sermons to tear down the erroneous teachings of the Schismatics.

He was most effective in bringing out the truths of the Catholic faith so that the Schismatics themselves might be convinced by quoting them from the teachings of the Holy Fathers of the Eastern Church and from the books of Scripture acknowledged and in use by the Schismatic churches to which the Schismatics never bothered to refer or try to understand. All during his sermons the Church of the Holy Trinity was crowded to overflowing not only by the faithful who came to strengthen themselves in the faith but also by the Schismatics who attended out of curiosity.

No one could resist his kindliness and persuasive eloquence; his teachings were fresh, clear and convincing, resolving all doubt in the greatest and simplest minds. He continuously moved the hearts of men unknown to him by the force of his genuine zeal and sincerity.

The Schismatics, seeing that many persons convinced by his teachings were returning to the Church, invited Josaphat to debate with the best of their speakers and preachers, but the mere opening of St. Josaphat's lips was enough to send them away abashed and ashamed pondering in their hearts the source of such power and force in his teachings.

When Christ is our one master, the spirit comes to teach us all things. St. Paul said, "He that raised up Christ from the dead, shall also quicken your mortal bodies by His spirit that dwelleth in you. Ye are built for an habitation of God by the Spirit."

He often came down from the pulpit, his face streaming with tears, to mingle with those who thronged about him. The subtle and manifold assaults of the heretics bore in upon him from all sides in the sacristy, the nave of the Church and the street. The crowds jostled, pulled this way and that but he never for an instant lost his smile, gentleness or the genuineness of his courtesy in responding. The truths rose almost miraculously to his lips when contending with the Heretics. For every clever argument he had an answer and for every obscure truth he had an enlightening explanation. He quoted the books of the Gospel with such humility and assurance that they were overpowered by its compelling clarity. "One could easily call him a walking encyclopedia, a 'living library' or treasury of the writings of the Holy Fathers of the Eastern Church," said one of his biographers. Both his sermons and his debates with the Schismatics bespoke the same earnestness and indefatigable zeal bearing the imprint of divine love. His disposition remained unruffled and he was at all times mindful of the amenities and niceties of life.

His greatest pleasure was to teach the simple people neglected by the Schismatic priesthood. Many of them hardly knew the Lord's prayer or any other of the prayers and truths of the faith. The faith of the multitude was sorely tried by the upheavel which ensued as a result of the purported cry of religious freedom raised by the dissident clergy and laity.

In addition, he went into the streets, the homes, into the fields, and meadows and everywhere taught the truths of the faith necessary for the salvation of souls. He spoke simply, avoiding obscurities, like Jesus in the Gospel, to make himself understood. Coming from a heart that spoke to the soul, his discourses turned men away from their sins and Schismatic contentiousness and revealed to them the happiness and serenity that one experiences in receiving the Holy Spirit through the body and blood of Christ in the Holy Eucharist and surrendering wholly to God.

Taking advantage of the unsettled state of the Eastern

110

Church, the confusion and separation which reigned supreme, the sects and Schismatics did all in their power to corrupt and terrorize men's minds against all restraint and compulsion in the name of liberty and cultural progress. A passion for liberty at all costs had spread among the people, arousing them to rebellion against all established, traditional powers, particularly that of the Church of Rome. If they were to throw overboard the traditional faith of their forefathers, how could an enraged mob know where to stop? Would not God be thrown overboard too?

Gradually people began to listen to the gentle monk who taught them the only road to happiness. His teachings germinated silently in many hearts, restoring hope to men and the strength to return to the Church of their forefathers.

Sometimes when Josephat remarked to a Schismatic banteringly, "Even you will return," that person discovered to his amazement that he also had received the grace of God to become a Catholic. Bewildered by the prestige and power of Josaphat, the Schismatic priests forbade their adherents to attend his sermons and lectures and even to speak to him. The Catholics with pleasure called him, "the rod of the Schismatics" and the Schismatics in turn named him, "soul snatcher."

They tried by every means possible to destroy his influence. They even painted a picture of him in which the Metropolitan Ipaty Poty and Rutsky were in the vestments appropriate to their station while at their feet Josaphat was depicted as the devil with horns protruding from his head, a horrible face and a hook in his hand with which he was shown grappling after souls and this was entitled, at the bottom, "The Soul Snatcher." When Josaphat learned of the picture, he rejoiced and mocked the Schismatics saying, "God grant that I may be able to draw all of your souls to Him."

His work did not concern itself entirely with the conversion of the Schismatics. With no lesser zeal, he occupied

111

himself with the strengthening of the faith of the Uniates. He realized that only that soul which is devoid of sin is willing and eager to serve God and can have a great love for Christian virtue and a hatred of evil. Thus he strove to persuade the faithful as soon as possible to avail themselves of the Sacrament of Penance so that the grace of God might nourish the spiritual life in the depths of the soul and help it in overcoming those desires which hinder the soul in its early steps towards God. The Schismatic priests did not trouble themselves overmuch about the cleanliness of the consciences of their faithful, hearing confession only once a year and then hurriedly for pay. There were no clear distinctions between what was allowable and what was forbidden. They were shallow in their fervor and careless as to the welfare of the souls of their faithful.

Josaphat not only did not accept money for confessions but gave to the penitents some little token of remembrance and aid to the needy. For the burden of sin which he absolved in God's name, he made atonement with his fasts and watchings and scourging. He heard confessions every day in the Church and when he had heard all their confessions, he would hurry to the fields and meadows and there he encouraged them also to come to confession squatting down on any handy stone. And when he had so many come to confession that he was physically unable to hear them all, he went to other priests and begged them with tears in his eyes to help the poor sinners.

At one time while on a journey, he had to wait some time by the River Nimnom as the ice had become too soft to make passage safe across it to the other side. With him awaited a multitude of people. Josaphat, believing that every moment is valuable for doing what pleases God, gave them a mission and after the sermons he heard their confessions. He cured souls and bodies, reading their hearts like a book. In a short time, all with clean consciences were able to get passage across safely.

When it came to the salvation of souls, Josaphat was always there first. He was interested in everybody and everything. The most affable of souls, he could put himself in the place of others. He approached all with love and consideration. He visited all the prisons and converted the evil doers. He gladly hurried to the side of criminals sentenced to death with spiritual consolation, and he did not leave them sorrowing until he had given their souls back into God's keeping. He was more eager to go and visit the unfortunate than some people are in seeking pleasures. He was able to assist the most degraded souls with words of such miraculous power, describing to them the joys of heaven that they awaited death impatiently.

At the hospitals he attended the sick. He made their beds, served their meals and medicines. He often dressed decaying puss-filled wounds, kissing them. He tenderly nursed the dying and helped them to die. He heard their confessions and gave them Extreme Unction. By prayer and the example of his own life, he encouraged them to self-denial and a great love for God.

Whenever he heard of anyone who was sick, whether in the city or suburbs, he went at once to visit them, not heeding the danger of infection, the stench or the distance. He had a whole treasury of compassion in him and this compassion gave him a power to perform countless miracles of healing. Once he came with a companion to a poor man who was sick with gangrene. In the small house there was such a stench that it was almost impossible to enter. He prayed silently for the courage to bear without disgust or uncontrollable revulsion whatever he might hear or see. His companion, however, was unable to tolerate the stench and stayed outside. But Josaphat took him by the hand, led him

113

into the poor hut, with the words, "It is easier to stand this human stench a few moments here on earth, than the eternal burning stench of hell."

The Schismatic priests said the Mass only once a week on Sundays and sometimes they omitted even that. St. Josaphat, since he had become a priest, celebrated Mass every day, as long as the Church custom permitted it and made the offering to God of the Bloodless Sacrifice. Before each Mass he prepared himself with scourging, self-mortification and confession.

While saying Mass he was so absorbed in his office, so deeply moved by the Real Presence that he could scarcely breathe or speak. From time to time he enjoyed the phenomenon of levitation, i.e., to rise into the air without support, remaining for several minutes as though in ecstasy, miraculously suspended in the air. Pious souls often saw Josaphat surrounded by light and angels. Frequently during the time when he said "As it was from the beginning, is now and ever shall be" (Roman Catholic, "All honor and glory, world without end, Amen.") when he turned with the chalice to the congregation, they saw the Child Jesus as it rose from the chalice and blessed the people while at Josaphat's side stood an angel clothed in the vestments of a deacon. As the Apostle said, "Ye present your bodies a living sacrifice, holy, acceptable to God, which is your reasonable service."

In the winter he arose at three o'clock in the morning and in summer at two. After scourging and prayer, he awakened his brethren. He sounded the Angelus and opened the door of the Church and the monastery. He sang in the choir. He held most of the offices. He was Rutsky's assistant, the prior of the monastery, father confessor for the monks and nuns, the master of the novices and the preacher. In other words, he was the heart and soul of the monastery. It seemed as if with the increase of his tasks there was more time for their accomplishment. His intense activity never slackened. He always found time for everything, and did not neglect in that his duties as a priest or monk. He fulfilled to exactness all his offices and duties. He increased the mortification of the flesh. He scourged himself daily. One day when he was scourging himself unmercifully the monks saw a great light in his cell. Thinking it was on fire, they ran to it with water to put it out, but when they had opened the door, they saw Josaphat laying flat on the ground after the scourging, as it was his custom in the form of a cross, absorbed in prayer.

In the midst of all his duties and constant work, no one ever saw him worried. The joy of the blessed never left him but suffused itself on all who came in contact with him. Everyone who came to him never went away without a more happy spirit, not only Catholics but also the Schismatics and Heretics. His face was a constant reflection of his inner joy, the reason which could be found in his constant attunement with God. The spirit dwells in the just constantly, manifesting itself in the individual as joy and love and peace. His joy was overflowing whenever anyone left the Schism and joined the Uniate Church.

God sent him such a great joy in 1610. In that year the Muscovite patriarch Ignatius came to King Sigmund with a young Greek, Emanuel Kantakuzen, a prince of the royal family of Palaeologus, who requested permission to stay at the monastery of the Holy Trinity. He was so impressed by St. Josaphat's holiness that after a few talks with him and Rutsky, he renounced schism and after having lived a life of holiness and sacrifice for six years, he passed away at the monastery. When Emanuel renounced schism he became very much attached to Josaphat and here in secret and in silence commenced that marvelous sharing of every burden from the moment of their meeting until death. He was more retired and more reticent than Josaphat. He had no particular views about the future. He seemed to divine that his field of destiny was not of this world.

During that period there appeared in Ukraine a great enemy of the Union and especially of St. Josaphat, Melety Smotritsky. Maxim Smotritsky (that was his name before he entered one of the Schismatic monasteries) was the son of Erasma, one of the best-known managers of Prince Ostrowsky's estates. The Prince was impressed by the boy's unusual intellectual gifts and wanted to train him to be an effective adversary to the hateful Union.

In the Academy of Ostrowsky, he learned Greek and Latin under the tutorship of Kirilo Lukarisa who later became a Byzantian patriarch and carried into the Greek Church the Calvinist heresy. In the Vilno Academy of the Jesuits, he studied philosophy and at the same time that Josaphat entered the Basilian Order, he entered the Protestant Academy of Leipzig and Nuremberg to complete his studies.

Brought up by his parents in schism and prejudiced against Catholicism by his Protestant and Calvinist teachers, in addition to the golden gift of speech and capability as a writer, he was richly equipped by knowledge of both heathen and Christian literature for the part of a learned foe against the Union and the Catholic Church. However, he was quick-tempered, an unreliable and undisciplined character, permitting himself to be led by custom and instinct. He was, moreover, not fully convinced of the truth of the faith of the Schismatics but preferred to seek the higher truth. Above all things, he thirsted for power, fame and worldly acclaim.

Returning to Ukraine, he settled in Minsk, forcing that city out of the Metropolitan's authority, organized a Schismatic brotherhood for the propagation of schism and built the Church of St. Peter and Paul for the use of the Schismatics. Then not seeing any further field for his energies, he came to Vilno to make his acquaintance with members of the most powerful Schismatic brotherhood located in that city. His reputation was already extensively celebrated and was still further increased by the publication, with their assistance, of a book against the Uniates entitled, "Our Afflicted Ukrainian Church." The book, written in a bitter and cynical tone, made a great stir among the Schismatics. It was reputed to be the greatest of literary treasures which, it was advertised, the dying venerated, requesting it to be buried with them. In other words, this book became a second Bible to the Schismatics.

What its actual value was in adding to the knowledge of the Schismatics when judged by the standards of a fanatic Schismatic himself, can best be understood when Smotritsky, after his conversion, criticized the book in his "Epilogue," calling it a compilation of error and vilification.

Gradually the discord aroused by the publication and circulation of this book subsided.

The Metropolitan, Ipaty Poty, now an aged man, could not efficiently manage all the affairs of the Church himself in the growing diocese. Therefore, he appointed William Joseph Rutsky as his assistant and successor, giving him the title of Vicar General of Halich. However, Rutsky did not leave the city of Vilno but continued also to keep his position as archimandrite of the monastery of the Holy Trinity.

Josaphat rejoiced that he could continue to work under the direction of his friend, but this rejoicing did not last long. God planned it otherwise.

CHAPTER XI

ST. JOSAPHAT AS PRIOR

The number of Josaphat and Rutsky's pupils had multiplied. There were many fresh young applicants for entry under their tutelage. But for the warriors of the Union the acquisition of holiness was not sufficient, they also needed to study and acquire practical knowledge. Rutsky and Josaphat could not by themselves supply them with this added armor of defense so they made a real effort to find a place for their pupils at various schools of learning. Some of the more sympathetic Latin bishops opened the doors of their seminaries to a few of Josaphat and Rutsky's pupils. The Jesuits proved their friendship for the Ukrainian Church by accepting several students at their monasteries. Then there arose a new problem. The rooms of the monastery which had stood empty not long before, were so full that there was no more room for the new companions eager for entry. It was necessary to plan a new monastery.

It is a peculiar fact in the history of monastic orders, which must be considered by every intelligent person, that if an Order should fall in its standards by not adhering strictly to the vows and precepts, even if it were wealthy and promised an easy, luxurious life, it would have but a very few or no new members. Although it would seem that in such Orders more should ask for admittance because the life is easier and would be more appealing to spoiled human nature, actually the reverse is true. It is the idealism and nobility of a system of principles that attracts men. Whenever an Order upholds its former strictness in demanding adherence to the primitive rule of prayer, penance and solitude in the monastic life, then at once new applicants announce themselves who gladly accept the hardships in sacrificing themselves to the service of God. How can this be explained? What will those persons say who do not believe in the divine calling to the monastic life? Is it not a demonstration of God's direct influence?

Every endeavor has its friends and enemies, most of all God's work. This was also true of Josaphat and his work. He had many and powerful enemies but he also had some powerful friends who either out of gratitude for his aid in guiding them to find the truth, or because of the love and respect for his holiness, did him and his Order many good turns. As already mentioned above, there arose a pressing need for new monasteries established by reform of the Order based upon the solid and enduring basis of sacrifice, suffering and total abnegation of self, and studies devoted to the Sacred Scriptures, where a number of monks growing up as a spiritual posterity under Josaphat's leadership could prepare themselves to carry out this ideal. The young priests prayed and studied together and were initiated into the various offices of their ministry. The idea of the place was to provide protection, mutual assistance as aids to moral and religious perfection. Yet contact was made and kept with the outside world in order that they might learn to understand the problems that faced them. They visited the poor, the sick and the prisons. They taught catechism whenever they could gather a class of children together and they gave missions.

Whenever men gather in the name of Christ to pray and render glory to Him, His bounty knows no limitations.

As if he had guessed Josaphat's problem, Jerome Khodkevich offered him the archimandrite of the monastery in Suprasel, but out of humility Josaphat would not accept it.

Gregory Tresna, the sheriff of the county of Sloninsky, gave Josaphat the monastery in Baeten which had originally been built for his daughter, a Basilian nun. Rutsky advised Josaphat to accept this monastery and made him its prior. Then in a short time another new home was open to the increasing number of monks, having no other thought or desire than to conform themselves to His mind and will; to convert and return souls to God. "Seek after God and your soul shall live." (St. John of Tuloss)

Not far from Baeten there lived a country squire and a Schismatic by the name of John Mileshko who was a courtier at the castle of Smolensk. Becoming acquainted with Josaphat, he was soon convinced of the error of Schism. After confession, he discovered the ease of mind enjoyed by a pure conscience which increased his confidence in God. He was granted the seemingly impossible and undeserved divine grace to become a devout and persevering Catholic, which because of the sins of his former unhappy life he considered an impossibility. Out of gratitude to Josaphat for his conversion he offered him the village of Zirovetz. There were only a few houses in the village each one enjoying its own little world, with a farmyard and orchard in back and a flower garden behind the picket fence in front, from which in the morning would wander out four or five cows, a few sheep, a dozen or two ducks lined in neat rows bound for the nearest stream. Here in a tiny Church was to be found the glorious image of the Blessed Virgin, noted for its miraculous powers since the year 1500.

Note: This image has a famous history in the Ukrainian Church which is as follows:

Around 1570 or 1580, the shepherds of the village of Ziro-vetz saw on one of the trees by the pasture land, a great light and running towards it, they found an image from which the light emanated. When the light had diminished so that they could approach it, they took the image and brought it to the owner of the forest in which the pasture was located, Alexander Soltana. This image was fashioned of mother-of-pearl and showed the Blessed Virgin holding the child Jesus in her arms. Around the image were chiseled the words in ancient Slavonic, "More honorable than the Cherubim and beyond compare more glorious than the Sera-phim, thou who without defilement bearest God the Word, true Birth-giver of God, we magnify Thee." Soltana hid this image in his chest, valuing it as a great treasure.

One day when he had a company of distinguished guests and wanted to show them the image, he was astounded that he could not find it even though the chest had been securely locked.

The shepherds informed him later that the image at that time had again been seen on the tree in the forest. He under-stood then the will of the Blessed Virgin, that she wished to remain in that place and so he erected a Church on the site and had the altar built on the exact spot where the image had appeared and placed the miraculous image over the altar. Then he built a monastery and brought monks to it to guard this treasure and the sanctuary.

A fire burned down the Church but the Blessed Virgin again manifested her miraculous power for the image was unharmed. Later when the Church was rebuilt it passed into the hands of secular priests until Josaphat on the 18th of October in 1613 restored it to the monastic Order.

Upon his arrival at Zirovetz, St. Josaphat set out to build a monastery together with all the other necessary buildings, enlarged and renovated the Church, furnishing it with all the essentials preparatory to celebrating the Divine Mysteries. A bell was hung and blessed. Inside, a chapel was opened to the right of the nave for use of the public and the image of the Blessed Virgin was set within handsome wooden panels carved in relief with sheaves of wheat and bunches of grapes. The result of these efforts was that people made pilgrimages to visit the sanctuary and those in the village came more willingly and regularly. Many wealthy gentlemen especially Leo Sapiha, the king's prime minister, lent their generous support to the building of this monastery. The rooms were low and airy. A square courtyard opened into a garden beyond which were the fields stretching down to the forest and the pasture lands.

From the time that Josaphat came to live in Zirovetz a lukewarm parish was recalled to fervor. He taught that labor is not an end in itself and incapable of assuring peace and happiness among men without the assistance of Divine love in the fullness of all its graces.

Men got into the habit of slipping into the Church on their way to the fields, leaving their tools outside the door and their flocks waiting in the road. When the bell sounded for vespers, the women and children would gather to sing the responses to the monk's prayers. Thereafter the heart of the village was the property of God. The place became the most famous in all of the province. It is sufficient to mention that through the use of the miraculous image of the Blessed Virgin some thirty persons were raised from the dead, without enumerating all the other lesser miracles.

The result of all these miracles was that Pope Benedict VIII sent as his personal gift, a golden crown with which the image was crowned by Rev. Athanasius Sheptitsky, OSBM, on September 19, 1730.

St. Josaphat believed that every moment is of utmost value for doing what pleases God. As he had done in Vilno and Baeten, he preached here also rousing the lethargic souls of the people oblivious to the future hope of freedom for their homeland. He penetrated their hearts and restored them to their ancient faith. He catechised them, heard their confessions and carried on disputations with the Schismatics and with his soul constantly nourished by sanctifying grace, the divine love that burned within him prevailed upon the Schismatics and Heretics to join the Union.

Here in Zirovetz he converted the nobleman Soltana, a descendant of the same Soltana who had first erected the Church of the Blessed Virgin. This Soltana was fanatically persistent in his heresy. From the moment people came into his presence it was impossible to keep anything about themselves hidden from Josaphat. He immediately perceived the emptiness of the man's soul. Though there was no explicit faith there, he discovered that there was good soil wherein he might plant the seed of faith. Therefore, one day he was invited by Josaphat to take a walk in the forest by the monastery. When the talk had turned to heresy and the Catholic Church, Soltana began to storm against the Church with the most abominable blasphemies and curses while Josaphat listened in consternation. He gently but unhesitatingly corrected the erroneous teachings of the Heretics, praying all the time in his heart for Soltana's conversion. It ended happily as usual, through Holy Patience which confounds Satan and all his wiles, that Soltana, touched by the grace of God suddenly fell at Josaphat's feet, renounced his heresy, made his confession then and there in the woods and cleansed, went back to thank the Blessed Virgin for this grace.

The confusion and separation which reigned supreme throughout the whole East also engulfed Ukraine. Schism arose because men revolted from the one great true and only King and God, our Lord Jesus Christ and His Church which was to embrace all nations and people in one fold as members of one body, "Ye shall all be of one fold," as Christ had said. Ukraine became so weakened by internal dissension that it was readily vanquished by the Mongol Horde. The towns were pillaged and entire villages destroyed, their harvest burned. The prisoners were mutilated and tortured with savage refinement. Quarrels and wars continued until the land was devastated, the Churches persecuted and the people reduced to serfdom under conquering foreign rulers. Whole villages fell into the hands of foreign gentry and the people were reduced to serfs attached to the land enjoying hardly any independence. It was the gentry who shared with the churches and monasteries almost all of the wealth of the time.

Time and again Josaphat gave strength to feeble souls to resolve to bear their sufferings in serfdom and to join the Uniate Church which alone is capable of upholding a disunited and disinherited people.

St. Josaphat thought that here, away from the busy world, in this isolated place in the depths of the forest with its silent grandeur, under the protection of the Blessed Virgin Mary, he could live out his life in peace, tilling, planting and harvesting the salvation of souls. But God called him again to another task. God's commands must be carried out, always pressing forward, reaching forth into the things ahead to press towards the mark.

Thus Josaphat expressed that care for the unity of the Church which his whole life exemplified. But his ideal of ecclesiastical obedience and of the greatness of the Church was far from being tyrannical or secular. He valued it for the sake of the holiness and freedom of the individual souls of his people.

CHAPTER XII

JOSAPHAT AS ARCHIMANDRITE

After the attack on his person the Metropolitan Ipaty Poty whose vigor for a man of his advanced age and saintly straightforwardness the Schismatics and Heretics feared, became more firmly established than ever. While Josaphat was occupied in the rebuilding of the monasteries in Baeten and Zirovetz, the Metropolitan was living out his life as the esteemed and venerated head of the Ukrainian Church. If he had been less preoccupied with the work in his diocese and were less humble, he might have enjoyed the triumph.

Divine Providence had sent this man at a time when tact, kindness and penetrating knowledge of men were most needed by the Ukrainian Church. A French biographer Jepin called him in truth "The father of the Union." He became the bishop of Volodimir not by the choice of the people or the clergy, nor even the appointment of the king but by request of Prince Ostrowsky and the gentry. Ostrowsky had thought to find in Poty a staunch supporter of his ambitions, but he misjudged the man. When Poty renounced heresy and returned to the Catholic Church, he became its most powerful protector. At that time Cyril Terlecky introduced the question of the joining of the Ukrainian Church with the Roman Catholic.

At first he hesitated as to whether or not he should join the Union but having once decided in favor of the Union he continued to hold to this determination to the end despite the worst sufferings, persecutions and calumnies by the Schismatics and the indifference of the Polish gentry.

He gained the highest reputation for his brilliant mind and Christian gentleness as a senator. He was an orator among orators and the king's favorite, so that his opinions carried weight. Combined with his extraordinary magnetic personality and large-minded good sense, he exercised a powerful influence in promoting the cause of the Union and maintaining the rights of the Church against the civil magistrates during the period of its direst need.

When he was appointed to replace the weak Rohoza, his first proclamation to the priesthood who refused obedience, was "You are now responsible tó me and not to Rohoza." He accepted no nonsense from those who wished to evade the rules. The endless struggle he had to wage against the uneducated clergy and the still more ignorant and illiterate people was described in previous chapters. His last days were somewhat lightened by the nimbus of martyrdom for the sake of the Union. It was God's will that this man also should give some of his blood for the Church, for whose distended misery he had made every sacrifice to alleviate for over eighteen years. He died on the 13th of July 1613.

Ipaty Poty was succeeded by his assistant, Joseph Rutsky. His friend and sponsor Benedict Woyna, the Latin bishop of Vilno brought him the king's formal appointment. He assumed his office as head of the Ukrainian Church on June 28, 1614. Having become the Metropolitan, he automatically resigned as the archimandrite of the monastery of the Holy Trinity in Vilno.

To whom could he relinquish this post, if not to Josaphat?

Although Josaphat in true humility declined the nomination, Rutsky commanded him to accept it. Regretfully, Josaphat left the monastery of Zirovetz but God comforted him in his true humility and obedience.

Who can describe his joy when on his return to Vilno he was greeted by sixty monks who were to work with him in carrying out his cherished ideal for the Union. It was not so long before, only ten years, that he had prayed for the fulfillment of his dream in his lonely cell. Now he could look forward to the future more hopefully. He realized that his work was inspired by God and God's plan never fails to come to pass.

With his usual zeal he began by enlarging the monastery. Through gifts from his many good friends he redecorated and enlarged the dormitory of the monastery within a short time so that all the monks could be comfortably housed.

His new position brought added duties and a multitude of cares. Having under him all young and inexperienced monks, he had to fill nearly all the important and minor offices, himself. He was the director of the novices, their preacher and confessor as well as the prior and economist of the monastery. As was his custom, he awoke all the brethren himself; carried the light in winter to each cell; rang the Angelus bell, opened the monastery and Church, directed and sang in the choir; taught and gave instructions to the novices, carried on discourses with them. Outside of the monastery, as usual, he heard confessions, visited the sick and comforted them; taught the nuns and carried on disputations with the Schismatics; visited the prisons and helped the poor.

All this he did with a cheerful disposition and light heart, as if these duties were no trouble at all but rewards for his efforts. It can truly be called miraculous that a man seemingly of so frail and delicate a constitution could undertake so much work, in addition to self-mortification, for so many hours each day, for the glory of God and the good of his fellow man. He entertained for himself the severest views of obedience to duty. No matter how busy he was as archimandrite, he did not seek to be relieved of any of his duties or to shirk any of them.

He dressed, lived and ate if not the same as other monks, then as one of the poorest and humblest but never any better.

At one time a gentleman sent him a suit of clothes made of good material and begged him to wear it in consideration of the dignity of his position but as soon as Josaphat learned that a few of his monks disapproved or were displeased by this, he at once gave the clothes to another and took his old suit for himself.

When Josaphat was leaving the monastery of Zirovetz, his friend Tresna ordered his cloak to be lined with the pelt of a wolf and placed it in the wagon and himself wrote a letter to Rutsky asking him to command Josaphat to wear it for the sake of his delicate health. However, Josaphat knew how to defend his views before the Metropolitan so that Rutsky did not have the heart to force Josaphat to obey the distressing command.

As soon as Rutsky had departed for his new office, Josaphat commanded the furs to be made into caps for all the brethren.

All his friars benefited from his affection, nonetheless, he showed a special indulgence to those who were apt in their studies. Frequently he would take their places in their tasks at the monastery in order to give them more time for their studies.

With the brothers who were in some ways at fault or who misbehaved, he was very gentle, avoided slighting anyone but showed himself respectful and courteous to all in word and manner. When once he lovingly corrected one of the friars for some fault, another scolded him severely for this same mistake and ridiculed him. When Josaphat learned of it, he called the strict monk to him and said to him only these words: "Watch while you stand that you fall not." He so stirred the monk with these words that from that time onward no one ever heard another bitter or mean word from him. At another time one of the monks, returning through the fields from an errand outside the village, carelessly lost his cloak on the way. When he came into the monastery, he reported it to Josaphat who instead of scolding comforted him for the loss and ordered him to go into the Church and say a prayer.

Soon afterwards, a villager found the cloak and recognizing it as belonging to a Basilian monk returned it to the monastery.

It is the custom in monasteries after dinner and after supper to get together for discussion, advice and recreation. To these gatherings Josaphat came along with the others as a companion and talked with them as a friend and not as the archimandrite. He had a wonderful ability to win hearts and instill into those about him the warmth of his inner life. Overflowing with love, enlightened by the divine light, Josaphat humbly revealed to them in terms that all could understand the requisites for a holy serenity that one experiences in belonging to God. His discourses were often picturesque and sublime, speaking direct to the souls of men. Himself a living channel through which grace poured into souls, he possessed a mysterious sense of infusing each heart as he spoke from the abundance of his heart with a desire to know and guide itself so that indwelt by God man might learn to understand the purpose of life. Humanity needs each other's aid and love so as to form the strength of links in a chain of unity and brotherhood. He taught them to pray without ceasing for the welfare of their souls, to seek God until having conquered all that could impede their union with Him they would acquire the gift of dynamic and enduring character with a tender compassion and charity towards their fellow men.

He opened his heart to show the love of God that was in it and if theirs was empty, he filled them with the grace from the stream which overflowed his own soul, so that it might nourish the life of God in the depths of their souls. He had a will quick to decision and action, guiding and guarding them all with his own spiritual strength and wisdom. Although he pardoned their sins and bore their burdens, his mind remained always clear. He forgot nothing that concerned others and had a word for everyone and could always put himself in the place of others.

Sometimes it so happened that Josaphat dozed off from overfatigue and overwork because of insufficient sleep at night; but as soon as the brethren began to discuss unessential matters, he would awake immediately and turn the discussion to subjects of a more profitable nature.

These few incidents are related here of Josaphat, during the period of his archimandrate to show his love and gentleness which the saints invariably extend to others, although towards themselves they are very strict. On the other hand, persons not possessing any real holiness or those only pretending by an outward show of holiness are always very indulgent and gentle towards themselves but towards others they are unreasonably merciless even in the smallest things.

The income of the Basilian Fathers was not very great, nonetheless, Divine Providence obviously cared for Josaphat, for he not only was able to support sixty monks but also several singers for the Church and caretakers.

One of the characteristics of the servants of God is their compassion for the poor. This characteristic was a hallmark of Josaphat's great love for God. While he was still a priest he was an earnest protector of the poor; now he became a real father to them. Beggars came in droves after him, crossed his path telling him their needs. For all he found unfailing counsel, cheer and aid. He fed them from the monastery provisions as much as he could or he went to the homes of the rich to beg charity for the poor and then divided what he had collected among them. If on some days he was unable to help the beggars, it was immediately reflected on his face, for he was sad all day. God desiring to show his pleasure at sight of such great love for fellow man often performed wonderful miracles.

Thus, one day a poor widow came to the saint begging help. She had a debtor who constantly nagged and pursued her demanding his money which she had borrowed and now had no means of returning. Josaphat listened to her pleas and told her to come back at an appointed hour, while in the meantime he gave himself to prayer. After he had finished praying and was coming out of the Church, some unknown young man came up to him and gave him a packet of money wrapped in a piece of paper, as if it were a gift of charity from some rich gentleman. When asked for the name of the benefactor, the young man made no reply but hurried away. At the hour appointed, the widow returned and Josaphat, without even unwrapping the package of money, gave it all to her. In a short time she returned with it for she had found more in the packet than she needed and wanted to return the rest. Nevertheless, Josaphat would not accept any of the money, saying, "God sent it all to you from heaven. Therefore, take all of it and use it for yourself!"

To speak truthfully, St. Josaphat in his zeal for charity was so shortsighted that the monastery itself was often short of supplies. Nonetheless, this over-generosity towards the poor Divine Providence invariably rewarded. It is said that where poverty reigns, there is no obstacle between men and God's gifts.

At one time Josaphat had given everything to the poor so that there was nothing for the monks to eat for dinner. But Josaphat was not worried about it, he simply ordered the friars to go to the Church and pray. They had not yet finished praying when five wagon loads of provisions rolled into the courtyard of the monastery. When they questioned the drivers from whom this gift had come the drivers made no reply, simply unloaded the supplies and drove away. At another time there was not even any fire in the kitchen for there was nothing to cook, but when the time had arrived for supper, some unknown friend sent food and drink already prepared as if they had ordered it.

The monks witnessed these miracles and glorified God.

Sometimes, as it was testified before the Commission later, whenever there was a shortage in the monastery, St. Josaphat appeared to the well-to-do at night in their sleep and asked for their charity. Such a vision appeared several times to Ipatia Dubovich, a wealthy magistrate of Vilno whose son later became a monk and archimandrite of the Order of St. Basil the Great in which office he effected a vast amount of good for the Order.

There was an outburst of diabolic activity by the permission of God. The devil began to frighten the monks in the monastery's Church of the Holy Trinity so badly that some of them lost weight, could not sleep and were afraid to go to Church alone.

Every night just before midnight, the outer and inner doors of the Church opened themselves despite the fact that they had been securely locked and into it trooped a company of devils pulling after them some creature in chains upon which there was such an uproar, howling, screeching, crackling and thunderous storm that the whole monastery quaked from the reverberations. At the first signs of daybreak the pack of devils left the Church with a tremendous noise, the doors locked themselves, a great whirlwind arose in front of the Church and carried the demons into the cemetery behind the Church where it all vanished.

One night St. Josaphat took one of the friars with him and

went to Church, lighted the candles, put on his ceremonial vestments, opened the royal doors of the sanctuary, went to the altar, took out the Holy Eucharist and calmly awaited the coming of the unclean spirit there. The monk whom he had brought with him he instructed not to be alarmed by anything when the frightful things appeared but only to kneel, call upon his guardian angel for protection and pray earnestly before the Holy Eucharist.

At the hour of midnight, suddenly with a tremendous bang the outer doors opened. Inside the Church arose such a wind that the candles were nearly all blown out and there appeared a hellish company dragging after them a black creature in chains all around the Church coming at last to the sanctuary doors as if with the intention of entering the presbytery, but there they stopped. Thereupon Josaphat grasped the Holy Eucharist in his right hand and a candle in his left, walked down the steps of the altar to the royal doors of the sanctuary and commanded in the name of the Holy Ghost present in the Holy Eucharist for the unclean spirit to depart from the Church and forbade it to further disturb the sanctity of the place.

At these words, the unclean company scrambled out of the Church and the doors locked themselves again with such a thunderous noise that it seemed as if the Church were collapsing. Josaphat pursued it through a side door, holding the Eucharist, to the spot in the cemetery where it all vanished. Josaphat marked the grave.

The next day, Josaphat learned that a woman from a well-known family was buried there who had an evil reputation during her lifetime and had died without making her confession and receiving the Holy Sacrament of Communion. He thereupon ordered her remains to be removed from the cemetery at night and buried away out in the fields. For a time the unclean spirit left the place. But after awhile it again returned to disturb the monks. Often at night when all the monks slept it frightened the panic-stricken monks by ringing the monastery bell, then it made a lot of racket running around the outside of the Church with another creature in chains.

St. Josaphat again dispelled the unclean spirit by prayer and exposure of the Holy Eucharist. At another time the unclean spirit attacked Josaphat himself as he knelt at prayer late at night, which he vanquished with the sign of the cross and holy water.

As Josaphat was himself a saint, he led those who were entrusted to him as well as his friends in the Order along the path of holiness. One could name a whole list of celebrated and holy men who were taught in St. Josaphat's school. Mention will be made here of only a few.

Bishop Susha mentions one brother who had the grace of God to be the first to die in the reformation of the Order. He was gentle and pure in heart and had a great love for Christ. As a true servant of God, he placed no store in the good deeds accomplished in his lifetime nor expected justification for his works, but put all his hope in the mercy of God. And God rewarded him with a vision before his death of St. Basil and St. Peter, the Apostle. The holy patriarch of the monks said to St. Peter, "This is the first flower chosen from the renewel of my garden." A few days later the pious monk died.

Another monk, Jerome Tisovich, also attained a reputation for sanctity. Because of his many virtues, the devil was much afraid of him. Robust and eloquent, he possessed energy and versatility as a preacher without rival. With his wonderful tranquility of mind he touched the hearts of men and assuaged their fears and anxieties with his peace.

He, like Josaphat, also had the power to dispel unclean spirits. He received from God the power of bi-location and could appear in several places simultaneously. He died in Zirovetz, near the miraculous ikon of the Madonna before

134

whom he was celebrating his usually fervent devotions. With tears in his eyes as if he were addressing the angels gathered about the altar, he prayed, opening his arms to the Blessed Virgin while she seemed to bend over him to help him in this last act. Upon examination of his tomb twenty years after his death, his body was found to be clean and white and unspoiled.

Then there was Simeon Yatskovich, a soul possessed of many admirable qualities and virtues as Josaphat, gentle, pure and modest. He was brought up from childhood under Josaphat's influence. The good that radiated from his small being attracted Josaphat's attention whom he admired and imitated. He came to reverence his priestly dignity. As he grew older he delighted in his company for his simplicity and gaiety and accessibility, and was entirely swayed by his spirit. He had given himself so entirely to God that he found his self-fulfillment in charity for his neighbor. He was an example to all, fired by the same earnestness as Josaphat, with his heroic zeal in practicing austerities. He denied his body the barest comfort in order that he might possess all that is most worthwhile for his soul. He endured weakness and tribulation that he might see the Supreme Good more clearly on which everything needful to the soul depends. The very pious and brilliant theologian Rev. Lenchitsky of the Jesuits said of him that no one excelled him in holiness in all of the Catholic Church of that period. His soul was accessible to mystical inspirations and these influenced a lifetime of great works. When it came time for him to leave this world and its vale of tears and he made a confession of all the sins of his life, there was found not a single serious or mortal sin among them. Despite his great weakness, he rose from his bed of sickness, dressed and knelt to receive his Lord and Creator for the last time in Holy Communion. After receiving Extreme Unction, he said, "I believe, I trust, I love and repent." He drew his last breath and died. Countless miracles afterwards were wronght with his relic. His body likewise did not rot, although it had been buried in a damp spot.

The lives of these monks and others like them bear witness to the greatness of Josaphat who taught them the way of happiness whose smile was sufficient praise and whose silence a rebuke to the secret evil in a man's conscience, which was impossible to keep hidden from Josaphat, and his genial conversation was always enlightening.

One from among them testified before the Apostolic Commission that Josaphat lived a life of great severity. He slept and ate very little and dressed poorly. His bed was meanly furnished and hard. He scourged himself and wore a hair shirt. In other words, he followed earnestly all the strictest practices prescribed for the most zealous monk. As a result he was so united to God that his life was an unceasing prayer.

He poured out all he had of ingenuity, happiness, love and strength to teach men the joy of a pure conscience, an active body, a life well-filled with service to humanity by keeping the heart open to every appeal and elevating the soul to God. He taught them how to acquire limitless patience, sympathy and simplicity in their relations with men. He listened to the confidences of the monks and instructed them in the delicate art of refining their souls by cultivating that which was highest in themselves. Here slowly but deliberately he commenced the amassing of that army of apostles to fulfill his farsighted ideal of a united Catholic Church throughout the land of Ukraine, before which regardless of its foreign occupants, all fantastic sects would vanish. By the expression of his face and the tears pouring from his eyes he taught them of the boundless love and great goodness of God. Of course there were disappointments, contradictions and opposition to be encountered but as the patriarch of the Order, St. Basil said:—

"As light transparent bodies touched by the sun become themselves aglow and send forth another splendor from themselves so souls that bear the Spirit, illumined by the Spirit, become themselves spiritual and transmit grace to others."

Thus Josaphat passed on grace to those whom he taught in person or by example. His counsels, wise, full of love and generosity, moved the hearts of men to continue steadily on the path. He had emptied himself to give place to the Being that guided all his actions.

CHAPTER XIII

ST. JOSAPHAT'S VISIT TO THE FAMOUS PECHERSKY MONASTERY IN KIEV

St. Josaphat, after becoming archimandrite often had to leave Vilno to travel either to see the Metropolitan or to visit other monasteries. And on these journeys he never forgot the words of the Saviour, "My meat is to do the will of Him that sent me and to finish His work. Say not, yet there are four months and then cometh harvest. Behold, I say unto you, Lift up your eyes and look on the fields, for they are white already to harvest." And "Ye shall all be of one fold." (St. John 4: 34-35)

Wherever he went, he never failed to draw attention to the acceptance of the Holy Union, preaching, catechising and confessing. The poor came to him, well-known citizens, even priests. Thus his fame spread widely throughout the country.

He would sit down in the midst of them, ask them questions, instruct and convert them. Whenever he met a soul that had lost touch with God, he opened his own soul and showed it the boundless love for God within in order to help it break through its wall of disbelief which hinders the soul in its early steps towards God and to renew contact with the

138

stream of divine grace, to nourish the life of the soul. He revitalized their hopes and faith in the resurrection, the enjoyment of the Beautific Vision and promised good things in the kingdom of God and in the life to come by obedience to the commandments of God and the Catholic Church, reception of the wonderful mystery of the precious body and blood of Christ in the Holy Eucharist. He often answered by intuition just those doubts, hopes and supplications which held the hearts of those who sat in the audience before him. Then he would send them to nearby churches to receive Communion; whether they were of the Eastern or Latin Rite, he would send each to his own Church.

For a long time Josaphat had wanted to see the famous Pechersky monastery in Kiev from which the monastic life had originally spread to all parts of Ukraine and which had given to the world so many Holy Men of God, to the glory of their homeland and which contained the relics of all these saints. But its fame had waned since Schism crept into it becoming instead the most infested center of that disease which brought about the decadence of the once grand and very devout land of Ukraine. Now his desire was to be fulfilled. The Metropolitan's jurisdiction extended over but one church in that See, that of St. Sophia, as the other churches were in the hands of the Schismatics.

Desiring to visit the ancient capital, he took Josaphat along as a companion because his gentleness and purity inspired and cheered him.

The church of St. Sophia was the gateway to the Uniate Ukrainian Church. It bore testimony to the people's continued faith in the Apostolic See. Yaroslav Mudry (The Wise) the one who refused to give recognition to Grecian Schism infiltrating Ukraine from the agitated East, ordered the Church in Kiev to be built as an exact replica of the one in Byzantium. When the building was completed, the pious prince who remained faithful to the Union until death, wanted to have it dedicated and blessed in the presence of a representative of the Pope of Rome. At his invitation, the Papal legate, Alexander, was the first to celebrate Mass in the new Metropolis, for the intention of bringing about closer unity with the Catholic Church.

Six decades had elapsed since Schism had over-run the country while the Church of St. Sophia, first from the onslaught of the Tartars and then through the schemes of worldly custodians gradually declined in fame and glory. This monument to the unity of the Catholic Church was necessary to retain at all cost for the Uniates. Since his authority was indeterminate, the Metropolitan counted chiefly on the virtues and miraculous aid of the future martyr to help him repossess it so that it would continue to bear witness to the ancient faith of St. Volodimir and Yaroslav in the One United Apostolic Church.

All during the long journey Josaphat devoted himself indefatigably to Apostolic labors thereby continuing his mission of winning souls for Christ. He recited the Gospel with such humility and confidence that those who were seeking solutions to their difficulties found in his answers the assurance they sought for the salvation of their homeland in the Union. People listened to the gentle monk who announced redemption with such simple sincerity to sinners and to those sick at heart of all the dissensions by being members of a united Catholic Church, unravelling their most difficult objections to their satisfaction, that there was a marvelous renewal of faith in each locality where they stopped. His purpose was to secure unity of the Church throughout the breadth and length of the diocese.

But as soon as they had arrived at Kiev, Josaphat went immediately to the monastery originally founded by the two very holy monks Anthony and Theodosius Pechersky at the behest of Grand Prince Yaroslav, the Wise. To no avail Joseph Rutsky tried to dissuade him, fearing for his life, as it was a well-known fact that the monks of that monastery burned with a fierce hatred towards Josaphat.

When Josaphat came in sight of the monastery, he met the monk Kurtsevich who was the scion of a noble Ukrainian family at exactly the moment when he was surrounded by his attendants and dogs, preparatory to going hunting. Realizing that he was speaking to Josaphat, he berated and insulted him, calling him a traitor to the faith and the homeland, a plunderer of souls and even approached him in the heat of anger threatening him with death. The comforting and placating peace of the saints frequently subdues people of uncontrolled temper. Thus it happened in this case. To this hateful barrage Josaphat answered quietly, "I am a lover of peace. I come not with any intention of evil, but as a guest, to visit the brethren and to speak with them.

"It is surprising to me, since I have not anywhere read in the precepts of the Basilian Order that it is permissible for a monk to go hunting?"

It is an amazing fact that these simple, earnest words and gentle rebuke changed the attitude of the monk Kurtsevich so that in his embarrassment, he admitted Josaphat into the monastery without further ado.

When Josephat had informed the prior of his presence, he immediately ordered the monastery bell to be rung for the monks to gather in their Assembly hall and meet the "soul snatcher" whom they had long desired to see.

At the news that the soul snatcher was in the monastery, a hundred monks gathered in the space of a few moments in their auditorium. But as soon as Josaphat appeared on the stage of the auditorium, there arose shouts of vehement suspicion from every side, "What did you come here for? Do you want to mislead us? Don't think you'll have the same success here as with the others!" One hundred angry monks some of whom wanted to beat him and others even to drown him in the nearby river Dnieper. Josaphat wanted to speak

141

to them but they would not permit him to say a word, the noise was so deafening. Filled with courage, Josaphat thought only of imitating Christ in his suffering, forcing himself to rival Him in love and goodness. When at Josaphat's request, the prior commanded them to be quiet, Josaphat made a polite bow before them and said, "I came here to visit this famous and ancient holy place to venerate the holy relics which are to be found here; and at the same time to enjoy the company of so many good monks. I cannot have any intention of doing evil, for as you see, I have come all by myself without a companion. I bring you my good wishes and will gladly remain with you if you can show me the way of truth according to the teachings of the Holy Scripture and the writings of the Holy Fathers and our Liturgical books."

Disarmed by Josaphat's gentle speech, they calmed down and the prior asked Josaphat to stay with them for dinner. Josaphat thanked him but excused himself saying that he had just eaten dinner in town and asked him to lend him their Liturgical books. When he had the books before him, he began to quote from them, laying down briefly, decidedly and beyond refutation, the doctrinal principles of the Catholic Church. He stressed the importance and necessity of Church unity and reminded them from the history of the Ukrainian Church of the fact that Ukraine had been Christened when the Greek Church was in Union with Rome and when there was but one Catholic Church and one faith and that the famous Pechersky monastery in Kiev had held out the longest in favor of the Union with Rome. There was no escape from the force of his logic. Finally he said, "If anyone among you can prove to me that all I have said is not the truth, then I will gladly remain with you. Let inspired Scripture be our arbiter and with whomsoever are found the doctrines which agree with the divine words these must have found the truth."

142

The monks were amazed at hearing so many rational proofs against themselves, contradictions to their beliefs, and taken from their own books, which they used every day in their services and they remarked to one another, "No wonder they call him soul snatcher. He knows how to draw people to himself with sweet words." But none among them dared to oppose Josaphat's statements. A deep thoughtfulness was reflected on all their faces. No doubt each in his heart sought for that higher truth to which he longed to dedicate his life.

The hated "soul snatcher" had won their respect, for having bade them goodby as brethren, he left the monastery in the company of several of the monks who respectfully accompanied him back home where the Metropolitan awaited him impatiently. Rutsky was astonished to see him not only alive and whole but in a pleasant company of monks, for in the long absence the worried Metropolitan had imagined all sorts of things and never thought to see him return alive from that hive of fanatical Schism.

While in Kiev, Josaphat succeeded in converting a magistrate, Batalia, and two priests. Later both priests became martyrs for the Union. Leaving the Church of St. Sophia under the guardianship of the converted priests, the Metropolitan, together with Josaphat, returned to Vilno.

As soon as the news had spread that Josaphat was returning, an inexplicable enthusiasm took hold of the crowd so that practically the whole city turned out to greet him. He was besieged by the gentry, townsfolk and the commoners and especially the beggars who regarded him as their special guardian and protector.

He blessed their images, and medals, settled differences, heard confessions and he taught them to become conscious of sin, the necessity of frequent confession and Communion to cure the diseases of the soul that would remedy sin. He persuaded them that they should believe those who are able to see into the state of their souls rather than to trust in their own insensibility and ignorance. Released from sin, the soul would then perceive the good and know the happiness of it and could enjoy the blessings of a light heart and unfettered soul.

At about this time Josaphat succeeded in converting a wealthy, but one of the most fanatically Schismatic, towns-woman. When he came to her house he tried with the most persuasive gentleness to win her over to the Union. The woman began by insulting him and when her anger was aroused, she grabbed a stick and wanted to hit him. But the saint said to her, "If I had known that I was to be the cause of so much anger and sin, I would never have come to your house." That stopped her. In a short time she had controlled her anger and ran after the holy man to fall at his feet, begging his pardon. Once converted, she became the most zealous of Catholics. She converted many other women like herself and even the Schismatic nuns with whom she had been on friendly terms.

With the help of God, Josaphat drew to the Uniate Church two senators, Michael Sokolinsky and Theodore Tishkevich the sheriff of Little Novgorod and his son Janushym, a secretary in the Diet. Both father and son became Josaphat's life-long friends and performed many good services for the Ukrainian Catholic Church.

What seemed impossible was made possible through the efforts of St. Josaphat by obedience and study and suffering in his own person for remission of the sins of men.

Divine compassion stored in him a treasury of holy patience with which to confound the wiles of Satan and which gave him the power gradually to convert nearly the whole city of Vilno together with surrounding villages and hamlets to the Uniate faith while there remained only a small group of Schismatics and this minority did not dare to oppose the saint in his work. As a matter of fact, Josaphat's apostolic labors fared so well in this city that the work was soon finished, that is why God called him to a higher office giving him a barren field to till for the harvest of souls and eventually to sprinkle it with his blood.

CHAPTER XIV

ST. JOSAPHAT AS ARCHBISHOP

The See of the Archbishop of Polotsk was occupied by Gideon Brolnitsky, a ninety-year-old man, who was no longer capable of carrying on the work.

Through lack of proper supervision of the priesthood, many discrepancies crept in from which the Schismatics benefited and thus were able to spread their heresy. The Union gradually lost ground so that very few remained Catholic. Rutsky was aware of the falling away of the Polotsk diocese but he did not care to interfere in setting things in order without first obtaining the approval of Rome.

While in Rome, in 1617, he described the grievous plight of the diocese to Pope Paul V who advised him to give the old archbishop an assistant with full right to succeed him upon his death. Who was more capable and deserving of this office than Josaphat? A great man was necessary and Josaphat could not be overlooked. It was hardly to be expected that such a man as he, so brilliant and eloquent a theologian should remain as archimandrite.

When the Metropolitan returned from Rome he did not mention his plan to Josaphat. However, Josaphat learned of it and was greatly saddened by it. The truly humble man shuns being placed in a position of power for he is afraid of it. This is how it affected Josaphat. Thinking that he might importune Heaven to spare him this responsible office, he fasted more frequently, scourged himself more strenuously and spent whole nights in tearful supplications.

A few days after his return from Rome Joseph Rutsky noticed the change on the saint's face and suspecting the cause of his haggard and drawn expression, he called him to his side and said, "The Church of Polotsk is like an orphan. The Good Shepherd's orderly management has ceased to exist. Many things are going on against the law of God and Christian piety. The Union in that diocese is practically non-existent. There are but a few Uniates left and these are holding on precariously to the Union while human souls perish needlessly, unheeded. It is God's will and mine that you should take over the office of this See."

Upon hearing these words, Josaphat crossed his hands on his breast, and kneeling at the Metropolitan's feet, begged him to be relieved of taking on the responsibility of such a burden. He promised the Metropolitan to work in the diocese unceasingly as a monk as long as his strength would hold out but he could not be the archbishop, as he did not feel within himself the power, courage and ability to hold such an office.

Rutsky did not wish to arouse his friend to further pleas, that would prove useless so he replied briefly that the matter was already settled and could not be changed. Under his vow of implicit obedience to his superiors, he was forced to obey. Josaphat turned away from his friend, grieved and in tears. Seeing that his pleas were in vain, he determined to flee to the wilderness and he would surely have carried out his design if the Reverend Valentine Fabrician, who had a strong influence over him had not dissuaded him from it.

Rutsky called an Assembly of the Basilian Fathers to Little Novgorod for the purpose of uniting all their monasteries as a single organization. At the close of the Assembly he spoke

147

briefly to the gathering about Josaphat, pointing him out as a leader. He called him to the platform beside him and there handed him the king's appointment as the bishop of Polotsk. Unprepared for the appointment as bishop at this Assembly, he fell on his knees before the Metropolitan and begged him to excuse him from this honor, pointing out his inability and aversion for such a high office.

But the Metropolitan would not heed his tears nor his protests but commanded him as his duty to accept the position, saying "The glory of God demands that you accept this office and it is already settled irrevocably."

All the assembled monks were unanimous in their approval of him. They were heartened by this appointment and thanked God for the selection with the feeling that he would not fail to effect a vast amount of good towards spreading the work of the Union for the glory and honor of God and the Church. Everyone felt that he was the ablest, most eloquent and the most capable man to take possession of the office. The intelligentsia and clergy, together with the monks, confirmed the choice. Only Josaphat, seeing that he could no longer protest against its acceptance, shed bitter tears of grief and suffering. He had on that day also determined that he would cede his place to Smotritsky as a more able and intellectually more eminent man that he, if he would accept the Union.

On the 12th of November 1617, the Metropolitan Joseph Rutsky with the assistance of his bishops and archbishops, ordained Josaphat bishop of Vitebsk with the right to succeed the archbishop of the See of Polotsk upon his death. The Catholics blessed this day, while the Schismatics cursed it possibly sensing prophetically that six years later, on the anniversary of the same day, he would accept the crown of martyrdom and they would curse the day they had become the murderers of the saint.

St. Josaphat did not immediately assume office after his

consecration. It was very difficult for him to tear himself away from the monastic life and to give up his friends and companions and pupils with whom he continued to make progress in holiness and in the attainment of Christian self-perfection. He also felt that he still owed them one last counsel in the secrecy of the sacrament and one last word of love. In addition to this, he wanted to prepare himself for the battle with the forces of darkness and to ask Almighty God for His blessing and Light for the difficult task ahead. For this intention he celebrated a ten-day retreat at the monastery with his friends and pupils before leaving them. Then he wrote letters of good will to the government officials at Vitebsk and to other officials in the various cities of his diocese to gain their friendship and through them the backing of the people.

When the time drew near for his departure from Vilno, practically the whole town hurried to the Church of the Holy Trinity to bid farewell to their benefactor. From all the surrounding countryside came the landed gentry to extend their good wishes and to thank him. The reception became nearly a riot and the entire affair turned into a personal triumph. All the assembled wept as if it were a funeral. A large company of them accompanied Josaphat for some distance out of the city, imploring God for his blessing for this angel of peace who having showed them the path of truth now hurried to carry the word of Holy Union to those regions still infected with the disease of Schism, whose intestine dissensions made them an object of sorrow to all good Catholics.

The arrival of the new bishop at Polotsk was set for January 9, 1618. Some of the peopleof Polotsk when they learned who was to be the new head of their Church rejoiced, others disparaged the new appointment.

When the time drew near for his arrival, the Catholics both of the Eastern and Latin Rite, informed of his holiness, zeal and love for fellow-man, determined to make a great festive celebration in honor of their new shepherd. The Schismatic parasites of the old archbishop were furious because with his arrival the power and wealth of the Polotsk Archdiocese would pass out of their hands which they had usurped because of the old age and weakness of the archbishop. They had already begun to arouse the people against Josaphat by spreading the false report that he intended to set up the Latin Rite among the Ukrainians of that region. But even they were forced to accept the new head of the Church as Yanish Tishkevich, the secretary to the Lithuanian prince whom Sigmund III had personally assigned to lead Josaphat to the chair of the See of the archbishopric in Polotsk, had sent instructions in advance to the officials of the local government, that it was by the command of the king that they were to welcome their new shepherd with proper respect and deference.

Josaphat's entry and welcome into the city was spectacular. The people of Polotsk had never before witnessed such a celebration, there was to be only one other like it which they were to see six years later but under very different circumstances.

This festive celebration is described by the biographer of the saint, his Excellency Bishop Susha as follows:
(Note: Susha, Chapter III, page 40-43, "Life of St. Josaphat.")

"When the boom of the cannons announced that Josaphat was on the way, the government officials, the city officials and the voyevod of Polotsk, Michael Sokolinsky, surrounded by a select company of the gentry and countless masses of humanity, marched to the gate of the city. As they neared the gates, the king's emissary, Tishkevich, stopped and spoke to the gathering:

" 'By the will of God and our king, I have brought a Uniate

150

bishop who is the light and jewel, and the proud boast of the gentry, a defense for the city and a shepherd for the flock chosen by God himself.'

"Thereupon, Michael Sokolinsky thanked Tishkevich on behalf of the gentry and the city for the introduction and his safe conduct to their city. Turning to Josaphat, he swore personal allegiance, respect and devotion begging him to take them all under care. St. Josaphat thanked them all briefly for their good will. The procession through the gates of the city was about to begin when Josaphat was suddenly approached by two venerable citizens, one of whom said to him, 'Hold firmly to the Ukrainian Rite' and the other, 'If you have come here with good intentions, trust in the Holy Name of God, but if with evil, then it would be better for you never to have come to Polotsk.'

"Tranquilly and humbly, the saint accepted the emotional warning from the proud old men, who at his very entry tried to show him what fate awaited him.

"Whenever a bishop first enters the Seat of his diocese, it is the custom in the Ukrainian Rite to set up an altar at the entrance to the gate of the city at which the shepherd prays for the first time for his flock and for the city of his diocese. Thus an altar was prepared by the people of Polotsk. Approaching the altar, St. Josaphat went down on his knees and knelt upright without support lifting his eyes heavenward to implore divine grace for the flock entrusted to his care.

"Those present watched the administrator of their churches praying and noting his angelic humility, humble appearance and face alight as it was uplifted in prayer, raised their own eyes and hands to heaven and thanked Almighty God who had sent them such a shepherd.

"After the prayer, the procession continued to the Church of St. Sophia. At the head of the procession came the school children pre-eminently of the Ukrainian Rite led by the Jesuits singing holy songs. After them came the citizens, the town officials then the Latin Rite priests, followed by Ukrainian priests, then came Josaphat clad in the bishop's vestments and surrounded by monks of the Basilian Order and escorted by the voyevod of Polotsk and the king's emissary, accompanied by government officials and the nobility.

"During the entire procession, the Church bells rang, the cannons thundered as if voicing their joy at the coming of the new shepherd of the Church. All faces were alight with happiness, only St. Josaphat, full of sadness, moved forward very slowly, possibly sensing that this feast day was for him the same march of triumph that Palm Sunday had been for the Divine Saviour. When the procession entered the Church of St. Sophia, St. Josaphat took the bishop's seat, presided at the Mass, and blessed the people. He said, "I bless you all, my friends, and I bless Ukraine," and at once went to see the old archbishop. St. Josaphat realized that the archbishop would probably be distrustful and not welcome him very cordially since he had been appointed as assistant without his request and was moreover led into the city with such pomp and glory into his Seat, but the humble saint wanted to also endure this unpleasantness. After a brief talk with the very old and eccentric archbishop, he was convinced that now the trial of his life would begin."

It was the custom at that time for the new head of the diocese to both entertain the supporters of the Church and to accept their invitations in turn. St. Josaphat was always hospitable to friends and strangers alike and desiring to make friends of them all for the sake of God's work, he accepted invitations for the entire week from the nobility, priesthood and gentry.

He listened to them, won their confidence and made them more docile, as one would tame wild birds. His heart overflowed with indulgence and tenderness thus drawing out the sting of evil in themselves. There was also always plenty of laughter, because Josaphat had a wise sense of humor. He was highly esteemed as a man of good faith with whom everyone was delighted to be acquainted. He attracted all by his simplicity and sincerity. Everywhere that he appeared people were amazed at his humble mien, his great love for God and personal dignity. Everyone saw in him a bishop such as St. Peter himself had wished for: (St. Paul to Timothy 3-2)

"A bishop then must be blameless, the husband of one wife, vigilant, sober, of good behavior, given to hospitality, apt to teach."

The greatness of Josaphat spread rapidly among the people. It was not surprising, therefore, that in the very first week he had converted many of them to the Union. Josaphat was invited not only by Catholics but also by the wealthier Schismatics and he hurried to accept the invitation to their homes more eagerly than to the others because it was a matter of utmost importance to bring them back to the fold for which Christ so ardently prayed. He determined to shun no humble word or deed that would bring this about. He began immediately to instruct them on the ugliness of sin and the reward of a virtuous life and the benefits to be gained by reception of the Holy Spirit in Communion, the gift of our Lord himself, that it might be the food of our souls. He heard their confessions and accepted them into the Church. Since God is the object of our search and all our happiness and we can find peace only in Him, then to know God is to live.

Thus it was that once when he was at the dinner of one of the Schismatics by whom he had been invited and to which his host had also invited other adherents of Schism, one among them, encouraged by Josaphat's affability said to

153

him, "It is rumored here in the city, your Excellency, that you were first to go to the Polish Church to hear the Services and then go to our Church."

"Nothing of the kind!" was Josaphat's reassuring reply. "I never even thought of such a thing!"

When they had heard these words, the Schismatics renounced Schism and joined the Church.

In this way, from the very beginning through his gentleness, gracious and mild manner, he obtained almost impossible results, the good will and respect of not only the Catholics but also the unruly Schismatics.

He was a keen observer of men and firmly convinced that no one can love God truly without also loving fellow-man. Man is a gentle and social creature by nature. He was interested in everything and everybody. He had the capacity to put himself in the place of others. This holy man of refined but dynamic and stable character, knew how to talk to artisans and villagers as well as great gentlemen, sophisticates and worldlings. He brought to all a cordial humaneness that won their hearts and through the balsam of his charity and knowledge disabused them of their errors and led them into the solace and joy of the true faith. He consecrated his time to promoting the reign of peace and persuading men to seek their salvation and to have a clear and definite conviction of the vital importance of unity in the Church. He realized with native acumen that there would be no obstacle to regaining the homeland if the Kingdom of God and His righteousness were sought first and all were united in a powerful and authoritative Church. When we love God, it is a natural consequence to also love our neighbor.

Many marvelous conversions were made by Josaphat. God could do anything through St. Josaphat's faith.

On account of the confusion and separation which reigned throughout the East, the fact was lost sight of that the Lord constituted St. Peter after Himself, Shepherd of the Church, saying to him, "Feed my sheep." What was most regrettable is that the rulers of the Churches themselves took part in the dissensions. Why was the Church united in one body? That discipline and order might be maintained in her of whom it was said, "Ye are the body of Christ and members in particular." (St. John 21-17) (I Corinthians 12-27)

CHAPTER XV

THE REORGANIZATION OF THE DIOCESE

St. Josaphat fulfilled the promise he had made to the old archbishop at their first meeting. At the beginning of their new relationship Gideon could not control the bitterness of jealousy. He was not at all cordial to Josaphat. But Josaphat was not offended by this behavior. He met the bitterness of personal enmity with perfect humility. Full as his days were with anxiety and pressure of troubled souls, they now had the added misery of harshness, reprimands, ceaseless contradictions. He continued to work in the Church as an ordinary priest displaying at the same time his grace of obedience and filial love towards Gideon to avoid making public the inability to effect a working friendship with the archbishop. But useful as Josaphat was, the archbishop did not like to see himself eclipsed by the forceful Josaphat.

Slowly by his patience, gentleness and many kindnesses, Josaphat won over the old man so that he finally called upon him for guidance and gradually relinquished to him the management of the diocese and came to love him as dearly as if he were his own son.

Gideon's deficiency in theology and inefficiency in Ecclesiastical affairs rendered it most necessary to have a trained theologian at his side as bishop to wield the authority for the excellent ends which he had in mind. Having learned wisdom by experience, Gideon finally contented himself with the semblance of honor and power. Thus a vast amount of work was thrust upon Josaphat.

Surrounded by Schismatics, Gideon was not strongly attached to the Union. St. Josaphat, having won his affection, tried his best to secure him firmly in the Catholic faith and did so without too much difficulty. He heard his confession several times, anointed him before his death and did not leave his bedside until the old man, reunited with God and the Holy Catholic Church, gave his soul into God's keeping through his hands. From a deep filial attachment, he gave a dignified funeral for his archbishop commensurate to the office of the deceased, although the treasury was almost depleted.

After Gideon's death, St. Josaphat automatically succeeded him as the archbishop. To his care were entrusted all the churches. The burden of vast administrative problems was laid on his shoulders including the reorganization of an extensive diocese. And this demanded the resources of an alert mind and vigorous body. Because of neglect and lack of foresight on the part of his predecessor, many errors had to be counteracted, many reforms had to be made both in the material and spiritual life of the diocese.

Recalling the words of the holy apostle, St. Paul, to Timothy: (Timothy I, 3-5) "For if a man know not how to rule his own house, how shall he take care of the Church of God?" He first set about to put his own house in order with the aid and inspiration of the Holy Spirit.

He displaced the lazy, quarrelsome and undisciplined domestic help with new servants. Into all phases of life he introduced order, economy and promoted diligence and better relations. For his own comfort he took very little pains. As heretofore, he lived in simplicity and poverty, rigorously denying himself human luxuries. All that concerned his person was clean but simple and humble. He kept only as many servants as he absolutely needed and these had to be pious and hard-working. The only time he was generous with expenditures was in commanding a superb choir for Church services. Realizing that the Ukrainian Rite depends very largely on beautiful singing and a music lover himself, he retained a number of fine singers but these had to either teach or occupy themselves at some trade. All of his servants he put under the management of Emanuel Kantakuzen who had come with him to Polotsk, but he continued surveillance of his servants from time to time. That he took a personal interest in them all is proved by the following incident:

At one time a silver urn was missing from the archbishop's house. The servants, hoping to discover the thief, gathered together and used an old-fashioned superstitious method. There was a superstition among the peasants that whoever is unable on an empty stomach to eat a piece of cheese on which is written the word "guilty," then he is surely the thief. This they did and when one of the boys could not swallow the piece of cheese, they all judged him to be the guilty one. When Josaphat found out about this, he reprimanded the servants severely for their superstitious practice and proclaimed the boy as innocent. And it so happened that in a few days, the real thief was apprehended.

The priests who remained with him in the residence he obliged to say Mass every day and in addition they were to attend lectures on theology and Catholic dogma given by the Jesuits. This command was not at all pleasing to some of them who, not wanting to study, excused themselves by saying that they didn't want to become latinized or to fall under Roman influence and become subject to its ways. He thereupon called them to a conference and put to them the following question: "Is it unwise to borrow fire when our own has gone out?" And when they made no answer to this simple question, he said again to them, "It is not a mistake to seek knowledge from those who possess it. Oh Holy God, some of them join up with the Schismatics, Heretics and even Jews, and they become exceedingly angry if I ally myself with enlightened priests of another Rite with whom in one universal Catholic faith, I am united in the same work for the salvation of souls!"

There was no reply they could make to his arguments; they had to obey the will of their superior.

Josaphat's entire household radiated with a new piety, diligence and discipline, above all the others in the city so that even his enemies admired and praised this wonderful harmony. A more refined demeanor and relationship was in evidence. Hired servants were well treated and cared for in body and soul so that the law of hearing Sunday Mass and rest was observed with absolute fidelity.

Josaphat also brought his property into the same efficient order. He placed the management of the Church properties into the hands of persons who had a reputation for honesty and sobriety instructing them to treat those in their employ with every consideration. For his trustees he chose persons who were kindly and honest. He would not permit his management to punish the transgressors too severely, either by exacting money or corporally, for he wanted those who served him to consider him as a father and good shepherd and not as a tyrant and robber. Purged of all selfishness by the inspiration of faith and love, he was not tempted by money. The taxes which those subject to him were obliged to pay, he often waived when he saw their poverty or inability to meet the obligations. When sometimes his wealthier subjects brought him valuable gifts he would use them to help the poor. Through the Christian method of dealing with his subjects with kindness and gentleness, he created in them a filial affection and devotion and obtained their genuine cooperation which certainly other stricter masters could never have achieved with their rigorous fines and punishments. He was not so much concerned with the acquisition of material possessions as with the salvation of the human souls entrusted to his care. To his administrators he often said: "For the passing value of their paltry offerings, we must return gifts of eternal worth. Since our short life is upheld by the fruit of their labors, we must provide for their eternal welfare so that after death they might all take on the garment of eternal life. A religious lives on the charity of Christ and in Christ his poverty finds maintenance."

True to his teachings, he invariably prepared those who served him for confession, heard their confessions and distributed Holy Communion himself and inspired in their hearts true devotion, the fear of God and earnest piety. He impressed upon them the importance of keeping the Sabbath, of attending Mass on Holy Days of Obligation, of paying careful attention to the Mass and listening to the sermons. He likewise instructed the priests in his diocese to so diligently concern themselves with the salvation of every soul entrusted to them that not one of them should stray from the fold and become lost. He reminded them of what the Apostle had said, "Ye present your bodies as a living sacrifice, holy, acceptable to God, which is your reasonable service. They which live should not henceforth live unto themselves but unto Him which died for them and rose again." The true servant of God should put no trust in his good deeds nor expect justification for his works but place his only hope in the compassion of God. (Romans 12-1)

If there were persons in the parishes of his diocese who were given to thieving, behaved badly or practiced witchcraft and who would not mend their ways despite being reprimanded, he ordered his administrators to discharge them from his service and ignominiously drive them away from the Church premises in order that they might not set a bad example to others. Thus it was that all the good and honest subjects loved St. Josaphat and gladly paid all that was due so that the treasury of the bishop's chancery might be full and so that it might again be expended on the poor. His heart was open to every appeal for he believed that the poor were especially dear to Christ.

Having established order in his household, he turned his attention to the temples of God. Persons who love and glorify God cannot tolerate ugliness, dirt and neglect in the Holy Temple of God but do their best to bring about the most perfect order, neatness and beauty into the dwelling of God Himself. What did not go to the poor was poured out generously for the beautifying of the Church and services in honor of God such as felonions (Chasubles), altar linen, candlesticks, ikons, etc.

By the appearance of the Church one can usually judge the people's zeal towards their God and just how much they care for the Church. Where people take more concern for the things of this world, their church will be neglected, ugly, devoid of the beauty and ancient charm of the Ukrainian Rite. This was the type of Church St. Josaphat found in Polotsk. It was bare, dark, dirty and on the verge of collapse. It was urgently necessary to repair and buttress the Church and if possible to enlarge it. Although the chancery treasury was nearly empty, nonetheless, trusting to Divine Providence, he began at once the work of remodeling the Church. In a comparatively short time, he had renewed it at his own expense, restoring it to its original beauty.

It was to be expected that the fanatical Schismatics would endeavor to discredit even his best deeds. During the remodeling of the Church of St. Sophia at the Seat of the Diocese in Polotsk, he ordered the old cupolas to be demolished, desiring to replace them gradually with new, better ones. There were five of these cupolas (Note: A Byzantine Church has five and sometimes seven domes which in Cathedrals and even in some parish churches are gilded. At the entrance of the Church there is usually a porch extending along the whole western width.) The people considered the central one as a symbol of the patriarch of Rome and the other four symbolical of the Eastern patriarchs. Josaphat ordered the central one to be renovated and installed first. The Schismatics seeing this complained all over town that Josaphat had cast out the four Eastern patriarchs from the Church and retained only the Roman patriarch.

This was reported to his Excellency who laughed and said, "I promise to restore the four patriarchs to the Church, provided they will not of themselves separate from the chief."

When the great church, majestic and pure in symmetry was renovated and the workmen were ready to set up the four other cupolas, St. Josaphat was so elated watching them work, that he shouted, "I would like to die when this work is finished." His desire was fulfilled, for when the work was in the final stages of completion, he received the crown of martyrdom.

Besides remodeling the Church of St. Sophia in Polotsk, St. Josaphat built several other churches in the smaller cities and towns such as in Vitebsk and Orshi and others, and remodeled or renewed many others in his diocese, everywhere restoring order, beauty and respectability. The result of these first efforts was that people paid visits to the sanctuary more willingly and regularly.

However, this zeal in beautifying the temples of God became very nearly the cause of his death. On a round of visits throughout the diocese, he stopped first at Vitebsk, which was the hornet's nest of Schismatic activity in his diocese and here he found the Church in a dilapidated state. To attract people to the Church and to make it less unworthy of God, he made up his mind to improve its appearance. Seeing the "Ikonostasis" (*Note:* A great picture screen which almost reaches the ceiling, separating the sanctuary from the nave. Upon it are ikons of our Lord, the Blessed Virgin and of many saints and prophets. At important parts of the Liturgy, three doors which pierce the screen are opened to disclose the priest at the altar. The center ones are the royal doors, the side ones are the deacon doors.) This Ikonostasis was so covered with cobwebs and dirt that the holy pictures were hardly discernible. He ordered it removed from the Church and brought outside in order to make it easier to clean and where necessary to gild the holy pictures. It served to stir up the story immediately circulated throughout the city by the Schismatics that His Excellency wanted to convert them all to the Latin Rite and that was the reason he had ordered the Ikonostasis to be removed from the Church. It acted upon unstable souls filled with untempered passion for speculation and dispute until the town was in a turmoil. They talked of taking his life and one among them ran up to Josaphat as he came out of the Church and publicly threatened him with death if the Ikonostasis were not immediately restored to its proper place. Their fury subsided only when they saw the clean Ikonostasis shining with new gilt in its original position in the Church.

During the war with the Muscovites much of the property of the diocese and the parishes was lost. Not only the land and the proceeds from its rental but also the parish buildings, churches, convents and monasteries fell into unscrupulous hands. Clearly it demanded a desperate remedy. St. Josaphat, the gentlest of hearts and most merciful of men, whose virtues, however, were allied with a remarkably keen business sense, now proceeded to take action to get all these properties restored of which the churches had become illegally dispossessed. He read over the deeds, searched the records, looked over the town archives and whenever he became convinced that the property in question belonged to the Church, he pursued legal action until the property was returned. Whenever he was in doubt as to his rights then he consulted persons of upright character, conscientious and just, well-informed in legal matters. He listened to their advice, taking care, nonetheless, not to injure anyone in any transaction. There were endless steps to be taken and opposition and disappointments to be encountered. However, whenever he was convinced that the property actually belonged to the Church then he swept aside all ordinary considerations, fought all obstructions, going from court to court until he reclaimed them. In this way he managed to effect the return of about half the Church properties that had been lost. Hatred, infamy, threats to his life, were heaped upon him for his zeal in reclaiming the Church properties. Thus it was that the Korsakiw family hired a murderer for Josaphat because he had taken away from them the monastery of St. Boris and Hliva of which it had taken possession illegally. Even though Josaphat knew that a paid murderer watched to slay him, he didn't let it stop him but reclaimed the monastery, remodeled the church and brought monks to occupy the monastery. He likewise reclaimed the monastery in Bratslav and Mstislav, which the Schismatics had converted for their purposes. In Polotsk there was a convent of the Sisters of St. Basil which had become totally neglected, forsaken, and impoverished materially and spiritually. St. Josaphat remodeled and renewed it, found ways and means of assuring support for the nuns and to rejuvenate the decadent monastic life. He brought a few nuns trained in his school as novices at Vilno and himself instructed and imparted proficiency by teaching them the principles of Christian self-discipline. In a short time his efforts were greatly rewarded for the convent soon shone with great virtue and became filled with pious virgins from the best families who vowed themselves to zealously serve God in the monastic life.

They visited the poor and nursed the sick. They formed Catechism classes for the children and taught to those who were apt the very fine and beautiful Ukrainian needlecraft.

It is necessary to see Josaphat not only as a very holy monk and bishop but also as a genial man of action, the friend of everybody and successful man of affairs.

Considering the total of Josaphat's works, we are forced to quote the words of his biographer, Morokhovia, "It is difficult for us to form any idea of how one man could in so brief a period of time perform so many good works, having so little time at his disposal. This is a mystery which is often repeated in the lives of saints. That which ordinary people are unable to accomplish in decades of time, the saints are able to perform apparently without difficulty and in a comparatively brief space of time, such as a few days, hours or even minutes. This secret of continued success cannot be otherwise explained than that the saints possessing a greater measure of divine grace, receive more support from God."

Some of his sanctity apparently remained in each Church and monastery he visited and upon those earnest workers who were to continue under his direction to care for the salvation of souls and to carry on the work of promoting the Holy Union.

Thus through his many phases of work and philanthropy which he carried on as archbishop to the last day of his life, St. Josaphat uplifted the ideal of the spiritual and religious life throughout the diocese.

Saints always seek the glory of God only and do His will after attaining that union which is the purpose of man's existence, led by the Holy Spirit step by step never thinking of the vast activity in apostolic labors on the way in which they would become involved.

As St. Basil said, "Everyone is a traveler in this life. All men run a race which carries each one forward, pressing on everyone towards the goal so that life possesses neither abiding joy nor unchanging grief. Neither the way nor the things present in it belong to us."

CHAPTER XVI

THE REVIVAL OF RELIGIOUS LIFE
IN THE DIOCESE

The most difficult change for man to undergo is his personal spiritual rebirth and even more difficult to accomplish is the religious awakening of whole groups or classes of people. This overhauling of the human soul cannot be accomplished solely by persons of great learning, of many talents, of powerful will nor those with a strong personality. These qualities may be of great value in the understanding of and in the orientation to the spiritual life in the individual himself but they cannot of themselves effect the actual change. It is not enough to understand human nature, the innate faults or weaknesses, the circumstances under which the individual lives or to understand the cure for all his waywardness and after deciding upon the proper remedy to bring about the necessary change in the spiritual life. For spiritual rebirth it is necessary to have the grace of God and it will suffice in itself without the concomitants of human wisdom and great learning. This grace of God and assistance from heaven Josaphat possessed in great measure and through this powerful grace was effected the phenomenal reawakening in his diocese.

His first efforts were directed to the rejuvenation of the religiously lax clergy. St. Josaphat realized that the pupils could be no better than their teacher. As the children resemble their father and the sheep are as good as their shepherd, therefore, the faithful could be no better than their pastor. When he took over the diocese of Polotsk, he felt that the words of the Holy Spirit had been fulfilled: (Matthew 26-31)

"Then said Jesus unto them, all ye shall be offended because of me this night, for it is written, I will smite the shepherd and the sheep of the flock shall be scattered."

It was first necessary to spiritually revitalize and to improve the conditions of the priesthood, which for centuries past had been spiritually and physically impoverished by lack of proper education and training and subjected to the princes and nobles who dictated to the Church and who cared more for their own personal aggrandizement while it took but lightly the Church's grave responsibility towards human souls.

The education of the priests in those days did not come under the surveillance of the bishop as we have it today in the seminaries. The Polish government would not consider the establishment of schools for the Ukrainian priesthood, but the education and training of future candidates for the priesthood began and ended in the home of the pastor. The pastor taught his son to read and write in the Slavonic language, a little of the Church music, that is ecclesiastical chant and the rudiments of the faith, the celebrating of Mass, and this constituted the entire education and training for the priesthood. The results of such training were that many Christians were servants of Christ in name only and this unenlightened priesthood was not capable of adequately instructing the people in the truths of the Catholic faith. Sadly many of the people easily fell away from the faith, were persuaded to join the Schism and the better educated families disdaining the uneducated priesthood, its faith and rite, forsook the ancient faith and rite of their forefathers and joined the various Protestant sects and sometimes the Latin Rite becoming Polonized and permanently lost to their people.

To make up for the inadequacy in the education and training of the priesthood, Josaphat published a more detailed Catechism in conformity with the Catechism written for priests of the Latin Rite, as approved by the authority of the Catholic Assembly. He distributed the Catechism to all the priests in the diocese and commanded them to study it and write an examination paper on it.

Another abuse resulting from this low estate of the priesthood was that it lived not in keeping with its status. St. Josaphat, desiring to remedy this evil situation, composed and published a body of forty-eight fixed rules for the clerical life and work with Scripture proofs which purpose was to improve the profession of the priesthood according to the laws of the Catholic Assembly. The over-all aim was to bridge over the gulf between the clergy and the faithful by breaking down the centuries' old tendency of indifference and even contempt by the people. Among other things it is stated in them:

The priest should make his confession on all the most important Holy Days of the year. He must say Mass at least every Sunday and Holy Day of Obligation, as well as the Church offices. During the Lenten Season and before Christmas, he should make every effort to visit all his parishioners who live at an inconvenient distance from the Church and prepare them for confession and Holy Communion. On every Holy Day and Sunday, he is to teach the faithful the various prayers and preach a sermon on the teachings of Christ. It is not permitted for priests to accede to worldly authority or listen to its advice in matters pertaining to the religious life.

In order to insure obedience to these laws he created a

system of fines for the disobedient and he set deacons in authority over them who would travel from parish to parish to oversee the scrupulous adherence to these new laws.

To uphold the religious zeal and at the same time promote further progress, he proposed to institute an annual session of the synod of the priesthood. Since his diocese was extensive and covered a large area, he ordered these Assemblies to convene in three places: at Polotsk, Vitebsk, and Mstyslav, to make it as convenient as possible for all the priests to attend.

He presided at these meetings himself, instructed them, supervised their examinations, where necessary reprimanded them, doing his best to make them real servants of God and the Catholic Church.

There was still another blotch on the life of the priesthood which was a scandal to the Ukrainian Church. The mutinous and arrogant gentry who shared with Church and monastery nearly all of the wealth of the time, treated the Ukrainian priesthood miserably. The serfs were attached to the land of the nobles, belonging to their master like common chattel, enjoying a minimum of human rights and decency.

The priest was considered to be on the same level as a villager, always dependent on the gentry to the extent that he was forced to obey it even in matters pertaining strictly to religion, for instance as in the sacrament of marriage, not considering the purely material concerns such as rentals, taxes, jobs and other essential services. The order most sacred of all had become the most ridiculous.

St. Josaphat could not tolerate such conditions in his diocese. This was to be absolutely altered for the future. Therefore, he forbade obedience to the supercilious gentry and advised the priests to resort to the courts of law when necessary to uphold their rights.

He realized, of course, that such a command would be the cause of hatred, anger and reprisals by the lawless gentry, but when it came to the rights of the priesthood and the Church, St. Josaphat considered no sacrifice too great. A few of the landed gentry built their own churches in their settlements and hired priests indiscriminately. This action created a priesthood independent of the bishop, completely ignoring his laws and fines. To offset this move, St. Josaphat forbade the erection of churches and chapels without his permission and instructed the priests not to serve in them.

Ordinarily he treated the priests who were subject to him as a father treats his children. Those who blundered he endeavored to set on the right path with his gentleness and loving compassion. Whenever he saw that this method failed, he ordered those who were incorrigible to be turned out of his diocese. Josaphat never relaxed his efforts or neglected distasteful tasks whenever he thought a wayward or blundering cleric would thus enjoy greater self-respect in his office and work if he exerted himself more diligently. He kept severity as a last resort to be used only when every means of persuasion within the power of a loving heart had been exhausted.

In this way the priesthood gradually forged ahead not only intellectually but also in respect among the people. The priests became the servants of God and not hostages or servants and pawns of the gentry. It is not the habit that is the glory of the priesthood but virtue. Living according to the proprieties of the priesthood, they became practical examples to their parishioners which is of more value than the most eloquent of preachers. The people, seeing the good resulting from the Union, gradually accepted it and became confirmed in it.

That was why St. Josaphat could answer Leo Sapiha boldly when he accused some of the priesthood of stirring up trouble and behaving in an unseemly manner. "If any of my priests have misbehaved and are not exactly perfect, the reason for it is that they were brought up under Schism and

171

not the Union; therefore, don't blame me for it but Schism."

One would think that while engaged in all this work, Josaphat neglected the conversion of the Schismatics. On the contrary, now more than ever as the shepherd of a flock, he kept in mind the words of the Master Shepherd, Jesus, "And other sheep I have, which are not of this fold; them also I must bring and they shall hear my voice; and there shall be one fold and one shepherd." (John 10-16)

Thus St. Josaphat's zeal in the conversion of the Schismatics increased. He used all available means to persuade them to join the Uniate Church.

He met with them often, sat down in their midst, allowed them to ask him questions and instructed them. He spoke of the Church and the faith. There was always plenty of laughter for no one could tell a story with more wit or give a hint more delicately in amusing the crowd. Often in his sermons he thrashed out the points of contention. Thus writes his biographer, His Excellency Susha:

"He had an extraordinary sweetness in his speech, dignity in quotation and power of conviction. He was prompt to reply and unhesitating in the advice he gave. His thorough knowledge of Scripture furnished him with enlightening answers to the most ingenious arguments of his opponents. He had at the same time a remarkably retentive memory and could quote exactly at a moment's notice from the writings of the Holy Fathers and books of Scripture so that he nearly always convinced the Schismatics and persuaded them to join the Union. His pleasant and courteous manner and kindness drew many more to the Union." (Note: "Life of St. Josaphat," Susha. Chapter III, Page 56.)

The people so loved to hear him speak that when once during a sermon he stopped and said, "My children, I will not detain you much longer at this sermon," the crowd answered, "Father, speak as long as you like even the whole day, we will gladly listen to you."

He often spoke in the Church of St. Sophia and his ardent and fiery sermons drew hundreds of both the faithful and Schismatics. During all of his sermons the Churches were crowded to overflowing. To counteract the subtle and manifold assaults of heresies, he published a booklet for the more enlightened class, "The Defense of the Faith," in which he explained the basic truths of the Catholic Faith and which he distributed free of charge. He ordered translations from the Latin into Slavonic of writings that treated on the Union. Whenever he noticed that a Schismatic feared him, he sent a priest or another Catholic to him to convert him to the Union. If he found it impossible to convert the whole family then he tried to convert at least one person from the household and through him to gradually bring the entire family into the Uniate Church. He welcomed graciously and respectfully all Schismatics who came to him. He drew them to himself with gifts, visited their homes, invited them to his table and at dinner spoke of the Union and the importance of the recognition of the Pope of Rome as head of the Ukrainian Church. His kindness to the poor and sorrowing was unfailing. Using all these methods, St. Josaphat brought back to the Catholic Church many of the intellectual gentry who had turned Schismatic or Calvinist. He softened hard hearts and brought to repentance hundreds of the elite and thousands of the rank and file. Nearly all of Polotsk was converted to the Uniate Church.

St. Josaphat was especially pleased when the people of Polotsk nicknamed him "Soul Snatcher" for actually it was he that tore thousands of souls from the claws of Schism.

Desiring to sustain his sheep in the Union, he often visited their parishes, listened to their requests and desires and tried his best to satisfy them to the best of his ability. To teach them greater piety and strengthen them in the faith, he issued a brief Catechism which he distributed to the faithful everywhere. His counsels, lofty and inspiring, implanted a desire in the hearts of men to strive for higher spiritual development.

Unmindful of the dignity of his position, he often visited the sick, regardless of whether they were Catholic, Schismatic or Heretic. He prepared them for a happy death, converted them to the Catholic Church, heard their confessions, gave them Communion or Extreme Unction. Although the Schismatics often did him great injury, St. Josaphat always returned gratitude for their hatred. He loved the Schismatics, but for Schism itself, he had no use whatever. He opposed it at every opportunity, preached against it and denounced the books and publications of the Schismatics. He forbade Schismatic churches to be established in his diocese. It needed strength and prudence to keep the peace while preserving the right balance of kindness and justice.

Thus it came about that the exiled Schismatic priests joined forces with other Schismatics outside the diocese and set up a howl against Josaphat that he persecuted and banished all Schismatics. That is why even to this day, the Schismatics and those who favor Schism wrongly accuse St. Josaphat of being their persecutor.

This self-sacrificing guileless work, these ceaseless efforts and Apostolic zeal finally succeeded in turning the diocese of Polotsk from Schismatic to Catholic unity. Very few Schismatics remained and these dared not to come out with their opposition openly. God's work conquered, the kingdom of Christ again reigned in the hearts of the faithful so that Rutsky could truthfully state later, "This good shepherd found everything overrun by the Schismatics when he came into office, but with God's help during the brief period of not quite three years, through his ingenuity, superhuman courage and magnanimity he so bound the hearts of all to himself and the Uniate Church that hardly a trace of Schism remained."

"Under Gideon, we were all Schismatics," testified Diahilevich, "but Josaphat converted us all to the Catholic Church."

Josaphat's joy was unbounded when he saw the scattered sheep returning en masse to the one fold under the One Shepherd and this joy seemed to strengthen him and increase his power in the work of further enlightening the souls entrusted to him. Schism in its retreat from his diocese left some deplorable after-effects which needed attention. It would not be possible to describe all his good works for the benefit of the faithful. However, there are two outstanding reforms which should be mentioned. After his arrival at Polotsk St. Josaphat noticed that the children were barred from the Holy Sacrament of Communion by the excuse that they were unprepared to receive it. This did not please St. Josaphat for this same excuse also prevented the adolescent boys and girls from receiving the Sacrament. St. Josaphat sympathized with the misery of soul of the children abandoned to their own perversity.

Therefore, St. Josaphat himself undertook to prepare the children. He started Catechism classes for the children and the adolescent boys and girls, taking place early in the morning before work. Those who were present regularly he would reward with some little gift. There was nothing he loved more than to awaken the young souls and implant in them the grace of God. He knew how to speak to children on their own level and they in turn adored him.

When they were properly prepared, he gave each innocent little soul Jesus Christ in Holy Communion himself. He likewise commanded his pastors throughout the diocese to start Catechism classes to prepare the children for the reception of the Holy Sacrament of Communion. A few stupid and possibly more likely, lazy priests rebelled against the new ruling but Josaphat was firmly convinced that if a child who has been properly prepared receives Communion frequently, it will be more likely to retain its innocence and holiness much longer than one who receives it in later years, for the Holy Sacrament of Communion is especially prescribed for toning down the fiery passions of youth and eliminating any inherited bad habits.

Christian parents who are anxious to bring up their children under divine guidance should try to have them prepared for the reception of the Holy Sacrament of Communion as early as possible before the passions and bad habits have had a chance to take hold on the innocent soul, but the children should be carefully and effectively prepared for sometimes the whole life and possibly even the attainment of eternal life is dependent upon the first confession and Communion of the child.

The other very important work of reform by St. Josaphat was his hearing of confessions. Schism doesn't like confession. The Schismatics made confession but once a year, as if they sinned only once a year during the Easter season. It would seem that having wallowed in sin for a year, they would become so accustomed to it that repentance would seem for them practically an impossibility, so that after confession, they would return again to the same evil. The same thing can happen to those careless Catholics who come to confession but once a year. An earnest Catholic, as soon as he happens to fall into sin hurries to confession not only to receive absolution but also to be given a cure for the sin so that he might be prevented from falling into it again.

St. Josaphat noted that in many places people had not been to confession for years, living in sin and transgressing the commandments without fear of God and His Holy Laws. This was the reason he had made it one of the forty-eight rules commanding the priests in his diocese to hear the confessions of their flock at least twice a year.

In the hearing of confession St. Josaphat was himself the best example for his priests. He was most courteous in his treatment of social inferiors and of the poor.

Rev. Kosinsky stated that on several occasions when he

was stopped on the street for alms-giving by destitute men, he asked them where they had made their last confession and their reply was "with our archbishop."

Gregory Ushatsky, one of the servants in Josaphat's household, testified that Josaphat was unceasingly evangelizing the people. He heard confessions everywhere, in the pasturelands, the fields, by the rivers, in way station cabins, anywhere that he could, he persuaded them to make confession, prepared them himself, and then heard their confessions, squatting on any convenient spot to do so. Whenever he was unable to persuade them with kind words, he used gifts and almsgiving to accomplish the same end. Just as he came to a knowledge of souls by the most diverse routes so by the same diverse routes he led them to salvation.

Thus one day an old beggar came to St. Josaphat asking for alms and St. Josaphat promised to help him if he in turn made a promise to make his confession. And the beggar who would not even hear of confession under ordinary circumstances was stirred by the persuasive sweetness and tone of authority tempered by grace to admit that he had never in his life made a confession. Having made his confession to Josaphat, he arose not only comforted but became a firm believer and he received, accordingly, very generous alms. A few days later, the servants learned that the old man had died soon after making his confession.

The consequences of more frequent confessions was that people became better Catholics and were more attached to the Holy Church.

Thus three years passed by quickly for St. Josaphat occupied in his work of securing peace and unity throughout the breadth and length of his extensive diocese, uniting it into one strong Catholic body, and restoring the ideal of a virtuous life. His fame shone out in its fullest splendor. The priests became true servants of God and the Church, leading their flocks along the path of God's commandments. From

177

the poorest and sometimes immoral class they became a devoted group working hard at their vocation in supporting the Union. Everywhere was order and peace so that it seemed the Union was safe at last from the violence of Schism, securing the peace and grandeur of the Church and that hell had no power to destroy the Union and there was nothing further needed except patient continuation of the work of maintaining the Uniate Church and Christian zeal in the service of God and the salvation of souls.

But it was not as it seemed. At the moment when success seemed assured all of St. Josaphat's work was cast into uncertainty. This was but the natural period of quiet before the advent of the storm which was soon to start and with letters in blood write its history of the Ukrainian Church.

CHAPTER XVII

THE SPIRITUAL LIFE OF ST. JOSAPHAT

Peculiar to the lives of saints, who, despite overwork and their untiring efforts in the salvation of the souls of others, still find time for recollection and study in the salvation of their own souls. The more zeal they display for the good of others, the harder they strive for their own progress. St. Josaphat was one of these. All those whom God has chosen to do great things for Himself seek Him until they are emptied of all other thoughts and desires which could impede their union with God, conforming themselves to His mind and will and thus receiving all that He wills to bestow upon them in overflowing charity and service to their fellow man.

After becoming archbishop, he not only did not alter his strict ascetic life but rather increased its rigour. For seldom less than twenty hours of each day he was on duty and never in that time lost communion with God. His prayer was unceasing and pervaded all his activities. He lived as a monk in the world, in the Basilian monastery and as a monk he remained as head of the Church.

Not to waste any time in his devotion to the care of other human souls, he arose even earlier at night, said his prayers, meditated on some great and simple truth which fixed his thought for the whole day and said his offices. Then recalling the words of the Saviour, "For whether is greater he that sitteth at meat, or he that serveth? is not he that sitteth at meat? but I am among you as he that serveth," he kept the keys himself, opened the door of the residence and the Church, rang the Angelus and prepared everything in readiness for the service of Mass. During the entire Mass he sang himself with his melodious voice the sacred chants so movingly that men were instinctively drawn to venerate the presence of divine love in this servant of the crucified, sometimes bringing tears of joy to their eyes. He was a living vessel from which grace flowed to the souls of men while he prayed.

Whenever he was on a prolonged journey and stopped at way stations and junctions, he hurried to nearby churches and there he celebrated the divine mysteries recollected in prayer and meditation. As at home so on his journeys his soul was constantly directed to God through his meditations. Whenever he was away from home, he invariably sought some quiet nook where he could meditate without being disturbed. When at home, he often went out into the garden and there giving himself up to meditation upon holy things he turned his eyes inward to contemplate upon the great Truth that is God and to become infused with the loving knowledge of Him who alone is able to enlighten the soul with direction and purpose. He prayed imploring almost unceasingly, "God grant us Holy Union, convert the Schismatics, Heretics and the heathen."

Before celebrating Mass, he prepared himself by long prayers and self-mortification. Such preparation sometimes occupied the whole night. While he was in Polotsk, he had the habit of going in the middle of the night to the Church to pray. One night two of his hired young men were led by their intemperate curiosity to see what he did at that hour in Church. Hidden behind a pillar they saw St. Josaphat kneeling before the ikon of the Blessed Virgin Mary from which streamed golden rays of light bathing the saint in a brilliance greater than that of the sun. At another time, watching him through the cracks of the door, they saw St. Josaphat flaying himself severely before the crucified Saviour, while clouds of fiery light enveloped him ever more closely in great brilliance.

Overawed by the mysterious splendors they had witnessed, the young men vowed to devote themselves to the service of God by entering into the monastic life of the Basilian Order. One of them soon became a monk but the other postponed his vow for a long time. And God punished his self-perjury for at one time while he was at a celebration he slipped and cracked his skull from which injury he never recovered. St. Josaphat was fervently devoted to the Blessed Virgin Mary and to Archangel Michael.

It is to be expected that out of reverence and humility St. Josaphat kept such favors jealousy hidden, yet certain phrases he let slip and from the observation of others of his household, there is reason to suppose that both the Church and his bedroom were frequent witnesses to visitors from the heavenly kingdom. Of mystical visions there is no proof except from the study of his eyes which saw through and beyond the things of sense and his spiritual exuberance which nothing could blight or destroy.

He liked best to pray before the ikons of the Blessed Virgin Mary. To her he offered all his self-mortifications, the wearing of the hair shirt and the scourgings. On Holy Days devoted to the Blessed Virgin Mary, he said Mass in her honor with great devotion. He mentioned her often in his sermons and spread and promoted devotion to the Blessed Mother of God.

After having become the archbishop he did not neglect

his self-mortifications but intensified them. He continued his fasts and not only avoided excesses in eating and drinking but often deprived himself of food essential for normal health. The scourgings he never neglected under any circumstances. Whenever he was absent from home he sought a spot protected from curious eyes, in a garden or in the woods or the fields and there he flayed himself until he bled. His archdeacon, Dorotheus, related the story of one of these scourgings:

It was while they were staying in the village of Usatien in one of the parishes of the diocese in January during the bitterest cold season. It so happened that Dorotheus blundered off the main road in the snow onto the path that led into the woods and a disturbing sight met his eyes. In a clearing among the trees knelt Josaphat, stripped to the waist and scourging himself so furiously that he was hardly able to breathe. After each flaying he lay on the snow on his face with arms outstretched, forming a cross and prayed thus for a long time. Dorotheus, unable to bear watching such suffering drew nearer to the saint and begged him to take care for his health and his life at least for the sake of the Church, but St. Josaphat answered him briefly, "Leave me in peace, dear Brother. Go home and tell no one what you have seen."

The obedient archdeacon with tears in his eyes was forced to leave his master who continued to punish himself. Nor did he take off his hairshirt. His loins he girded so tightly with a belt of prickly chains that one time he fainted from the sheer pain while celebrating Mass and after Mass when he was unable himself to take it off, he asked his archdeacon to do it for him, at the same time forbidding him to speak of it to anyone.

He underwent these self-mortifications in order to subdue the four natural passions until he attained such mastery over his being that not a trace of sinful inclinations remained in him and his purity was comparable to that of the angels. This ascetic practice prepared his soul to receive the gift of contemplation so that for Josaphat the divine and heavenly joy was constant and in this he moved and lived and did all his work untiringly, unmindful of recompense, hindrances or hardships. He denuded his soul of all that might hinder its capacity to be recreated in its original unity and give place to being itself.

He loved everyone but especially towards the poor and neglected he showed his great tenderness and hospitality. At his table there always sat at least one beggar while he ordered food to be served to others in another room and after dinner he gave them alms personally. His heart was open to every appeal. If ever any money came to him, he at once distributed it among those who had asked for aid.

On one occasion when he had nothing to give to a poor widow who came to beg alms, he ordered his omophorion, the symbol of the episcopal office, to be pawned and the money thus obtained to be given to her. The poor always went away comforted, cheered and satisfied for the income of the archbishop he considered not as his own but as placed in his keeping by God to be used for the good of the Church and the poor even to the extent that he refused to use this money to help his own family. As soon as he had become the archbishop his brother came to visit him with the idea in mind that now that he had a brother as archbishop he could begin to live comfortably. But St. Josaphat understood the spirit of Christ when He said: (Matthew 10-37)

"He that loveth father or mother more than me is not worthy of me: and he that loveth son or daughter more than me is not worthy of me."

Therefore, giving his brother some money and two suits of clothes, he said, "The proceeds of the Church should be used for the support of the churches and the poor. You must find ways and means of supporting yourself in the manner to which you are accustomed."

As he was generous to the poor so he was economical and even niggardly in satisfying his own needs.

Forced out of his monastery cell by obedience to his superiors to live in the palatial residence of the archbishop, to be attended by many servants, making use of fine carriages and horses and such other luxuries in connection with the dignity of his office, he nevertheless never forgot his vows of poverty. Alms-giving, the remodeling and renewal of old churches and the building of new ones and the many other needs of the diocese exhausted his income. He continued to live as simply as a monk, with his attendants. Although as the archbishop he could dress in better and more comfortable clothing, he retained only the habit which he wore as a monk and nothing he held was too old or worn out. Even the cape of the archbishop was of ordinary material so that it could hardly be distinguished from that of an ordinary monk. On his table appeared only the plainest fare. In other words, the archbishop's residence had changed into a miniature monastery. His life was that of a monk, tranquillity of mind directing the eyes of his soul to things eternal instead of distracting them with superfluous cares.

The second most important virtue of a good monk is his obedience to his superiors. Although as an executive of the Church, he was not obliged to obey the superiors of the Basilian Order, nonetheless, he adhered to this virtue until death, obeying the Metropolitan in all things, just as if he were an ordinary monk and Rutsky his archimandrite. To understand the high degree of his development of the virtue of obedience, it is sufficient to report the following incident. When by the will of God the residence of the archbishop in Polotsk burned down, together with all the other buildings on the property so that there was not a decent carriage left nor a pair of good horses, Rutsky not being informed of this, just then ordered him to come and discuss some important matter of business with him at New Novgorod. Although the journey was long, some seventy miles and he had not a decent carriage, St. Josaphat did not postpone the trip but hired an ordinary wagon and horses and without further ado traveled thus to visit the Metropolitan. The Metropolitan was amazed to see St. Josaphat arrive in a plain wagon and having learned the reason for it, he remarked that he could have remained at home and was not obliged to make the journey under the circumstances, if a proper carriage to travel in was not available in keeping with the dignity of his office. But Josaphat replied briefly, "I could not ignore the request of one who is my shepherd after God and so I came." By this strict obedience to the rule, St. Josaphat proved the value of his ideal of love and understanding of the spirit of the monastic life particularly in the Basilian Order for the sake of the holiness of individual souls.

It has been noted how much time and effort he had devoted to the renewal of the monasteries and rule and direction of the monastic and mission work in his diocese, which work he did not neglect even up to the time of his death. He attended all the assemblies of the monks held in the Metropolitan See at Ruta and in order to instill a stronger faith in some of them and to revitalize the ideal of the spiritual life throughout his diocese, he renewed his monastic vows. "They which live should not henceforth live unto themselves but unto Him which died for them and rose again."

True obedience must be impregnated by humility. A proud man or one who thinks too well of himself will never be obedient. Therefore, the man who is obedient must also be humble. St. Josaphat had resolved to live a life of severe self-discipline and austerity, but this did not estrange him from enjoyment of life and taking an interest in his fellow man. He lived his daily life in brotherly love and anxiety for his neighbor. St. Josaphat harbored no grudges or personal hatred towards anyone. He was equally at home with the poor as with the rich, even more so with the poor. He considered himself of lowly birth and unworthy of the high position which he held. He saw himself as mere nothing. It is not only God who loves the humble and is unsparing in His blessings as He promised, but people also love them and that was why St. Josaphat was able to draw out the sting of evil in so many of the Schismatics and to win the hearts of those about him by his affability and simple, unassuming behavior and to share his joy with them.

He was always ready to forgive his enemies for their evil deeds and reward them with gratitude. He was devoid of all hatred towards anyone. All the people were aware of this. Some of them unable to obtain from him what they wanted purposely did him an injury or persecuted him in order to obtain what they desired. He was especially successful in settling disputes, reconciling those who had quarrelled. Often he would go to visit them himself or invite them to his residence and work with them in finding the solution to their differences. In his work, he did not make a distinction among Schismatics, Heretics or even Jews but was constantly ready to give the aid that was required of him to counsel and compose their differences. He kept in mind what the Blessed Saviour had said: (Matthew 25-40)

"And the King shall answer and say unto them, Verily I say unto you, inasmuch as ye have done it unto one of the least of these my brethren, ye have done it unto me."

There was nothing he strove harder to attain than purity of conscience. Almost without exception he went to confession before every Mass. He had two confessors. Whenever he left home on a journey he usually took one of his confessors with him saying, "I want to have a confessor with me all the time so that I can make my confession more frequently."

What profound respect the confessors had for St. Josaphat can be gotten from the statement made by his confessor the Rev. Konsinsky who under oath testified to the Apostolic Commission, "I am fully convinced that the life and works of St. Josaphat followed closely the lives and works of other saints and martyrs in the same rank of bishops and monks. All his preachings and teachings and deeds conformed to the inspiration of the Holy Spirit and the will of God. He united to the highest advantage the life of contemplation with that of intense activity in the Order. He distinguished himself, to my way of thinking as well as in the opinion of others who knew him, by heroic virtues, for God wanted to make of him an example to persons of all ranks and especially for the benefit of the black-robed monks of the Basilian Order and bishops of the Church." (*Note:* In the Eastern Church only monks are eligible to become bishops.) In like vein spoke those who lived with and served Josaphat and who thus knew his life intimately. Gregory Ushatsky, one of St. Josaphat's attendants, for whom he entertained the sincerest affection, when questioned by the Commission if he had noticed any unusual virtues in St. Josaphat, burst into tears and said: "I have served with the archbishops of Polotsk for fifty years but I have never seen anyone who could in the slightest degree compare with the person of St. Josaphat."

This brief outline of the spiritual life of St. Josaphat shows us that although he left the monastery cell and worked without ceasing for the good of his diocese he never neglected the constant cultivation and pruning of his own soul and perfection in all the virtues but persisted in forging ahead to greater heights of holiness.

187

CHAPTER XVIII

A NEW STRUGGLE WITH THE SCHISMATICS

St. Josaphat had labored for three years in the extensive program of Catholic Action of his diocese during which time his work brought forth tremendous fruits. Everywhere peace reigned as the Union took root; piety flourished. It seemed that the Schismatics, having lost their power, would abandon their fruitless struggle with the Uniates. However, the devil was not asleep. He soon sent upon the unfortunate Ukraine a new and more frightful storm which would rock it to its foundation.

It was the year 1620. From Moscow came the Greek Theophanus, the self-appointed patriarch of Jerusalem. As it is written by historians, a Turkish Sultan had sent Theophanus to Moscow on a secret mission to persuade Moscow to declare war against Poland at the same time when the Sultan would attack it with all his forces. On his return journey, by invitation of the Kozak Hetman Konashevich, he stopped at Kiev where Kozaks and Schismatics welcomed him ceremoniously. Theophanus having been given full power over the Church in Moscow and Ukraine by the Byzantine patriarch, wrote letters after his arrival in Kiev to all the leading authorities in the Ukrainian cities announcing his arrival and at the same time calling upon all Schismatics to hold fast to their Orthodox faith, to organize and unite themselves for its defense and to look to him as their shepherd.

The king also heard of his arrival and guessing the purpose of the visit sent him a personal guard from among his courtiers, as a courtesy, and a letter in which he expressed the hope that Theophanus had come to Ukraine to visit only his own faithful followers and would try his best to keep the peace. It was impossible at the time for the king to act otherwise than to accept the spying patriarch in his kingdom, as he feared an uprising in Ukraine.

Poland was in a precarious position, threatened by war on every side. It needed the help of the Kozaks who at that period had a powerful, numerous and well-trained army and who had but recently helped to defeat the Turks. The Schismatics were also aware of this and took advantage of that opportunity by asking Theophanus to ordain Schismatic bishops. Theophanus whose concern was to bring about chaos readily complied with their wishes.

For each of the Sees occupied by the Uniate bishops and Metropolitan, he ordained Schismatics. As Metropolitan he appointed the fanatical Schismatic Jona Boretsky, for the diocese of Polotsk, Smotritsky and for the diocese of Volodimir, Kurtsevich, etc.

They all rebelled at the audacity of the Turkish emissary and spy who had the courage, without the permission of the king and without the participation of the other Church dignitaries, to ordain new bishops. However, the deed was done. It is true that the irate king sent an order to all the towns of Ukraine to seize the new Schismatic bishops and sentence them according to the existent laws of the land but these letters had no effect for Turkey had already declared war on Poland and the attention of all was distracted by the meeting of the Diet which was to consider the various matters in connection with the war declaration. Theophanus, having accomplished his plan of creating disorder fled, fearing his own possible imprisonment.

At the Assembly of the Diet in 1620, the Kozaks, conscious of their power and the weakness of Poland, made a request through their Hetman Konasevich to exile all the Uniate bishops and replace them with the bishops Theophanus had ordained. In return for this favor, they would supply sixty thousand fighting men who would faithfully serve the commander.

To this the king replied briefly, "We are assembled here to consider a matter of war and not religion." Therefore, they were forced to wait until the following Assembly which was scheduled for the first month of the year 1621.

The Schismatics prepared themselves well in advance by organizing a powerful group of partisans to rise up in protest against the Uniates, while the Uniate bishops had no one to back them up except the Apostolic Nuncio, Diotalevio, and King Sigmund who remained faithful to his oath by repeating, "I would rather die than permit anything in my kingdom that is contrary to the will of God."

When the Schismatics in a public hearing demanded the exile of the Uniate bishops, then Rutsky, having listed all the wrongs done the Uniate Church, closed his famous speech thus: "Seventy murderers have been set on my trail and that of my bishops, who persecute us everywhere, intent on displacing us from our Sees, but I call upon God as my witness that it will be easier for them to take our lives than to take our offices from us. In a Catholic country, under a Catholic king, our lives are threatened and for what reason? Just because we are Catholics!" The Schismatics could make no answer to these accusations and the defense of the Uniate cause. Fearing to be ridiculed, they made no reply, especially since after the speech the king ordered his chancellor to answer the Schismatics. "His majesty, the king, will sooner give up his crown than do anything to interfere with the interests of the Catholic Church. If there are any disputes to be settled, between the Uniates and the Schismatics, let them be postponed until the following session of the Assembly."

In the meantime, while the Diet was in session in Warsaw, the wolves had gone about their business among the Uniates. Those ordained as bishops by Theophanus used all the forces at their command to instigate the faithful against the lawful shepherds in order that they might themselves occupy their places as soon as possible. The Union was not yet firmly established, therefore it was not surprising that many unstable souls were duped by the empty promises of the Schismatics to turn against their rightful leaders.

The most zealous of the instigators against the Union was Melety Smotritsky, appointed by the false patriarch Theophanus to the diocese of Polotsk. They took advantage of the unenlightened public mind to spread among the people and especially the Kozaks the prevalent democratic notion of the disturbed East of liberty of religious worship at all costs corrupting the people against the "tyranny" of the Church of Rome and terrorizing the peasants in the name of liberty and progress and the national need. Under the pretext of religious duty they distributed to the homes of the gentry, the townspeople and the commoners throughout the diocese contentious literature against Josaphat's tyranny of Union with the Church of Rome, attacking in God's name all the customs and discipline of the Catholic Church.

To satify his desire for ostentation and publicity, in these letters and literature, he set himself up as a model product of the great Eastern Church, the true archbishop and their real shepherd and called upon the Schismatics to banish Josaphat as a traitor to the nation, a Papist and heretic and to obey only his own commands.

He closed the communications by urging all to spread the ancient Orthodox faith in which they were born and brought up in and to destroy the Union that had been unknown to the Holy Fathers. In order to arouse the greatest possible hatred towards the Catholic Church he had his agents distribute throughout the cities and towns books full of hatred, invective and calumnies against the Papal See at Rome and the Catholic Church.

Evil spreads much more rapidly than good, just as falsehood finds more followers than truth. Thus it happened in the diocese of Polotsk. At Smotritsky's instigation nearly all the cities rose up against Josaphat, Mstyslav, Orst, Vitebsk and even the greater part of Polotsk sided with the self-appointed leader. The diocese which had but recently accepted the Union and in which as stated by Rutsky, there was perfect unity, rebelled against its shepherd. The Schismatics were aware of the unreliability of the public, therefore, in order to assure themselves of its backing, one of the leaders prepared a book for the signature of all who had left the Uniate Catholic Church by which they would be bound under oath to remain faithful to Smotritsky until death.

The devil's work of disunion made rapid strides forward. In Polotsk itself, which had but recently been entirely Catholic, were found several thousand persons who signed their names in that book. Schism invariably thrives on calumny and slander as it is not possible for clean water to flow out of an unclean source. It was to this diabolical method that the Schismatics resorted in accomplishing their maniacal scheme. The news was spread that while in Warsaw, St. Josaphat had adopted the Latin Rite because he had celebrated Mass in a Latin Rite Church and in the Latin vestments and manner. This meant a great deal to the common people who seldom understand the deeper and true meaning of problems which must be adapted to the circumstances at hand. They had now found a reason by which to placate their outraged consciences. Thousands of them left the Catholic Church. Do not the present opposers of the Catholic Church resort to the same cheap methods, by placing more value in external form than the Christian faith itself? Do they not also in these times frighten the Uniates with the Latin Rite or the plot of the Pope against the State?

St. Josaphat and Rutsky were in Warsaw during the meeting of the Assembly in order to defend the threatened Union when the disturbing news was brought to them as to what was transpiring in Lithuania. What went on in the heart of the saint when he saw all his great work for which he had labored so earnestly to accomplish as in one breath destroyed is not difficult to imagine. It is certain that he must have been heartbroken at the realization that all his efforts were not enough.

Persons of pusillanimous character who seek only their own gain and not the glory of God under such circumstances usually succumb to despair and torment. But Josaphat was not one of these. His disappointment in mankind was counterbalanced by his great love of God and His mercy. He put all his troubles and sorrow in the hands of God. He immediately notified the king of what had transpired in his absence and delayed his return until he had received letters from the king by a special messenger, reaffirming St. Josaphat in his position as the rightful shepherd and commanding all to show him proper respect. Thereupon Josaphat hurried from Warsaw to his sheepfold. The outlook was a lot worse than he had expected. It seemed as if the Union had expired. The Churches became empty even though the priests who were faithful to Josaphat would not relinquish them to the Schismatics. Very few persons frequented them whereas the Schismatics had constructed shacks outside the city and gathered there for services which were performed by Schismatic monks and those unworthy priests who had been suspended and exiled by Josaphat and whom Smotritsky now pressed into service and sent abroad to rouse to rebellion against Josaphat and the Union. The extent of the hatred which Smotritsky was able to arouse against Josaphat can best be understood by describing the tumult which arose after the reading of the king's letters in Polotsk.

After his return from Warsaw St. Josaphat accompanied by the voyevod Michael Sokolinsky, Michael Tishkevich and other lay friends, set out for the public square where according to the instructions of the king, his letters to Josaphat were to be read as a public proclamation. The voyevod commanded the bells to be rung for Assembly of the elders. At the ringing of the bells not only the elders gathered but nearly all of the city's population, for they all knew what was to be read there. Thereupon the voyevod directed the king's letters to be read, which proclaimed St. Josaphat and not the self-appointed Smotritsky as the true head of the Church and commanded the public to show him due respect as their leader.

After the reading of the communication, St. Josaphat spoke to the gathering urging them to return to the Uniate Church. As soon as Josaphat finished his speech, the assembly hall echoed with the threatening shout, "We are not Uniates and do not want to be. In the whole city there are to be found hardly more than ten Uniates. Away with the traitors! Kill the Papist soul snatcher!" At this shout the maddened crowd of men and women, armed with knives, ropes and stones, stormed into the assembly hall and it would surely have resulted in bloodshed, if it had not been for the quick-witted action of Sokolinsky and Tishkevich who immediately perceived the difficulty of the situation and to what it would lead. The voyevod called the elders John Terlikowsky and Peter Wasilevich and said to these leaders of the rebellion that if they did not quiet the storming crowd they would be the first to suffer punishment by death. Tishkevich, armed with a pistol, pointed it at the chest of Terlikowsky and said, "If you are the ungodly man who has aroused this mutinous crowd, then you won't escape out of my hands and may God keep us and the archbishop under his protection." At this Josaphat threw himself between them and saved Terlikowsky. The frightened leaders of the rebellion thereupon held back the crowd explaining that if anything untoward should happen, if there were any violence, they would, according to the law of the king, be punished by death. Gradually the crowd quieted down, in the meantime the voyevod led Josaphat and his companions out of danger. In the assembly hall only the notary public remained, John Dahilevich a good Catholic, whom the Schismatics planned to torture to death and for this purpose closed the gate; but God himself saved him, for as he prayed fervently within his heart for deliverance, by some miracle he suddenly found himself behind the crowd in the public square. Thus by the grace of God all of them had escaped certain death.

Having come out of this danger, St. Josaphat did not go into hiding, seek revenge on his enemies nor demand punishment but on the contrary he realized the need of great patience, and sympathetic consideration, therefore, he exerted a marvelous benevolence and brotherly love towards them. Whenever he met any of them, he spoke to them kindly and invited them to his house as friends. In this way, he drew to himself and converted to the Holy Union the chief of the rebel leaders, John Terlikowsky. Terlikowsky, together with other companions fearing arrest and subsequent punishment for their part in inciting the rebellion that had arisen, came to Josaphat to beg his forgiveness.

Just as soon as Josaphat noticed them coming across the courtyard of the residence, he ran out to meet them himself, shook their hands as with his dearest friends and embraced them, calling them his sons. Expecting to be accused and thrown out St. Josaphat's unexpected reception and kindness so overcame them emotionally that they requested him of their own accord to accept them into the Catholic Church. When people know with full certitude that they are loved and prayed for by their spiritual leaders who bear with them in charity and suffer with them, they invariably turn to them in all their problems and must needs return to the fold no matter for how long they have strayed. St. Josaphat himself was so overjoyed that as soon as they had left, he ran to the Church to thank God for their conversion. It was his pious custom whenever any person was converted to hurry immediately to the altar of Almighty God in Church and with tears of joy to pray, "My God, I have found a lost sheep and bring it back to Thee and leave it in Thy keeping."

Although it was a very trying period for St. Josaphat and many of the converted who had fallen back into Schism never returned to the Union, nonetheless, St. Josaphat was not daunted by it. Because sanctity, complete detachment from self, companionship with souls at every instant were the pillars of his work, he continued to preach, recalling them to the Catholic Church. All during this troubled time amid the calamities which had befallen his Church he did not neglect his duties. He wrote pamphlets combatting the insidious dissident literature and managed the affairs of the diocese, lending a helping hand wherever it was needed. Men were again to be irresistibly drawn to the faith through this great man of God who knew no limits to patience and love.

The saints have such great fortitude in matters pertaining to God and Church that their enemies can in no way discourage them. A man who has access to the divine strength is never found wanting in courage before men who must depend on mere human strength alone.

The Schismatics were soon to discover in Josaphat an unshakable power and resistance that was to dash their wicked plots and connivances.

CHAPTER XIX

THE REBELLION OF THE SCHISMATICS
AGAINST JOSAPHAT

Through Josaphat's unceasing efforts, the city of Polotsk gradually returned to Unity. Gathering his little flock closer about him, he saw it grow again by new souls every day. On Sundays, he got them to frequent vespers. After vespers they recited the rosary or he would bring them together in one of the rooms of the residence and give them a lecture or tell them the marvelous history of some saint.

Aware of this, the Schismatics became fanatical in their hatred towards the Union. Religious quarrels tend to be more violent and bitter than others for the issues are so much more personal. It has no regard for family relationships such as marriage and even friendship. This was the state of affairs in Polotsk and in all of Ukraine. With regard to the faithful Uniates the words of our Lord were fulfilled. (Matthew 10-22)

"And ye shall be hated of all men for my name's sake: but he that endureth to the end shall be saved."

Susha writes that the mother of Dorotheus Archemovich did not speak to him for seventeen years because he had accepted the Union although they lived all that time under one roof. The same happened in other families. The Schismatics became adamant in their heresy and deaf to all instruction and admonitions.

Their greatest hatred was of course directed against Josaphat. Whenever and wherever they could, they made up slanderous stories. They spread rumors that he attracted girls to his house for immoral purposes and spent nights in debauchery that being the reason, as they triumphantly pointed out, for his slight constitution and pallor. They annoyed him, were publicly disrespectful on the streets, in the public square, in meeting halls and religious processions. They wanted to be rid of Josaphat at any price. But he did nct bother to deny the slanders nor cease his efforts. He would permit no one to undo the good work he had accomplished in the meantime. He continued with his good deeds, prayers, fasting, and severe scourgings.

In his diocese, the greatest blasphemies were committed. Baptism, the visitation of the sick, consolation of the sorrowing, confession, teaching of children, all these duties which constituted the ordinary obligation of the priesthood were performed by the Schismatic laymen themselves. There was, for instance, one Peter Wasilevich, a city magistrate, who without fear of judgment of God and man himself Christened, heard confessions and celebrated Mass just to keep the people from going to Catholic priests for the performance of these Rites. There were those who preferred their children to die unchristened and themselves left the world without receiving the Holy Sacraments of Communion and Extreme Unction rather than call in Catholic priests. There were times when the dying begged with tears in their eyes for Catholic priests to be sent to them but the hardened hearts of the fanatic Schismatics would not permit themselves to be softened by anything. Hatred destroyed in them all decent human emotions even in regard to their own families. This awful state of affairs was brought about by the Schismatic priests whom Smotritsky had ordained and who in their malevolent ignorance taught their adherents that it was better to make confession to a deaf man or the stump of a tree than before a Catholic priest.

Josaphat was most hated by the people of the city of Vitebsk. Ever since Josaphat had taken over the Seat of the archbishop they were averse to the Union. Schism had taken root deeply there so that even the most zealous efforts of St. Josaphat had not been able to uproot it. Aroused by the Schismatics, the monk Sylvester and the priest Rev. John Kamin back in January 1621 had publicly renounced their allegiance to Josaphat and accepted the self-appointed Smotritsky as their bishop. The good shepherd hastened to the lost sheep; but when his persuasions and admonishment turned off the evil path but a few persons, then Josaphat ordered the king's proclamation to be read publicly in the town hall commanding all to obey St. Josaphat as the rightful head of the Church. During the reading the rebellious crowd began to throw their caps to the ground denoting death and yelled: "We don't want to recognize Josaphat or the Union!" St. Josaphat barely escaped with his life from the angry crowd of Schismatics.

The people of Vitebsk continued their wanton destruction and plundering. When on one of the following days St. Josaphat was celebrating Mass, they fell upon the Church and robbed it of its treasures and then they drove the Catholic priests from the other Churches. Not until after a month's time and forced by the king's official command did they return the denuded and impaired churches to the Catholics. The Schismatics took the same action against the Uniates in other towns. The Polish city administrators, instead of putting a stop to this vandalism at the outset and punishing the evil-doers publicly, passed over these sacrileges heedlessly, thereby encouraging the Schismatics to grow bolder in their opposition. It seemed that the elite had apostatized in a body.

Nonetheless, to camouflage their actions and escape their deserved punishment, the Schismatic leaders of Polotsk and Vitebsk joined forces and wrote their pretended grievances to the king against Josaphat. They accused Josaphat of being the cause of all the uprisings because he persecuted them without cause, punished them and took vengeance on them. Some of these falsehoods were believed readily enough by those of the Polish gentry who were unfriendly to the Union as well as by the king's chancellor Leo Sapiha a man who had done many favors for the Uniate Church during his lifetime. Because Sapiha was well-acquainted with Josaphat he wrote him a personal letter asking him to reconsider his actions and tone down his enthusiasm because the Kozaks were taking advantage of the resultant chaos and were ready to withdraw their support from the weak Poland under the present offensive circumstances.

St. Josaphat's large-minded good sense furnished him with a very thorough answer to the shrewd arguments of the Schismatics and he replied at once listing all the wrongs done by the Schismatics to the Catholic Church and at the same time pointing out that it was both unnecessary and improper to mix politics with religion. Politics can and do concern themselves with a wide variety of interests but it is not proper to sacrifice matters pertaining to religion and the Church for the good of the State and then as in this case for the price of an uncertain peace. He closed the letter by warning Sapiha not to believe false reports brought to him until he had himself first verified the truth of the matter under consideration.

Upon receipt of the letter Sapiha felt offended by Josaphat's reply as he never expected that a common Ukrainian bishop would dare to dispute the matter with such a great gentleman as himself. Therefore, he wrote St. Josaphat an angry letter thoughtlessly accusing him of being the actual cause of the chaos and confusion in Lithuania, through his over-zealousness and strictness to the extent that the common folk preferred to be under Turkish rule and enjoy their religious beliefs in peace rather than to suffer such religious intolerance as in Polotsk; also that he should make friends with the Kozaks who were serving Poland and not do anything to offend them. In addition, he requested St. Josaphat to turn over his Catholic Churches in Mohilev to the Schismatics.

St. Josaphat replied to this letter with proper respect but at the same time with Apostolic dignity and fearlessness. The entire message was permeated by the spirit of truth by which Josaphat lived. He was unyielding on matters of principle as he was unwearied in his love for men. Pitiless to himself, he never failed to display gentleness and reverence to his neighbor. Let us quote some of the passages of the letter: "That which concerns my character God is my witness who sees into my heart and knows the purpose of my actions that by no evil example or uncompromising actions did I drive away from me any citizen of Polotsk or any other person in my diocese. There is not the slightest indication of severity on my part which might have become the cause for rebellion. The same applies to my priests whom the Schismatics accuse of being evil and stupid because they obey me; but if they should join the ranks of the Schismatics, they would at once become good and wise. I do not force anyone nor drag anyone against his will into the Union and there is no proof of it. Whenever I defend the rights of the Church which the Schismatics threaten to take from us by force, I do that which my position as head of the Church obliges me to do. Nonetheless, I do all of this in a legal, peaceful way, taking for my inspiration and ideal St. Ambrose and St. John Chrysostom who accomplished so many great works for the glory of God unmindful of any obstacles. If these saints had seen in their times as much wrong done to Almighty God as I now see, they would do much more about it than I. I know of no other motive for the action of the Schismatics except their jealousy and possibly the fact that we sail in the bark of the greatest captain, the successor to Christ himself. This ship never did sail on peaceful waters but always in the storm. Whether we ourselves are going to continue in it or not, it will never be free from attack. If it seems to anyone that the fury of these storms is caused by some fault in us, then let them bring us to judgment and according to the law sentence us to be cast out of the ship with John. Even the fisherman of Tarsus did not cast John out of the boat until they were convinced that the storm had been caused on his account.

The Schismatics do the fighting and then complain that they are being beaten. They rebel themselves and accuse us of being the cause of the rebellion and in addition some of our own Catholics blame us for the chaos. Is this not directly opposed to the love of one's neighbor as preached by Christ?

"It is good to have national peace but of the kind of which Christ spoke: (St. John 14-27) 'Peace I leave with you, my peace I give unto you: not as the world giveth, give I unto you: Let not your heart be troubled, neither let it be afraid, but the kind against which He said: (Matthew 10-34)

" 'Think not that I am come to send peace on earth; I come not to send peace, but a sword.'

"How can there be perfect accord between forces of light and darkness? How can there be peace between Christ and Beelzebub? Between Catholics and Schismatics or heretics? Between Catholic Churches and the Schismatic meeting halls? How can there be peace when God is offended, when God's laws are disregarded which had been given to St. Peter and his successors for safe-keeping, when bishops are unfairly attacked in an effort to displace them from their posts and there are those who dare to try to force the Catholic Churches out of the hand of the highest authority of the Church established by Christ Himself in order to turn them over to the schismatics?

"St. Peter, together with all his successors, the Popes of Rome, will surely call upon God for vengeance against such mistreatment, nor will the founders of our Church, St. Volodimir and Yaroslav and the Metropolitans, archbishops and dignitaries of the Church keep silent for their hopes have been interfered with. They were good Catholics and not Schismatics and it was for the purpose of being transmitted to the Catholic Church dignitaries that they prepared their Sees in the Ukrainian Rite. Is this not sufficient cause for the wrath of God. Can God bless such peace which can be attained only by offending Him?"

He wrote further that Schism was and still is the cause for all the wars in Poland, with quotations from history to prove that it was in reality the Schismatics and no one else who invariably joined forces with the enemy against Poland and he also thus prophesied about the Union and the Kozaks, "We may be sure that this work of the Union almighty God will bless unto the end and all obstacles, not only those created by the Kozaks but even by hell itself, He will remove without injury to the Union and comfort the hearts of the Uniates. All Schism arises because men have revolted from obedience to the one, great, true and only king, Jesus Christ, and the See of St. Peter, whom the Lord constituted after Himself shepherd of the Church, and have taken up the veneration of personalities rather than preserving the ancient worship of the Holy Trinity of God.

"It has long been observed that peaceful agreement among nations could be brought about much sooner, regardless of political differences, if the rulers of the Churches would themselves obey in common the one chief shepherd. Why was the Church united in one body? That discipline and

204

order might be maintained in her of whom it was said, 'Ye are the body of Christ and members in particular.'

"If the satisfaction of the Kozaks is of greater importance than the Holy Union and their will obeyed in preference to God's then we must live in fear of God's just wrath for our country on account of the Kozaks just as long ago the chosen people of Israel were punished because of the Philistines whom they had tried to please. The Union must not be destroyed just to win the favor of the Kozaks. The self-will of the Kozaks will not be satisfied with this one privilege but will continually demand more and more until in the end it will have no respect left whatever for God or Christ or their conscience and will have only increased its power to dare ever greater misdemeanors than were committed once upon a time by the story book 'Naliwayko.'

"They who will not accept the ordinances of the Churches elect of God, resist the commands of God."

This prophecy was fulfilled. Although Poland later turned over to the Kozaks most of the Sees of the bishops, together with their Catholic Churches to pacify them, they were never satisfied and continued to war with Poland from the year 1648 until they caused its downfall and partition and thus they repaid those who were for giving-in to them on the advice of the Schismatics and at the expense of the Uniates.

Those Churches separated from the Apostolic Church no longer possess the grace of the Holy Spirit, the communication failing as the Apostolic succession had been cut off. They have really no power to baptize, ordain or to communicate to others the grace of the Holy Spirit from which they have themselves fallen.

To this letter Sapiha made no further reply and did not again demand the Catholic Churches in Mohilev to be turned over to the Schismatics. That he regretted his haste in believing the lies of the Schismatics was evidenced by the fact that as if desiring to correct his error, he remained thereafter truly respectful of the person of St. Josaphat and performed many valuable services for the Catholic Ukrainian Church and after the martyrdom of St. Josaphat, he became the avenger of his death by punishing the murderers without mercy. So St. Josaphat was more firmly established than before the effort to dislodge him from his jurisdiction.

To demonstrate how unrighteous were the accusations and calumnies directed at St. Josaphat by the Schismatics, we will quote here the words of a few witnesses who knew Josaphat well and who were often with him and they all without exception testify to the purity and holiness of Josaphat's life, so that the Schismatics can find no proof whatever for their slanders: Thus testified Diahilevich:

"I never heard an impatient or angry word from Josaphat which might have offended the Schismatics and incited them to demonstrate with such violent hatred; and even though he could have proved them in the wrong and by entirely legal means brought about punishment for their misdemeanors, he preferred not to make use of such methods but always declared instead quite frankly that he would rather have them join the Union."

The archdeacon Dorotheus, eyewitness of all of St. Josaphat's struggles with the Schismatics said, "St. Josaphat realized very well that nothing could be accomplished by trying to use force for the propagation of the Union among the Schismatics to accept the Union, that was why he approached them kindly and addressed them with loving words. His sermons were infused with Apostolic zeal inspired by the Holy Spirit and fatherly good will."

Emanuel Kantakuzen who lived with Josaphat for several years said: "I am certain that the saint was never angry or hateful and when he wanted to convert everybody to the Union he did it not by striking fear into them but with gentle entreaties, suggestion and admonishments."

Michael Tishkevich, a gentleman and scion of a noble

family, had this to say: "All that I state I vow to be the absolute truth for I witnessed it with my own eyes. Because of St. Josaphat's gentleness and piety I found it of personal benefit to meet him frequently. I hereby testify with a clear conscience that as long as he was archbishop he lived an exemplary holy life. His eyes looked out beyond the honest daily toil of men towards the supreme goal so that his least gesture, step or word was capable of moving men's hearts. The poor came to him, famous noblemen, even priests made special arrangement to hear him.

"It is true that he had a hatred for the teachings of the Schismatics but not for the Schismatics themselves whom he drew to the Church with his goodness and gentleness, for as great as his enmity was for the error so great was his love for the person. I never noticed in Josaphat any displeasure at the wrongs done him by the Schismatics. He never showed annoyance with them by words or deeds."

One of Josaphat's confessors said thus of him: "I know that in order to convert the Schismatics St. Josaphat never threatened them, mistreated them or persecuted them, but tried instead to draw them to the faith with kind words, hints and instructions and was so successful in his methods that seldom did he fail to convert some Schismatic. He displayed no dislike for the Schismatics but only objected to their false teachings."

The Rev. Kosinsky also confessor to St. Josaphat said that he knew thousands of ways in which Josaphat succeeded in converting the Schismatics to the Union but all of the methods were full of tenderness and divine love.

Finally, John Khodiha, a city counsellor of Polotsk and a Schismatic, who had taken part in all of the rebellions against Josaphat confessed thus: "God forbid that I should have anything to say against Josaphat of any ill-treatment suffered by any of us Schismatics, neither of any wrong committed against us nor of any reason he might have given us for hat-ing him. On the contrary, I was there and was eyewitness to it all, when during the tumult in the town hall, Mr. Sokolinsky voyevod of Polotsk threatened one of our leaders, John Terlikowsky, the burgomeister, with an iron bar while Josaphat seized him by the hand and would not permit him to injure what he was perfectly aware was his own greatest enemy. Thus did Josaphat behave who had a friendly and fatherly heart for all."

All of these witnesses testified under oath publicly before a commission chosen for the purpose, in the place where Josaphat had lived and labored and at a time when they still remembered Josaphat and his work. They unanimously praised the saint so that not a voice was raised in opposition. Then why did the Schismatics hate and persecute St. Josaphat? Let an eyewitness give an answer to this question:

"St. Josaphat gave no cause for the hatred of the Schismatics. Their hatred towards Josaphat was one of religious intolerance. The reason of it was their hatred for the Union with the See of Rome."

Michael Tishkevich states that the Schismatics called Josaphat a saint and they persecuted him only because of their hatred for the Pope of Rome. It was not uncommon to hear Josaphat's enemies say, "If only Josaphat would be willing to conform to us we would shower him with gold and would worship him as an angel from heaven."

Even the Jews called him "Father" and said of him that Josaphat was a true Christian because he worshipped God only and obeyed his commandments, was pure and that his life was exemplary and without blemish and if he did not go straight to heaven then who could ever hope to attain to it?

Therefore, in the light of such concrete declarations, the false accusations of the Schismatics who try to discredit his work through their calumnies and lessen the glory of St. Josaphat in the past and present are of little consequence.

We must not be amazed that although he was a saint he was so persecuted and is still persecuted for as Jesus Christ Himself had said: (St. John 15-20)

"Remember the word that I said unto you, the servant is not greater than his Lord. If they have persecuted me, they will also persecute you; if they have kept my saying, they will keep yours also."

Amidst this stress of sufferings, persecutions and vilifications, St. Josaphat did not lose heart, but acted as if nothing at all happened, while he continued to preach and spread the blessings of the Holy Union. He would come down from the pulpit his face streaming with tears and his frame shaken with the force of his entreaties. To him eloquence was but a secondary consideration to his earnestness to be severed from the material world and to be with God earning the celestial joys by suffering and acquiring by degrees the heavenly mansion awaiting those who are worthy.

God blessed his efforts and sent him comforts by softening the hardened hearts of the Schismatics so that many more of them were converted as if to reward him for the relapse of many of his followers. Let us mention a few such conversions which brought St. Josaphat great joy:

While passing through the town of Duda St. Josaphat stopped at the house of the local priest. However, the parish house was so tiny there was no room in it to put him up overnight. Therefore, he advised Josaphat to call at the house of a well-to-do gentleman but one who was a fanatic Calvinist. Placing his trust in God to help him convert the man to the Catholic Church, Josaphat gladly went to the house of the Calvinist family whose name was Soroka. But Soroka did not appear at all anxious to welcome the "soul snatcher" in his house. Having learned from his own lips that he was a Calvinist, Josaphat so thoroughly convinced him of the falsity of his faith that Soroka was unable to deny the truth of his teachings but as it was the habit of heretics, he persisted in the heresy and would not think of accepting the Catholic faith. Soroka had three daughters who also listened to Josaphat and were converted. They begged the father to renounce their heresy together but the proud man would not even hear of it. However, when Soroka left the house to oversee the work on his estate, the daughters took advantage of the opportunity to fall at the feet of the archbishop to renounce their heresy and to make their confessions of their whole lives.

When Soroka learned what had transpired during his absence, he began to abuse the saint and became so angry that he ordered him to leave his house at once and at his departure, called his dogs to give chase after him. St. Josaphat bore this indignity quietly and humbly comforted by the fact that he had gained three souls for the Uniate Catholic Church.

After he had ejected the archbishop from the house, Soroka's anger cooled down while his daughters scolded him for his disrespectful behavior towards the pious bishop. He suddenly realized that he had behaved in an ungentlemanly manner. Thereupon he jumped on a horse and caught up with the archibishop, fell to his knees before him and begged his forgiveness for his breach of good manners.

"You have not done me the slightest harm, friend," said Josaphat. "I have only one request to make of you, permit your daughters to follow their faith in peace."

Profoundly impressed by Josaphat's good will, he begged him to return to his house with him promising at the same time to accept the Catholic faith. St. Josaphat excused himself, stating that he had a long journey ahead of him but desiring nonetheless to gain another soul, he got out of his carriage, sat on a handy stone by the roadside, heard his confession of his whole life, accepted him into the Catholic

Church and bestowing upon him his Apostolic blessings, he set out on his journey anew.

The parish priest was astonished when he learned of the conversion of the fanatic Calvinist which he had failed to accomplish with pleadings and persuasion over a period of years and which Josaphat was able to do in one evening.

Susha writes of another similar conversion. The Polotsk voyevod Christopher Zenovich had a wife Theodora of Volovich who was a fanatical Schismatic. St. Josaphat was on friendly terms with the voyevod and wanted to convert his wife also to the true faith. He came, therefore, to visit them often and with great tact and gentleness tried to convince her to accept the Union. These persuasions, however, so irritated Theodora that she ordered several vicious dogs to be let loose in her yard who would be sure not to permit Josaphat to enter her house. When Josaphat came again to call on them, the dogs not only did not attack him, but upon seeing him, they sidled up to him and rubbed themselves against his legs. Seeing this, Theodora was so ashamed that the dogs showed him more respect that she that she straightway was converted to become one of the most zealous Catholics.

While Josaphat was staying in Ruta with the Metropolitan he heard that a heretic nobleman was dying. He hurried to his bedside at once, converted him to the Catholic faith and gave him Extreme Unction, and assisted him with words so moving and supernatural, showing him the joys of heaven with such ardent earnestness, tempered by grace that just before his death the man said, "Now I believe that God sent me his angel!"

With such conversions God encouraged his faithful servant whose companionship with souls at every instant were the mainstay of his work, preparing him for the heroic suffering which God would soon demand of his chosen servant.

211

The saint poured out all he had of ingenuity and love and it was his gentleness combined with the tireless propaganda by pen, word, example and action which gained these souls for God. He thanked Him and prayed without ceasing, asking Almighty God to help him further spread acceptance of the Union. He did not, however, for a moment imagine that he had finished with trials.

CHAPTER XX

THE PERSECUTIONS OF ST. JOSAPHAT AND THE PLIGHT OF THE UNIATE CHURCH

The hatred and jealousy of the Schismatics towards St. Josaphat continued to rise and gather force. Throughout every city and town there were plots being devised to take away his life. The crown of martyrdom was promised him in heaven and earth. The saint was fully aware of this and thought of nothing but death. His greatest desire was to give his life for the sake of the Union. He did not run away from death but yearned for it all the more. He held his ground courageously to the last, not losing sight for even a moment of his mission in life.

If we admire a man who courageously faces death on the battlefield, with an avowed enemy, then how much more we ought to admire St. Josaphat who had to be prepared for death at any moment at the hands of a maddened blood-thirsty mob and for whose salvation he was ready to pay with his life.

As a last resort, when every means of persuasion within the power of a loving heart had failed, St. Josaphat exclaimed to the Schismatics, "You hate me,, and want to murder me, but I hold you in my heart and I would feel myself privileged if I could die for your sakes." But these words full of divine love did not soften the hardened hearts of the Schismatics. Just as upon the Jews before the death of His Son, so now upon the hopeless Schismatics God sent the most dreadful punishment, hardening in evil. (John 9-39)

"And Jesus said: For judgment I came into this world that they which see not, might see; and that they which see, might be made blind."

Unfortunate indeed are they who have earned themselves such a fate. Their jealousy devised many different ways by which to annoy St. Josaphat. For instance, when the Polish prince, Wladislav, was preparing for his journey to Moscow to take over the Sees offered to him, the citizens of Polotsk sent a deputation to St. Josaphat which, pretending friendship, advised him to go along with the prince to Moscow where he might with his holiness and eloquence be able to convert the Muscovites to the Union.

Josaphat recognized their purpose and replied quietly, "For the Union I am ready and willing to given even my life, but you can go home now and not tempt me."

At another time they came to St. Josaphat and promising to pay the expense of the journey begged him to visit the patriarch of Byzantium. To all of which the archbishop answered, "I will not go to visit the patriarch but will continue my obedience to the Pope of Rome. If I were ever to visit him, it would not be for the purpose of declaring my allegiance to him but to convert him to the Holy Catholic Church."

The worst annoyances were experienced by St. Josaphat in Vitebsk. To irritate him, the Schismatics held their services directly across from the archbishop's residence on the opposite shore of the river Dwina and sang as loud as they could on purpose, not the better to glorify God but to vex the saint. But Holy Patience would not permit the saint to be confounded. Whenever St. Josaphat heard their singing he

214

knelt down and prayed fervently with tears in his eyes pleading with God not to be angered by the noisy display and count it as a sin against them. He said, "My God I count my merits as nothing but yours are infinite. May they win for me the grace of suffering to save their souls."

The endless domestic squabbles of the city of Vitebsk made it an object of ridicule and sorrow to all good Christians. When the townspeople observed that the Polish government was lax with regard to their demonstrations, they grew constantly bolder in their attacks upon Josaphat and his servants.

Whenever one of the archbishop's servants showed himself in the city on some errand they threw sticks and stones and mud at him, hitting and injuring him. They attacked St. Josaphat in public on his processions and in churches.

On the day of Pentecost, St. Josaphat was leading a feast day procession to the Church of the Holy Spirit. When the procession had started crossing the bridge, a nobleman by the name of Basilowsky fell upon Josaphat, insulted him and having a troop of soldiers with him, threatened to throw the archbishop off the bridge if he would not turn back with the procession. The gentleman was very boastful of his conquest afterwards but not for long, for by the will of God, he was eaten alive by worms and thus finished his worthless life.

The citizens of Vitebsk did not restrain themselves from committing a still greater evil on the day of the Transfiguration of Our Lord in the year 1622. During Mass, at the Great Entrance, when Rev. Maxim Turchenovich, a monk of the Basilian Order, was coming out of the deacon doors in ceremonial vestments, the Schismatics, heedless of violating the sanctity of the place, fell upon him and beat him up almost to the point of death. They also wanted to attack St. Josaphat but some of the faithful gentry who were present at the Mass surrounded him and would not permit him to be touched.

Another time, when the archbishop heedless of threats

boldly came out into the pulpit to preach against the false teachings of the Schismatics, one of them, Adam Kosiw, wanted to shoot Josaphat down in Church but God Himself prevented the evil intention for in the moment that he proceeded to aim his gun, God punished him with total blindness.

St. Josaphat often had occasion to cross the river Dwina by ferry. The people of Vitebsk persuaded one of their townsmen, a fisherman and ferry owner, to drown Josaphat while taking him across. When they bribed him, he agreed, but as he did not know Josaphat well and there were other priests on board, he had to postpone his plan. After he had taken a good look at St. Josaphat in Church and when he again had occasion to ferry him across all alone, he was about to lay his hands on him when turning around he noticed his small son whom he had taken with him on board that day watching him and fearing that he might give him away sometime he did not at that time carry out his evil design.

Other towns did not behave any better towards Josaphat. The agents of Smotritsky had long since spread the fire of hatred towards the Union and Josaphat. There were rumors in every town of a plot on his life. Evidently it seemed to the fanatical schismatics that with the death of St. Josaphat, the Union would be dissolved.

When St. Josaphat on a visitation to the Churches of his diocese came to the city of Mohila, it shut its gates as if against an enemy and the townspeople gathered on the walls and in the ramparts, rolled out their cannons and aimed their guns threatening him with death if he should dare to try to enter. Despite this, St. Josaphat insisted upon visiting his lost sheep. Only the fervent pleas of the faithful Catholics, who had come out to meet their shepherd and who now surrounded him for protection, kept him from carrying out his plan and meeting certain death.

The townspeople, with the desire to be rid of him as speedily as possible, sent a delegation offering His Excellency three thousand gold pieces if only he would not demand the return of his churches and cast out from them the Schismatic priests. Sorely provoked by such a mercenary proposition, St. Josaphat cried out, "It's not your money that I want but the salvation of your souls! And as it is forbidden to sell salvation, I cannot accept your proposition!" He departed sadly deploring their want of understanding and restraint.

When on his continued visitations St. Josaphat came to the town of Mstyslav, one of the Schismatics of the influential family of Masalsky planned to kill him. But St. Josaphat's hour had not yet come. On the day planned for the murder Masalsky was himself mortally wounded by an enemy. When Josaphat learned of this, he recalled the words of our Saviour: (Matthew 5-44)

"But I say unto you, love your enemies, bless them that curse you, do good to them that hate you and pray for them which despitefully use you and persecute you."

He hastened to the bedside of the dying nobleman, made friends with him and by his sympathetic words of comfort and simplicity of person so softened Masalsky's heart that he voluntarily renounced Schism, made his confession to St. Josaphat, took Communion from his hands and with the hope of obtaining eternal salvation he left this world in peace.

Also the citizens of the city of Orshi planned to get rid of their shepherd by drowning him in the river Dnieper but they were prevented from carrying out this evil intention.

It was not only St. Josaphat whom the Schismatics persecuted but their hatred was directed against all Uniates. Taking note that the Polish government did not or could not punish the lawbreakers, there was an ever-increasing oppression of the Catholics of the Ukrainian Rite. The people were

217

lawless, their wickedness immeasurable. Everyone walked by the will of his own heart. It was not enough that they forced the Churches out of the hands of the Uniates and cast out their priests but to satisfy their monstrous hatred they also spilled innocent blood.

In the year 1618, the Kozaks fell upon the Rev. Anthony Archemovich, OSBM, the Vicar General of the Metropolitan in Kiev, pulled him out of bed and drowned him in the river Dnieper, calling out to the drowning man, "Call on the Pope now to come to your rescue!"

In the year 1620 when the incarnation of the evil spirit, Theophanes, appeared in Ukraine on Easter Sunday, one of the Schismatic priests accompanied by his brother killed with an axe right at the altar the Rev. Anthony Rutkevich, Basilian monk and visitant from Peremysl.

In Kiev, Jonah Boretsky had put to death several innocent Uniate Catholics. The burmeister, Batalia and the two priests converted by Josaphat while he was staying in Kiev became martyrs to the cause of the Union. Later on the Schismatics made Jonah a "saint" but it must have been solely because he was a blood thirsty murderer of the Uniate Catholics.

In the year 1622 the Kozaks attacked Matthew, the deacon of Sharhorodsk, beheaded him and threw his body into the river. In that same year on the 8th of September on the feast day of the birth of the Blessed Virgin Mary, the Kozaks fell upon the Church of St. Sophia, seized four Basilian fathers sent to administer the Church by the Metropolitan, put them in chains and after beating them sent them off to Trechtimirov where they were cast into prison for six weeks. Brought before the court marshall of the Kozak Hetman the monks were released on the promise that they would not set foot again in Kiev.

Josaphat was grieved when he learned of these martyrs and said to Basil Khotelsky, "If only my superiors would release me from my position as bishop and send me to Kiev, I would gladly die and sprinkle the barren field with my blood, if it would only produce historic fruit." At another time he said to Emanuel Kantakuzen, "Let us go to Kiev and spread the true faith and the Union there." And when Emanuel replied that he did not want to die there, St. Josaphat replied, "We will then reach heaven the sooner."

Despite all the maledictions, the murders and all the injustices committed by the Schismatics, the Uniate Church did not find many defenders. An increasingly darkening cloud hung over it.

Persons of little faith and weak spirit saw its approaching end. For it was really necessary to have a faith strong as steel in order that seeing all the obstacles which the Holy Church had to conquer not to expect its downfall.

It is true that the Union had a defender always in the past as in the present in the Pope and his nuncios and in the cooperation of the king whose efforts, however, were for the most part made impotent by the mutinous gentry but for all that, it had against it all of the Latin priesthood with but a few exceptions, all the gentry, Roman Catholic as well as Schismatic and Heretics. A false notion had turned the heads of all. They had the idea that if the Uniate Church fell, the enmity of the Schismatics would cease and they would convert the Uniates to the Polish Latin Rite and thus assimilate the Ukrainian people to strengthen the weakening Polish nation. They raised the good of the earthly paradise above natural and divine law. This was not the first nor last error made by the Polish gentry and priesthood. Disregard for God's work and God's will, however, never did and never will produce good results. "They who will not accept the ordinances of the Churches elect of God, resist the command of God."

In vain did Rutsky, like a wounded lioness her young, defend the Union before the Polish Diet, and visit the more enlightened persons to plead their aid for the tottering Uniate Church. Invariably he was arrogantly and superciliously turned away with comic answers or else they wrote letters to Rome full of calumnies against the Union and its leaders. But this Rutsky's alert mind had forseen. Sometimes in advance he had sent Basilian monks to Rome to present to Pope Gregory XV the truth about the deplorable state of the Ukrainian Church.

Rutsky had strength and endurance, an intellectual vigor with a grip on reality and a spirit of enterprise that admitted of no obstacles. His fiery activity and superb good humor fitted him admirably to meet this trial of the Ukrainian Church. There was no one else who could have withstood it. He was tall in stature with a massive brow and piercing eye. He had the ability to deal with others without giving offense and a sensitive perception of the character of men. To worthily hold the place of authority given him by God and to check the persecutions of the Church he had to reflect much, meditate and pray and purify his will to achieve the serenity of being which he possessed in great measure. He was a man of discernment with whom every honest citizen might be delighted to be able to associate. He avoided hurting anyone and showed himself to all solicitous in manner and speech. His indefatigable zeal and uncommon constancy marked him as a born prince of the Church. He tried in so far as possible to imitate the ideal of the Blessed Saviour as an unresisting lamb.

The Uniates could not and cannot complain of a lack of fatherly protection and interest in the good of their Church on the part of the Popes of Rome. They are the only real friends who fearlessly defended and defend the interests of the Ukrainian Catholic Church.

Pope Gregory XV, having had everything properly explained to him by the Basilian monks, wrote Rutsky a fatherly letter encouraging him to endure patiently and in addition sent other letters to the Diet which was to hold its Assembly in the year 1623, with the recommendation to back his Nuncio Lanceolotti and defend the Ukrainian Church by assisting in restoring her to her old power. He also wrote a letter to the king, to the Polish archbishop and to a few powerful noblemen requesting their cooperation in defense of the Union. Nonetheless, neither the Polish priesthood nor the gentry would accede the asserted supremacy of the successor to Christ in the matter.

The Schismatics likewise impatiently awaited the session of the Diet and prepared themselves for it well in advance. With powerful defenders from among their own ranks as well as that of Heretics, having collected in addition large sums of money for bribing the representatives and senators, they determined once and for all to write a final finish to the Union. Much can be bought with money, justice and even the conscience of men. This is what actually happened.

"It is regrettable but true," wrote Jepin, "that gold played an important part in the battle of the Union.

"The leader of the Diet, the representatives and senators, even the ministers were not beyond being bribed."

To Warsaw also came Boretsky and Smotritsky, certain that they would leave it victorious. The Uniates also made an effort, it is true, with empty purses but for all that with honest hearts. What transpired during the session of the Diet? What suffering was endured by Rutsky? How with no qualms of conscience whatever did the Schismatics proceed? How did the senators discuss the matter? Instead of recording these details, we refer the more inquisitive to the annals of the Polish Diet. Suffice it to state that no humiliation and no malign persecution was spared Rutsky and that if it had not been for the statesmanlike behavior of King Sigmund, his sense of justice and immense compassion for the fate of the Uniate Church, its survival would certainly have been doubtful. After many speeches and conferences,

221

the committee on the Union gave the report that the entire matter must be postponed for another time.

St. Josaphat was unable to be at this Session at Warsaw for the disturbance in the diocese by the Schismatics demanded his constant presence. He simply wrote a letter to Rutsky explaining all the needs of his diocese and that he was occupied in the strengthening and propagation of the Union.

Picturesque and sublime, in his sermons he spoke with such persuasive eloquence and enlightenment dissolving all doubt on the controversial subjects, especially on the seniority of St. Peter and the proceeding of the Holy Spirit from the Father and Son, certain of which expressions had been tortured into plausible proofs by the Schismatics so that no one dared or could oppose his proofs. However, there were those Schismatics who, setting out from the same principles as he declined to follow them to their logical conclusions just because they were hateful to the ears of the populace.

The Schismatics, not knowing what else to do about it, forbade their adherents to frequent Josaphat's sermons and lectures.

At one time while expounding the truths of the Catholic faith, he cried, his voice and eyes full of tears, "Christ wept over Jerusalem. I weep over you! How can I help weeping, my brethren? For the truth of the one, holy, Catholic faith, I would gladly die!"

He recited quotations chosen from the Gospel with such charm, humility and assurance that it again found its original freshness and power of conviction in replying to those who questioned him. Through his diligent mastery of the Bible he was winning the hearts of those who had persecuted the Uniate Church.

Crushed under the maledictions he was suffering, he often also repeated the following: "Grant, O God, that I could, for

Christ, the faith, the Church and for the seniority of the Pope, give my life!"

He desired death more than others desire long life. He yearned most passionately for the unity of the Church and to secure this was the object most prominent in his mind. His wish for martyrdom was a supreme proof of the love he could give to God. And when he spoke of his approaching death it was with such deep emotion and great inward joy that the entire congregation wept. At the sight of such saintly straightforwardness and so ardent a desire to sacrifice his life for the sake of the Union many more Schismatics were drawn to marvel at the manifestation of divine love in this servant of the Living God and to be converted to the Holy Catholic Church.

He seemed sad and was joyful so that his desolations were as nothing compared with the consolations God showered upon him. Of mystical visions and mysterious splendors which shone for him at night in the Church and his bedroom there is no other concrete proof than already related, except in his glance and the tears of joy at the prospect of his martyrdom. All such great favors are jealously guarded by the saints. In that last marvelous state of his soul on earth, he was piercingly happy and seemed no longer to be of this world.

The lesson St. Josaphat teaches to all is the outpouring of the human soul in love of his own kind and his neighbor in an effort to better the lot of all by promoting the divine Saviour's Kingdom of Peace.

CHAPTER XXI

ST. JOSAPHAT'S LAST VISIT TO VITEBSK

The test of a good shepherd is that he not only cares for those of his sheep who stay with him but also tries to find those who have strayed away and become lost, and when he finds them, he rejoices over them and carries them back to the sheepfold. A good shepherd does not heed the safety of his own life and does not run away like a hired hand but boldly goes forth to meet the danger approaching and would rather give his own life than allow any of his sheep to be killed.

(St. John 10: 11-12)

"I am the good shepherd: the good shepherd giveth his life for the sheep. But he that is an hireling and not the shepherd, whose own the sheep are not, seeth the wolf coming and leaveth the sheep and fleeth; and the wolf catcheth them and scattereth the sheep."

That kind of shepherd according to the Christ Spirit in him was St. Josaphat. In his heart there was such a longing for the peace of the Church that he could willingly shed forth his own life to extinguish the flames of hatred which certain evil Schismatics had kindled.

Polotsk by the grace of God and the very active character

of St. Josaphat changed back again to the Union. Only Vitebsk remained a nest of godless Schismatics. Josaphat often visited those lost sheep in an effort to win them back to the fold even though he realized that the sly wolves had designs on his own life. Once more, before his martyrdom, Josaphat visited the hapless citizens of Vitebsk in March 1623. He thought that through the sheer power of his own goodness, love and holiness, his kind words and unmindfulness of his own life, he would be able to rescue them from Schism. He was not aggressive or intolerant in his faith, which would cause him to condemn permitted leniency in laymen. Far from wishing to subject the wills of others, he left each to follow the inspiration of the Word of God. He would not permit the austerities that he imposed on himself to make others suffer. But God had closed their hearts and the devil locked them in his chains. The deadly enemy omitted no opportunity of calumniating him. It murmured loudly and indignantly against him. But opposition and calumny did not hinder him from a strenuous administration of his diocese. It was a battle to be carried on forever without hope of ever being finished. All his good deeds, persuasions and pleadings not only did no good but made them more hateful and perverse.

And this last visitation was not without its consequence of new sacrileges on the part of the more fanatical Schismatics. Full as his life already was of anxiety and pressure from the Schismatics who in spite of all his efforts to win them over, paralyzed his actions, it now had the added worry of unexpected attacks upon his priests.

For instance, when on the feast day of the Ascension of the Blessed Virgin Mary the archdeacon Dorotheus, together with Emanuel Kantakuzen were hurrying to the Church of the Blessed Virgin Mary in order to prepare the priestly vestments for the feast day Liturgy, the Schismatics when they saw them, attacked them with a hailstorm of stones so that they barely escaped with their lives. That same day, during Mass, which the archbishop celebrated, there was a new outbreak of malevolence. When during the Great Entrance, the archdeacon came out from the presbytery, carrying on a tray the blessed bread, one of the Schismatics present hit him in the face so hard that the discus, together with the sacrificial lamb, fell to the ground.

After all, anyone who sets up a daily battle against Satan openly as he had done, must expect reprisals sooner or later and he knew it. This incident plainly indicated to Josaphat that the time was approaching when he did not have long to wait for his own death, therefore he returned to Polotsk to give his final instructions.

When he was back in Polotsk there came to him many friendly persons begging him to beware for his life as it was threatened everywhere. To this the saint replied cheerfully, "I desire to be freed to be with Christ." The closer he was to death, the more often and happily did he speak of it. Before his final departure for Vitebsk he announced in the pulpit publicly to the people of Polotsk, "Your plans and preparations for my death are not secret to me and therefore, be convinced that I desire nothing better than death for the cause of the Union, for Christ and the head of His Church."

Because Josephat was invariably lighthearted, he demanded good humor from those about him. When one of the guests present at a dinner with Josaphat begged him not to speak so often of his death, because it saddened them all to listen to it, the saintly archbishop answered him by saying, "Brother, no one interferes with your eating, then let no one prevent me from dying for my God and the Holy Union."

To Polotsk came increasingly frequent rumours that the people of Vitebsk had determined to murder their archbishop. Heedless of this, St. Josaphat announced towards the end of October his departure for Vitebsk. As soon as this news had spread, there came visitors from all sections. All the better-class townsmen, gentry and friends counselled him to postpone his departure from their city. However, their pleadings and persuasions could not dissuade Josaphat who was insensible to the distinctions which he had earned among his subjects. To all of them he replied, "I am not afraid of death. For martyrdom I am prepared, if only I am worthy of giving my life for God." Evidently Josaphat sensed prophetically that God was ambitious to make him a star of great brilliance in the eternity of his glory. Some of the gentry offered to accompany the archbishop to Vitebsk and to guard him there but St. Josaphat refused to allow them to make this sacrifice.

On the day of his departure, there arrived in Polotsk, Michael Tishkevich, a great friend of the saint who remonstrated with him for risking his life in unnecessary dangers instead of protecting it for the sake of the Church. When he was unable to persuade Josaphat to remain in Polotsk, then he begged him to allow him to accompany him to Vitebsk but even this offer St. Josaphat refused. He thanked him for his kindness and said: "I do not want to risk anyone's life in danger but my own. Friends and companions I do not need, my servants will be sufficient. I am not afraid to lose my life, as I have ordered my coffin prepared." Then he raised his eyes to heaven and said, "Grant, O God, that I may be found worthy to sacrifice my blood for the Union and obedience to the Apostolic See!" Only the strong can immolate the self in martyrdom for the truth.

Upon hearing these words Tishkevich did not attempt to oppose him further but with tears in his eyes took leave of his friend and spiritual director.

Just as once the Son of God going to His trial in the Garden of Olives took only three of his best beloved Apostles and left the others at the bottom of the Mt. of Olives, desiring to demonstrate to them in this way that he was volunarily going to His death, thus now his follower, St. Josaphat in

227

preparing to give his life for the teachings of Christ, took only the archdeacon Dorotheus, Emanuel Kantakuzen and one of his servants with him.

Just before his departure from Polotsk he asked the Rev. Hennedy Khmelnitsky, his confessor, to see to the finishing of his burial place which he had ordered constructed sometime earlier at the right of the altar in the Church of the diocese. When a few days before his death, the Rev. Hennedy informed the saint that the work of preparing the crypt was finished, he seemed very pleased.

When all was in readiness for him to enter his carriage, he hurried to his Church to say a last prayer in farewell. He prostrated himself, spreading out his arms in the form of a cross at the altar before the Presence of the Almighty and prayed fervently and said, "My God, although my merits are as nothing compared with yours which are infinite, grant in thy gracious goodness to me the grace of offering my life for the salvation of my Ukraine." Then he arose and turning to those assembled, he said: "I am fully aware of the plot of the Schismatics on my head. I am glad that I am going to certain death for Christ." Those remaining behind began to weep and the attendants were frightened lest any evil should befall them. Then the saint comforted them by saying, "If it happens at Vitebsk, then only I will die, no one else besides me will perish."

Again another similar scene in the life of Christ comes to mind. The Saviour hurries to Jerusalem, prophesying to the Apostles his own death and they dread following Him there. (St. Mark: 10-32)

"And they were in the way going up to Jerusalem; and Jesus went before them: and they were amazed; and as they followed they were afraid. And he took again the twelve and began to tell them what things should happen unto him." As the time approached for his passion, Jesus comforted them:

(St. John 17: 12)

"While I was with them in the world, I kept them in thy name: those that Thou gavest me I have kept and none of them is lost, but the son of perdition; that the Scripture might be fulfilled."

Are other words necessary to point out the similarity of these scenes, how closely St. Josaphat followed the steps of his master?

With tears and lamentations the city of Polotsk bade farewell to their shepherd and with tears and lamentations it was to greet his return. St. Josaphat made the journey uneventfully. The dignity of his authority had not diminished from his powerful magnetic personality and interest in life. He rather enjoyed seeing the peasant cottages he passed scattered about the large-sized farms or estates of the country squires where the people were employed at work. His heart was filled with simple kindness. Nor did the prospect of the meanness of the Schismatics and bleakness of his residence in Vitebsk discourage him Although it needed superhuman strength of character to keep peace within his soul, God's presence prevailed and he went cheerfully forth to meet his tragic destiny. Every man cast in the heroic mold seeks self-fulfillment. He blessed eternal life which triumphs over death and evil and thanked God for having created the earth with opportunity for each of us to share His life.

"Blessed are they who peacefully shall endure, for Thou, O most high shall give them a crown!"

Although the entire city seethed with anger and hatred towards him, he set about his work peacefully, as if he were not the cause of all this malice. To all that returned to him, he preached the word of Holy Union with confidence. His activity never slackened. Nothing made the slightest alteration in the miraculous evenness of his temper, while he continued his pastoral work amongst the city's poor and serfs of the village.

Although the evil which prevailed did not escape him, rather than lingering over it, he consecrated his time to promoting the reign of what was good in persuading men to their salvation in the Union. He avoided especially hurting their feelings to maintain as peaceful a courtesy as possible. He reconciled differences, taught, heard confessions and celebrated Mass. When on the feast day of St. Demetrius, he preached a sermon to his murderers, he took for his subject the words from the Gospel for the day:

"They shall put you out of the synagogues: Yea, the time cometh that whoever killeth you will think that he doeth God service." He took them to task from the pulpit: "You people of Vitebsk are seeking my death; on the rivers, bridges, roads and streets you were awaiting to ensnare me. But you see, I have come to you myself, voluntarily so that you may be convinced that I am your spiritual leader. God grant that I should for your sakes, the Holy Union, Holy See of St. Peter and infallibility of the Popes of Rome whom I venerate, lay down life itself!" St. Josaphat wanted to rouse his faithful from their spiritual lethargy and bring them to repentance, just as the Son of God had once tried to stir the heart of Judas to prevent him from carrying out his plot to betray Him. But evidently there is no cure for the hardened sinners. The following is another demonstration of St. Josaphat's divine love. Four days before his death he invited to dinner his greatest enemy and murderer, Naim Wowk, a magistrate of Vitebsk and one of the chief civil officials of the town, who was constantly investigating his activities on the pretext that he was plotting with the Pope against the state. Josaphat, having greeted him as a friend, tried to persuade the man by employing his most admirable power of eloquence to dissolve his doubts in becoming reunited with another man with whom he had quarrelled. When Naim would not permit himself to be persuaded he prophesied that if he would not agree to it in a short time he would die a violent death. But Naim would not heed or obey him. When haughty characters are treated with respect it is their nature to become still more disdainful. Prejudiced by false suspicions they neither know the truth nor care to learn it but are jealous of those who tell them the truth about the consequences of their own actions. In a couple of weeks afterwards for his part in the murder of the archbishop, he finished his life beneath the executioners' axe.

His face streamed with tears under the force of his entreaties as he stood in the pulpit suffering from the maledictions which he pointed out exist as a vast impassable gulf between the creator and human beings crushed by sin.

CHAPTER XXII

THE MARTYRDOM OF ST. JOSAPHAT

The people of Vitebsk had long ago formed their plot to take the life of St. Josaphat. It was only necessary to find some excuse which would cover the evil deed. Sometime before the arrival of the saint in Vitebsk, it was voted at one of the violent and contentious town meetings to provoke the archbishop's servants and when His Excellency reproves them for it, to openly fall upon the residence and fulfill their devilish intention.

Therefore, immediately after the arrival of His Excellency, when the servants appeared in the city or went someplace outside of the residence, the Schismatics were disrespectful, threatened them, beat them and threw stones after them. St. Josaphat instructed his servants begging them to bear all the wrongs which their master's struggles for the Union brought upon them all patiently and not to display their resentment.

Under these circumstances St. Josaphat managed to live with his servants through two difficult weeks of his stay in Vitebsk. This was too long for the Schismatics to wait for the fulfillment of their malevolent plan. The city was plunged into a tumult of intrigue. They raged with the determination to get it over with as soon as possible.

On the 11th of November, on a Saturday, they gathered once more in the town hall and under the leadership of Naim Wowk and Simon Nish, the greatest of all of St. Josaphat's enemies, they decided not to postpone the matter any longer but on the following day on Sunday to fall upon the residence and murder the detestable archbishop.

The Schismatic priest Ilia was to annoy St. Josaphat's servants and if his servants were in turn to beat him or seize and hold him, then on a given signal from the town hall all the bells were to be rung and the people, led by the priests, were to attack the residence in a body. Under the advice of the town magistrates, who were the instigators of the plot to murder, they were to leave town so that they would not be suspected of any part in the plot.

That day, the 11th of November, when the citizens of Vitebsk definitely decided to commit the murder, Josaphat was not in the city of Vitebsk, but had ridden out to one of his farms to settle a dispute over a boundary line with a gentleman named Krupevich. The archbishop desired to return by evening to Vitebsk for vespers, but he was unable to finish the business as quickly as he had planned. As he was returning home in the company of Emanuel Kantakuzen and his servants, the Schismatics were coming out from the evening services in the shanties they had constructed for this purpose. Seeing Josaphat surrounded by his servants, they jeered at them saying, "You have not much longer to be in the service of your lord!"

When he had returned to his residence, he learned that all day the Schismatic priest Ilia had annoyed the household with all kinds of mischief and blasphemies and ridicule but despite their resentment and command to stop, he purposely hung around the residence and did not stop calling them names. Dorotheus insisted that Ilia should be punished.

Josaphat agreed to this, for as the archbishop he had the right under both Canonical and civil law to punish one of a rebellious priesthood.

In the evening of the same day there came to the residence, Peter Ivanovich, one of the town officials and a great friend of St. Josaphat's who told him of the plan set for the next day and urged His Excellency to leave the city as soon as possible. But St. Josaphat would not hear of it, saying: "I have sent the horses to the stables. My life is in God's hands. I want to bear all that God has destined for me." Peter again begged him to depart but without result. Then against St. Josaphat's will, he went into the city, brought back some gunpowder and his servants and insisted upon remaining in the residence to guard the archbishop's safety, but St. Josaphat would not agree even to this.

In the Garden of Olives, Peter had wanted to defend Christ. Here another Peter wanted to render the same kind of service to the servant of Christ, St. Josaphat. But neither Christ nor Josaphat wanted human defense when their appointed hour had come.

As long ago the divine Saviour had gathered before his death all of his Apostles, to take leave of them, to comfort them and to prepare them for the coming trial, thus now St. Josaphat also sat down for the last supper. There were present with him only the archdeacon Dorotheus, Emanuel Kantakuzen and five of his servants. He did his best to cheer them and draw from them the gloom in which they were enveloped by repeating that if there should be any real danger it would threaten only his own person. He talked happily all evening of death so that Dorotheus implored him to let them eat without fear of death hanging over them. Then His Excellency turned to him lovingly and said, "What harm is it to you that I want to die for Christ and the holy faith. Even if there were no such thing as life after death, which we know there is, it would still be a great privilege to

234

share life with God and to serve him by doing something to increase His glory in helping our fellow man. There is no ambition more worthy than to enter into the service of God."

After supper they separated. The servants went to take their rest and Josaphat retired to his room to prepare for the trial. Faithful to the last moment to the example of Christ, he wanted those few hours which separated him from death to be sanctified in prayer. He had with him a beggar by the name of Tiphon whom for the sake of Christian charity he accepted into the house and sometimes permitted him the use of his bed overnight. Thus Tiphon observed everything that St. Josaphat did all of that night.

As long ago Christ had done in the Garden of Gethsemane thus Josaphat prostrated himself extending his arms in the form of a cross offering his blood for the salvation of ungrateful men. Tears of joy rolled down his face and from the depths of his heart tore great sighs. His soul was lost in sublime ravishment as he communed with Jesus Christ. A heavenly light covered him throughout the period of prayer.

But even this night he did not forget about humbling himself by chastising his flesh to remove any trace of vanity from his soul and more than usually he tore his flesh with the scourges. And over the residence the people saw for a radius of three miles around Vitebsk black clouds forming over it and in their midst a flaming cross to which St. Josaphat lifted his soul so fervently in prayer.

The sun had not yet risen when Josaphat went to the Church to say his offices. Dorotheus awakened all the servants and under the recommendation of Emanuel Kantakuzen, he ordered them to detain the priest, Ilia.

When the archbishop was on his way to Church, Ilia was already stationed in front of the residence and began at once to hurl insults at Josaphat, but the saint continued peacefully on his way to Church. However, Ilia did not stop his name calling, whereupon the servants seized him and locked him in the kitchen. At the moment when Kantakuzen had seized the priest, there was a Schismatic crossing the road who, when he saw the commotion, began at once to run towards town and to yelp for help with all his might. John Husnechiw, one of the murder plotters, seeing that the opportune moment had arrived, ran into the town hall and rang the bell for assembly. This was just what the Schismatics had been waiting for. At the same time there was an answering peal of bells from all the Churches except that of the Archbishop calling the plotters to the fulfillment of their dark enterprise.

The whole city was in an uproar. The streets thronged with milling crowds, pressing towards the bishop's residence, who had hastily armed themselves with sticks and stones, poles, guns and any weapons that came at hand, as if the Tartars had suddenly attacked the city. Among the crowd were the leaders of the murder plot busily inciting them to fury by stressing the fact that one of their priests had been disrespectfully treated by being manhandled and detained in the bishop's residence.

A group of the Schismatics now hurled themselves into the yard before the residence and in a moment overpowered the servants standing guard while a volley of stones showered the house and a cry arose as if all hell had been loosed for the accomplishment of bloody murder. The servants hid themselves behind the fence around the residence. When Josaphat heard the blood-curdling howl in Church, he guessed the cause of it and immediately sent word to the residence ordering the priest Ilia to be released. But even though Ilia was released, the suspicious mob did not depart but continued to loudly threaten the archbishop and his attendants.

At dawn he said his Mass slowly almost with tears. Sometimes a smile was seen to pass over his face as though he were addressing the angels gathered about the altar to assist him in his final offering of self in place of the Lamb. Joy or suffering? They are so closely intermingled in the sacrificial chalice, his heart was full and he said his prayer of thanksgiving.

When the morning services were over, the archbishop returned peacefully from the Church to the residence. The whole yard between the Church and the residence was filled with fanatic Schismatics. According to human reasoning certain death awaited the archbishop. But as in the Garden of Gethsemane at the voice of the Saviour, "As soon as he had said unto them, I am he, they went backward and fell to the ground." A similar mob was stilled and fell to the ground now as if they had seen the Holy Spirit at the appearance of the shepherd who with his silent reproach quieted the mob of Schismatics. Their arms hung limply by their sides and Josaphat passed through to the residence unharmed. This was a victory of holiness over evil.

The noise stopped. They disbanded and dispersed, some of them returning to the city while others remained by the house. St. Josaphat called his servants and assuring them that none of them would die, he forbade them to load the guns with gun shots and permitted them to shoot only with paper wads just to frighten them off. Even in his last moments the divine love welling in him would not permit the shedding of the blood of the strayed sheep. He went to his room and prostrating himself in prayer thus spent the time until eight o'clock in the morning.

When around eight o'clock the sun arose and with its dazzling blood-red rays lit up the city, there gathered new groups of Schismatics in front of the residence armed with axes, mallets, poles and shot guns. Their faces were clouded and eyes bloodthirsty, their lips pouring forth streams of revengeful threats and curses. There were again a hailstorm of stones over the roof and fence of the residence. Someone had made a fire beside the fence but fearing the conflagration of the whole city, they tore down the burning fence and thus got into the yard. The servants locked the gates of the residence and to frighten the mob they shot off the muskets with blind shots. However, the murderers, noting that the shots did not wound them, hurled themselves with axes and mallets upon the gate and tore it down in a moment and reached the inside corridor. The servants hid themselves so that there remained only the archdeacon Dorotheus, Kantakuzen and Gregory Ushatsky who intended to block the way to the archbishop's room.

The murderers fell upon Kantakuzen and he fell senseless to the ground, streaming blood. Then they inflicted eighteen wounds upon the valiant head of Dorotheus, pushing him away from the path and fell upon the last, Ushatsky. One of his Schismatic acquaintances recognized him and said, "So you are one of them! Didn't you know that sooner or later such a fate would overtake you?" And he dealt him a blow with his mallet so that he fell across the doorway of the archbishop's room.

Here again one is reminded of a similar occurrence in the Garden of Olives. Accompanying the Saviour there were only three of the most faithful followers. One of them wanted to defend him, but the Saviour gave himself up into the hands of the revengeful Jewish mob and begged it to permit his followers to depart in peace. A like scene took place now. The mob was about to tear itself into the room when all at once the door opened and St. Josaphat came out into the hall and raised his hand in benediction and having made the sign of the holy cross over them, he spoke to them gently, "My children, why do you kill innocent servants? Let not any man slavishly mutter against me in the corner but come out into the open boldly to convict me. If you have anything against me, here I am!"

At these words of the saint, the murderers stopped, none of whom dared to open his mouth and even those in the front

238

ranks turned round to return. However, all at once from the next room there hurled themselves two murderers, yelling, "Mow down and murder the Latinite, Pope-sucker," and fell upon the saint.

One of them hit him over the head with a mallet and the other split his head open on the left side with an axe. The archbishop fell to the ground covered with blood and the Schismatics, as if they were starved wolves fell upon their prey, beating, pounding and punishing him so that the face of the saint was changed into an unrecognizable mass. Not one complaint or cry escaped his lips. Thinking that he was no longer alive, the murderers fell upon his servants but in that moment St. Josaphat lifted his head streaming with blood and turned his eyes full of blood heavenward and raised one hand as if trying to bless his murderers for the last time and said softly, "Oh my God!" But they would not let him finish, for one of the murderers screamed, "He is still alive!" and springing to the side of the archbishop shot him twice through the head.

St. Josaphat uttered three sighs in honor of the Holy Trinity and gave up his soul to God.

The maddened mob thereupon fell to plundering the residence. Whatever they found was in a moment torn among themselves, gold and silver utensils, money, clothes, arms, brass vases, kitchen and table ware, everything vanished. They tore down the door to the storeroom and all that had been stored away of supplies for the entire winter fell into the hands of the ransackers. They got into the basement, rolled out barrels of wine and beer and getting drunk, they made merry by rolling the barrels off the hill named after the Blessed Virgin on which the residence and Church were located. The whole place was pillaged, the windows and doors torn out, the wagons and carriages demolished. The official papers, various documents destroyed; chairs, tables and other furnishings broken up.

In the meantime, when there were no servants left, there sat beside the body as if on guard, a dog whom Josaphat had sometimes petted. An animal has more sensibility and sense of gratitude than a human being overpowered by his passions. The dog would not permit anyone to touch the body of his master until they killed him and cutting him into pieces, placed him on top the relic of the saint. A man who has lost the true faith becomes when angry more maddened than the wildest animal and equals only the devil.

They dragged the body of St. Josaphat outside into the yard among the crazed and bloodthirsty mob of Schismatics and heedless of the instinct of shame, they tore off his clothes and bared the virgin flesh. How amazed they were when they saw on the naked body the hairshirt and his loins girded with a prickly belt. They thought at first it was but the body of a common monk and not the archbishop, especially since it was hard to recognize the face. Then they dragged out the seriously wounded Ushatsky and Kantakuzen and the servant John Edlinsky and by beating them forced them to tell them who was the dead man. They refused to believe the identification of the servants that this was actually the archbishop himself. Not until the Jews had affirmed that St. Josaphat never wore a shirt did they believe and rejoice that they had rid themselves of the "soul-snatcher." It was a very gay devilish celebration.

Some sat on the naked body of the saintly martyr and thus ate and drank while others pulled the archbishop by his feet and yelled "Get up, your Excellency, this is Sunday. Why don't you give us a sermon. We are all waiting to hear you!" Others jumped back and forth over the holy body and spat on it, while still others pulled the hair out of his head; others with sticks and clubs beat the bruised flesh while still others kicked the saint in the face with the heels of their boots. Even the women and children revenged themselves on the blood-stained archbishop. There were songs and wild beatings of pots and pans so that the persecution of his body was thorough.

The devil who is legion had taken possession of their souls. Whatever the fiend suggested they did to the body of the saint. They were so blinded by their hatred that they failed to heed the miracles God performed for their awakening. One old woman while pulling the hair out of the head of the saint became blind right beside his body. The very heavens wanted to awaken the crazed evil-doers. Over the property of the residence there appeared a black cloud and from it shone a great light covering the naked body. But even this phenomenon made little impression on them. Truly it is a dreadful thing to come to the hardening of the heart.

While one group of the murderers revenged themselves on the body of the saint, the others plundered the residence and beat the servants. When they observed that the archdeacon Dorotheus had revived, they began to beat him with their walking sticks and then rolled him down hill after the barrels, with great howls of joy. It was a miracle, said even by the Jews that Dorotheus falling down that steep hill was not killed at once. However, the Jews proved themselves to be more humane than the irate Schismatics for having found the half-dead body of Dorotheus at the bottom of the hill, they took him in and nursed him back to health without being paid. The servants had managed to carry Kantakuzen and Ushatsky to a place of safety. Although they had been so seriously injured that there was no hope for their recovery, they miraculously returned to their former strength and health thus to remain alive long enough to bear direct witness to these events and to fulfill the prophecy which St. Josaphat had made before his death when he had said to them, "Except for me, no one else will perish."

When they were satisfied with their diabolic amusement on the premises, the evil thought occurred to them to make a parade with the body. Therefore, they tore off the hairshirt from the body and tying a rope to his feet, amidst horrifying howls and demoniac blood-curdling yells and curses, they dragged the body of the prince of their Church through the streets of the city. Thus the blood of the saint sprinkled the streets of that hardened city. In one place where the body had hit a wall, a trace of blood remained which it was impossible to remove by any means available. Finally they dragged the holy body of the archbishop out of the city to the top of a steep incline overlooking the river Dwina and having filled the hairshirt with stones, they tied it to the body and pushed the body down the bank yelling, "Hold fast, your Excellency, hold fast!"

It was indeed a miracle that the body, catapulting downhill over the protruding stones was not torn to bits. The words of the psalmist were fulfilled: (Psalm 33: 21)

"He keepeth all his bones; not one of them is broken."

In memory of this miracle a cross was erected at this place from which the body had been thrown with a placard reading, "God who had protected the body of the martyr from harm because of the undefiled purity which he had observed, let it down the hill uninjured."

As soon as the body had fallen to the shore of the river, the Schismatic fishermen who were awaiting it ran to it and after having first tied to his neck the hairshirt filled with stones and a big rock to each foot they placed it in a canoe and rowed it up the river and drowned it in the deepest part.

No wonder this spot had been known from time immemorial as "the sanctuary of the saints" for actually it became sanctified by the body of the martyr.

To the first Commission the witnesses testified under oath that at the time the martyr's body was drowned, they saw descending from heaven a great light over the spot where the body went down and in the midst of that brilliance could be seen the form of a dignified being who stepped into the water. Immediately afterwards the body was seen floating to the surface despite the fact that there were tied to it so many heavy stones. The frightened evil doers began to run away while the body floated after them. Finally the fishermen returned and grabbing the body they again weighed it down under the water.

When the body had become hidden beneath the waves of the river, there fell over Vitebsk and environs such a heavy fog that people could hardly recognize each other at close range. This fog lasted until the body had again floated to the surface. The sun was hidden and the heavens veiled with black clouds as if it were unable to look upon the monstrous crime of the people of Vitebsk.

Beneath the cross of the Saviour had stood the godless Jews with hatred and vengeance in their hearts and diabolic joy at His suffering. Not until darkness had enveloped the earth, with fear and regret did they flee from the cursed place, fearing the righteous wrath of God. Thus it was now as soon as the relic of the saint was hidden beneath the water and the fog covered the city of Vitebsk, they all silently, as affirmed by eyewitnesses, in the Acts of Beatification, fled into the city. After the murder, when the fog had extinguished the flames of hatred which the evil one had kindled, there came upon them the shocking realization of what they had done. In the city which had but a short time before been so lively and noisy, there was graveyard stillness. The murderers, with bloody hands hid themselves to reflect with deep anguish of mind upon their crime and to bear witness to the punishment of Cain after the slaying of the innocent Abel.

CHAPTER XXIII

POST MORTEM ACCLAIM AND FUNERAL
OF ST. JOSAPHAT

The world repaid St. Josaphat in its own way. For years of continuous effort, hard work, suffering and love with which St. Josaphat had tried to draw the ungrateful earth closer to heaven, not only did it forsake him, but also hated, persecuted and in the end destroyed him. This is the usual reward of the world to those people who earnestly strive to glorify God by the accomplishment of a worthy service to humanity. What happened to the Saviour is repeated in the lives of those who follow Him. That was why the Saviour addressed Himself to the chosen in this manner: (St. John 15: 19)

"If ye were of the world, the world would love his own: but because ye are not of the world, but I have chosen you out of the world, therefore, the world hateth you."

Nonetheless, heaven knows how to compensate for the injustice and neglect suffered by his beloved while on earth. As a rebuke for depreciation by the earth, God bestows such great honors upon His chosen that even the earth which lies in evil is forced to recognize the greatness and power of those whom God desires to glorify.

Thus heaven began by visible ways and means to demonstrate the greatness and holiness of St. Josaphat. From the time of St. Josaphat's death to the burial of his relic in the tomb there were continuous miracles created before the very eyes of thousands of not only Catholics but also Schismatics, murderers and idolaters. These miracles, verified under oath to the Commission for Beatification of St. Josaphat, bear the best testimony to the glory of the martyr.

The day of the murder was drawing to a close. It began to grow dark. The civil and Latin Church authorities had kept their eyes and ears closed all day to the illegal act of the Schismatics. Not until a graveyard stillness had covered the city did the sheriff John Usenetsky and his assistant Philip Osipowsky dare to go in company with others to view the destruction of the archbishop's residence and to write out their report. It was said by some that it was their fear of the Schismatics that kept them from defending St. Josaphat while others said that they had been bribed by the Schismatics. Upon entering the Church they found a locked trunk which the Schismatics had abandoned because they could neither open it, although they had the key, nor break it open with their tools.

When the assistant voyevod learned that in it were the archbishop's vestments, he ordered the chest to be carried to the residence. Hardly had they arrived at the spot where the blood of the martyr was congealed when the chest as if pushed out of their hands fell to the floor, opened of itself and from it fell the stikharion unto the spot where there was a pool of blood. After it rolled out the chalice, the discus, the star and cross. The chalice in falling overturned and dipped itself into the blood, whereupon it arose and straightened itself, as if it wanted of itself to offer the blood of the martyr as a sacrifice in place of the usual bloodless sacrifice which he was obliged to offer to God within each seven days. All the other garments and objects thereupon arranged themselves as if the archbishop were about to put them on for

245

celebrating the Mass. Everyone present saw this miracle. No one dared to touch any of the things until the faithful servant of the archbishop Timothy Chechersky, with trembling hands gathered them up and folded the holy and now blood-stained garments of the martyr back into the chest. It was then carried to the chapel.

On that same day, after the murder was committed, the people of Polotsk saw over the city of Vitebsk, which is about twenty-four miles distant from them, a fiery column reaching to the very heavens.

In Polotsk itself, Simeon, the two-year-old son of Dorotheus Archimovich, a city official, having awakened early the day after the murder, began to exclaim in a sad voice in the presence of his parents and the servants, "Oh Father, the holy one has died!" They were all amazed, for the child up till then had been unable to speak intelligently. And when they asked him, "Which holy one died?" The child replied, "The one who built the White Church." This was what everyone called the Church which had been rebuilt by St. Josaphat. After that speech the child returned to baby talk until he reached the proper age to speak intelligently. It was not until the following day that word was brought to Polotsk that St. Josaphat had been murdered.

The authorities of Vitebsk desiring to minimize their guilt showed a great earnestness in finding the body of the archbishop. Despite the fact that they offered one hundred gold pieces to the fisherman who would find the holy relic, no one was able to find it on account of the dense fog which had covered the river. Not until the sixth day did the fishermen see a great light through the gloom over the place in the river where they found the body.

As soon as news of this fact had spread throughout the city, the people hurried to the riverbank. Ahead of them all came a city official and magistrate of Polotsk, John Khodiha, who had been a great enemy of the holy martyr, together with the nobleman Khrapowitsky. When they came to the spot indicated, they saw the body in the water with the feet pointing shoreward. The archbishop's servants brought rugs and clothing and after pulling the body out of the water, they began to clothe it with which Khodiha assisted by holding a sheet over the naked body to shield it from the curious eyes of the onlookers, while Khrapovitsky drove back with a club the crowd which tried to force its way to the holy relic.

As soon as the body was on shore, the clouds dispersed and the fog lifted itself. The sun shone once more upon the earth after six days of being hidden. The clothed body was thereupon carefully placed in one canoe and covered with a spread while the hairshirt and stones were placed in another canoe and thus began the mournful procession.

Along the bank of the river ran a numerous crowd of people to the place where they were to make the landing. The canoes stopped at the riverside pier of the bishop's residence and the body was placed on the bank where the priests were waiting to receive it.

When the people actually saw their shepherd, there arose among them a great wailing and they began weeping. Then the relic of the saint was placed on a stretcher, covered with a fine coverlet and amid the clanging of bells, Church songs and loud laments of the crowd, it was carried on the shoulders of the priests to the Church of St. Michael.

Upon their arrival at the Church, the crowds were dismissed. They preceded the archdeacon, Dorotheus, who was then hardly able to stand on his feet but who had in the meantime sufficiently recovered so that he might for the last time serve his master as he had served him faithfully all his life.

With tears in his eyes and a broken heart, with trembling hands he dressed with the assistance of the priests, the relic of the holy martyr in his archbishop's vestments. On his finger gleamed the episcopal ring, the crosier was in his hand

247

and over his shoulder flowed the white omophorion embroidered with its four crosses.

Then it was placed in the center of the Church where it could be viewed the best. Here the body rested in state for nine days. During the entire period the Church was filled to overcrowding with those who came sometimes from great distances to pay their last respects to their archbishop, to pray and cry over him. For truly there was something to see here, to be amazed at and cry over. God desired the body not to be spoiled. Although it had lain in the water for five days, it was not spoiled at all, but on the contrary, was made more beautiful. The face did not have anything repellent in it of the dead. As it had been in real life fair, it became only fairer in death. The lips were red, as if ready to open to announce, "Let there be one fold!" The eyes were gently closed as if in sleep. The entire expression of the face which in the past had awakened souls to repentance now became magnetically attractive, pleasant, smiling softly. It seemed as if Josaphat would in a moment arise to give a sermon and teach. Not any part of the body was newly injured although the fishermen had grappled for it with iron hooks. The great wound in the head made with the axe was open and from it flowed fresh blood. As many blows as the murderers had dealt St. Josaphat, so many red marks remained on his flesh. On the face remained the marks of the heels of the boots with which the women had kicked him. The entire body was soft and pliable.

Many conversions were attributed to this miracle. The Schismatics who came out of curiosity returned home with tears of repentance, converted to the Holy Union. Among the first to be converted was Khodiha himself who later testified under oath to his personal experiences of all that had transpired.

When the news of St. Josaphat's martyrdom had spread throughout Polotsk, all the Catholics, Heretics and even the

Jews mourned his death. Now they fully realized what a good shepherd they had lost and how unjustly they had treated him in the past. People always value the good most after they have lost it.

It was thereupon determined to bring the body back to the city in state, and a deputation of the city officials headed by Rev. Hennedy Khmelnitsky the confessor to St. Josaphat and his companion from the earliest days of his monastic life was sent to Vitebsk.

The city of Vitebsk did not have the right to hold the body of St. Josaphat, first of all because they were his murderers, secondly the Seat of the archbishop was in Polotsk and also because St. Josaphat had himself expressed a desire to be buried in Polotsk after the completion of his tomb.

Two weeks after the murder, the delegation arrived at Vitebsk and at once repaired to the Church of St. Michael to view the body. It is hard to describe the lamentations and floods of tears. Later Dahilevich testified before the Apostolic Commission about their official examination as follows: "We saw St. Josaphat looking as beautiful as an angel with a greater sweetness and holiness expressed in his face than in real life."

The delegates thereupon placed the body in an expensive coffin which they had brought with them and decided to transport it by boat to Polotsk. They planned to take the body of their shepherd back on the third day after their arrival. This was a day of tears and lamentation for Vitebsk. The people who had formerly not even wanted to know St. Josaphat were now unable to part with him.

While St. Josaphat still lay in their Church, they felt that they had him with them, but now that they were to lose him, the pain of their grief was reflected on all their faces.

The people of Polotsk wanted to carry the body themselves to the pier of the river but the citizens of Vitebsk would not permit it. They realized very well that they were unworthy that the relic should remain with them. Nonetheless, they wanted to render it at least this final service. They all pressed forward to have the bier of the saint at least touch their shoulders for a moment. Even the murderers themselves had to force the stretchers out of their hands on which rested their sacrifice. Everyone considered it good luck merely to touch the coffin with his finger. The people thronged the pier sobbing to do homage to their shepherd. The weeping and lamentations were so loud that they almost drowned out the peals of the bells and the chanting. Some beat themselves on the breast, others raised their hands to the heavens, still others cursed the murderers.

The wailings were heard all over the city, "They killed the good Father; murdered our shepherd. Oh God, avert our punishment; Josaphat, forgive us our wickedness!"

When the procession passed by the Calvinist house of worship, the minister, standing in the doorway exclaimed, "Woe to those who killed an innocent man!" And in that moment a strange thing occurred. The chalice which had stood upright thus far on top of the coffin and which was securely attached thereto now turned itself away in the opposite direction from the Calvinist meeting house. Even after death St. Josaphat affirmed the fact that the true sacrifice is made only at the altar of the Catholic Church. That was why the chalice in which the sacrifice is made turned itself away from the meeting house of the heretic Calvinists.

When the relic was placed in the canoe and the people of Polotsk were making ready to pull off, everybody began to weep. The priest wept, the Catholics, Schismatics, Heretics, the murderers and Jews. There was not a dry eye among them all. And when the boats began to move, the people ran along the river bank following them for some distance.

Again God glorified St. Josaphat with a new miracle. At that time it was very cold and frosty but the river was frozen only half-way so that the canoe with the relic and men could float along easily. But as soon as they had arrived in Polotsk the entire river froze over at once.

Throughout the entire journey down stream from nearby towns and villages which they passed along the river route gathered crowds of noblemen, citizens and peasants waiting to see St. Josaphat or at least to catch a glimpse of his form and to pay their respects to him as a martyr. Those who were able to get a closer look at the body of the saint were amazed by the fact that although so much time had elapsed since the death of the archbishop, his body was not yet spoiled and looked handsomer than during life.

Who can describe the reception of the holy relic by the people of Polotsk? When bidding him farewell upon his departure for Vitebsk they had not expected that he would return under such circumstances although the saint had prophesied it.

The news about the marvelous preservation of the body, report of the holiness of the murdered shepherd of the Church, the love of the Catholics, respect of the Schismatics and Heretics, prompted all to turn out to greet the holy relic. The bier had scarcely arrived when it was besieged. The riverside was thronged with folk who regardless of their religious beliefs had come to see the archbishop and offer him special reverence. Unable to deny the pleadings and wish of the multitude the cover of the coffin was raised. When the people saw the face full of gentleness, holiness and sweetness, their hearts were softened and touched with grief they fell on their knees while the tears flooded their eyes and they all prayed the saint to remain now as ever before their protector and spiritual director and intercessor at the throne of God.

With due reverence the relic was carried to the archbishop's own Church of the See of Polotsk, newly finished just as St. Josaphat had desired and here displayed for public veneration, so that all might marvel at the work of God which He performs on His holy ones.

The actual burial, because of the various obstacles and difficulties, took place fourteen months after his death, that is, on the 18th of January 1625. God in His divine wisdom had so planned it, in order to glorify the martyr more. During all that time the body did not change but remained as if alive, retaining the coloring of live flesh. By the relic took place numerous miracles. God wanted also on earth to compensate His servant for the indignities to which the people had subjected him before his death.

When the set time came for the funeral, throughout the entire week preceding it, the bells rang in all the Churches for an hour in the morning, noon and night. Three days before the funeral, the relic was carried out of the Uniate Church and placed in the Church of the Saviour in the center of town in order to in the meantime decorate and prepare the Church of the See for the funeral.

The day before the funeral, there arrived in Polotsk, the Metropolitan Joseph Rutsky, the bishop of Pinsk, Gregory Michalowsky and the newly appointed archbishop bought by St. Josaphat's blood to the See of Smolensk, Leo Krewza. To greet them rode out Anthony Silawa, the successor to St. Josaphat accompanied by the gentry, city officials and other notables. After their arrival, the three princes of the Church went straight to the Church where the relic of St. Josaphat lay in state, celebrated vespers and afterwards repaired to the residence of the archbishop.

The next day the bells of all the Churches began ringing at dawn, calling the faithful to pay their homage of respect to their archbishop.

At eight o'clock in the morning salvos were fired from the fort's guns announcing the start of the procession. The procession began with the citizens of the city forming themselves in long rows carrying lighted candles. In their midst marched the school children under the direction of their teachers, the Jesuit Fathers, singing the funeral songs as they marched. After them came the Latin priesthood in their red vestments followed by one hundred twelve Ukrainian priests in their vestments of various colors. After the Ukrainian priesthood came the nine pastors of Polotsk in their richest vestments carrying the stikharion and chalice crusted with the blood of the martyr, the hair shirt, ropes and stones which were the paraphernalia connected with the martyrdom.

On the hearse, covered with a fine red cloth, rested the coffin in which was the relic covered with a red silk scarf, while beside the hearse marched the curates in red vestments carrying lighted torches. On each side of them marched one hundred fully armed soldiers also dressed in red. Following the hearse came the princes of the Church dressed in the richest vestments of the Rite accompanied by the gentry and civil authorities.

Looking upon this festive procession, anyone would say that this was more in the way of a coronation of a king than a sad funeral procession. They were all so fully convinced of the holiness of St. Josaphat and overwhelmed by the power of his spirit which went rushing through the crowd to struggle with and overcome sin in men in order to make them become conscious of God, that they did not even wear the customary black mourning vestments but the red vestments of martyrdom.

When the procession entered the fort, the guns thundered five volleys of shots. The walls of the Church were covered with red damask and in the center stood the catafalque covered with the same red damask cloth, illumined by numerous lighted candles. When the coffin was placed on the catafalque, the Metropolitan, assisted by the archbishops, celebrated a festive Liturgy, accompanied by the melodious singing of the choir which St. Josaphat had loved so well. The fervor of devotion and the beauty of holiness reigned throughout the Assembly. After Mass, the newly appointed archbishop to the See of Smolensk gave such an impassioned sermon that tears streamed down the faces of the Catholics and the Schismatics renounced their heresy. The children sang songs of eulogy composed in honor of St. Josaphat and finally after a few words by Joseph Rutsky, the greatest friend of the martyr, they placed the coffin in the crypt he had ordered prepared for himself in advance.

Everyone present regardless of Rite paid their final respects to the saint. It was the day of his glory, a day of victory, a day of triumph for St. Josaphat's indomitable spirit, who immolated the Saviour in his work for the Union for which he had worked all his life and for which in the end he paid with his life.

CHAPTER XXIV

THE RESULTS OF ST. JOSAPHAT'S MARTYRDOM

The death of St. Josaphat brought about various reactions throughout Ukraine. The Schismatics were jubilant; a few weak Catholics grieved. They all thought that with the death of St. Josaphat, the work of the Union would cease as there was no longer a powerful fighter against Schism and mighty defender of the Union. But the task of the Union was God's work and God's work is never neglected. The prophecy of the divine Saviour was fulfilled:

(St. John 12: 24-25)

"Verily, verily, I say unto you, Except a corn of wheat fall into the ground and die, it abideth alone: but if it die, it bringeth forth much fruit. He that loveth his life shall lose it, and he that hateth his life in this world shall keep it unto life eternal."

During his life, St. Josaphat was to the Schismatics a Samson and this he remained after death. What the Holy Spirit said of Samson can be repeated as applying also to St. Josaphat.

(Judges 16: 30)

"And Samson said, Let me die with the Philistines. And he bowed himself with all his might; and the house fell upon the lords and upon all the people therein. So the dead which he slew at his death were more than they which he slew in his life."

St. Josaphat converted more by his martyrdom after death than he had ever done during his lifetime. His worst enemies and murderers who while he was alive did not even want to hear St. Josaphat speak of the Union, after his death begged with tears in their eyes to be permitted to join the Uniate Church for which he had given his life. And how could it be otherwise? How could St. Josaphat forget in heaven about the work for which he had sacrificed his life? How could God disregard the prayers of the beloved?

It has already been described what sorrow and remorse was displayed by the Schismatics at sight of the relic of St. Josaphat so that even that hardened city of Vitebsk to which St. Josaphat had so many times spoken in vain, after the removal of his body was plunged into deep mourning and repentance. For truly, it was difficult, according to human reasoning, to look upon all the miracles by which God glorified St. Josaphat not to see in them the hand of God, demonstrating the holiness and innocence of the archbishop as compared with the sin and evil will of his persecutors and murderers. Therefore, it was not surprising that thousands of Schismatics became converted among whom were in the past some of the most powerful enemies of St. Josaphat. One among them had been John Khodiha a city official and magistrate of Polotsk who had hated St. Josaphat and the Union to such an extent that he could not bear to look at the archbishop and during sermons fled from the Church in order not to hear the words of the soul snatcher. He had been a party to all the plots devised against the life of the holy archbishop, himself inciting the people of Polotsk to rebellion. In other words, he had been one of St. Josaphat's worst enemies.

"God wanted to show through me," he said afterwards,

"that Josaphat could convert after his death those who had refused to listen to the words of their shepherd, while he lived."

Having come to Vitebsk after the murder of St. Josaphat for the purpose of attending to some business in that city, he had run with others out of curiosity to the river bank when they had found the holy body. Here, already touched by the grace of God, he helped with the dressing of the body of the archbishop and later accompanied it to Church. "That sight of the relic," he testified before the Apostolic Commission, "made such a profound impression on my unworthy self that I at once renounced Schism and after a period of eight days, I received the Holy Sacraments of Penance and Holy Communion in the Church of the See of the archbishop of Polotsk."

From that moment he became one of the most ardent Catholics and at the same time the greatest apostle and greatest venerator of St. Josaphat. St. Josaphat rewarded him for this by granting him many favors and graces. The following is a record of one of the favors received:

In the year 1636 John Khodiha was returning to Vitebsk with two boat loads of valuable merchandise. At night he was viciously attacked by his determined enemy, John Hlinsky who inflicted on him twelve wounds. In order to escape certain death, he jumped into the river and cried, "St. Josaphat come to my aid." His call was answered, for despite the fact that he lost a great quantity of blood, and the river was wide and full of dangerous whirlpools, he managed to reach the shore safely and got well quickly. Such conversions as that of Khodiha were repeated daily. All during the time the relic was displayed for public veneration in Vitebsk and Polotsk, there was not a day in which some of the most powerful enemies of the Union were not converted to the Uniate Church. Every touch, moving of his body, even just the sight of the holy relic of the saint served as a means of conversion of the Schismatics. From among many such conversions it might be well to mention the following:

In Vilno lived a fanatical Schismatic, wife of the Catholic Stephen Ripnitsky; one of the civil officials of the city. When at one time he was preparing for a pilgrimage to Polotsk, to fulfill a promise he had made to St. Josaphat for granting a favor, he begged his wife to accompany him but at first she would not even hear of it; then she consented with the understanding that she would not be made to look at the relic of the saint. When she came to the Church of St. Sophia, she stood on purpose behind one of the columns in order not to see the relic. However, what she had not desired happened. The blood of St. Josaphat flowed upon her in a spiritual way for mentally illumined by the grace of God she suddenly came to the realization of the unfortunate state of her soul and with the softening of her heart she began to sob so bitterly that she attracted the attention of all in the Church. The people thought that she had been taken sick and came over to help her, but she would not be comforted until she had renounced Schism and made friends with God.

There was a much greater and more glorious conquest by St. Josaphat over his murderers. Their crime was great. They felt themselves that proper punishment was their due and had to be in keeping with the enormity of the crime, for the Schismatics, noting that a few murders went unpunished, continued to increase in their malevolence. It was impossible, therefore, to keep silent on the matter. The blood of the innocent cried out for justice. The Uniates demanded it.

The news of St. Josaphat's murder was brought to the Metropolitan Rutsky by one of St. Josaphat's servants. Rutsky was very much pained because he had lost a companion and true friend, but strong in his faith, he did not succumb to grief but rather with joy offered this sacrifice to Almighty God for the sake of the Union. He immediately called his bishops for a conference as to what action they were to take in the matter. The martyrdom of the saint had its effect. They were so inspired that the bishops agreed unanimously that they also would willingly sacrifice their lives for the Catholic faith and the Union.

The Metropolitan at once informed Pope Urban VIII of St. Josaphat's death, at the same time reassuring the Holy Father that all the other bishops were likewise ready to sacrifice their lives for the sake of the Union. In addition, he sent letters to the king and his ministers by a messenger, who had been one of the eyewitnesses to the martyrdom of St. Josaphat, demanding justice and defense. "What else is there for us to do but appeal to the king and put the matter into the hands of his ministers who are the guardians of the public peace, the defenders of the lives of the servants of God." He also wrote to the Chancellor's assistant:

"Do whatever you think best in the matter. If you fail to punish the crime I will not complain except to God to whom I will pray, telling him of the injustice that is done to us."

The king wanted to investigate the matter at once and mete out proper punishment but evidently the lawyers had been bribed and they advised, supposedly for the sake of obtaining more evidence, to postpone the punishment with the idea in mind, of course, of letting it become gradually forgotten.

In the meantime, the king received a message from Pope Urban VIII who requested justice through his Papal Nuncio, Lanceolotti and Leo Sapiha, the prime minister, demanding adequate penalty for the criminals. The king appointed a committee which was to gather and investigate the facts and punish the guilty ones without delay. Those appointed to the Commission were: Leo Sapiha, the king's chancellor, Samuel Sanhushko, voyevod of Vitebsk, Christian Sokolinsky of Mstyslav, Alexander Corwin Goncewsky, secretary to the king and Alexander Sapiha Orshon, elder. The Commission set out for Vitebsk accompanied by a powerful guard of soldiers, as they feared that the Schismatic Kozaks might defend the murderers and thus interfere with the carrying out of proper justice.

The court began its session on the 17th of January 1624. Here was revealed the innocence and holiness of St. Josaphat. All of the murderers not only confessed their guilt but also the motive for the murder. They admitted that it was not anything St. Josaphat had done that led them to the murder but only their hatred for the Union backed by Smotritsky's letters and the persuasive literature of his agents, especially of the monk Sylvester.

"When St. Josaphat first became bishop," they said, "in 1618, we accepted him as our shepherd. We could see that he was a saint, ardent and zealous in teaching the good life, that he followed all the customs of our Rite exactly and that he administered the Church according to canonical laws and the precepts of the Holy Fathers. We loved him and respected him as our shepherd, admired his gentleness and appreciated his fatherly concern for us. Thus it went on for three years until by God's will and our own sins as well as that of our forefathers, Smotritsky sent us his monk Sylvester with literature which incited us to rebellion." There could be no better or more enlightening proof of the innocence and holiness of St. Josaphat given by anyone than that attested to by his murderers. Thus they admitted their guilt and brought not a single accusation against St. Josaphat. On the basis of these facts, the Commission passed a very strict sentence not only to adequately punish the guilty ones but also to discourage a repetition of any such crime in the future.

Their decision announced on the 23rd of January 1624 was as follows: Vitebsk ceases to be from now on a free city, losing all the rights given it by the kings and is to be henceforth under the rule of the voyevod. The townhall is to be

260

closed and the use of the bell to call town meetings is forbidden. All the bells in all the Churches which were used to call the Schismatics to their crime were to be taken down and brought to the armory, melted and made into one bell on which was to be engraved their act of disobedience, the sentence of the guilty and the bell was to be placed in the Church near the scene of the crime. Other churches would not be permitted to ring their bells without permission from the bishop. Nineteen murderers were given the death sentence and seventy-four accomplices were to be exiled beyond the borders of the country, suffering the loss of all their rights of citizenship. This stringent judgment was put into effect without delay.

Through the prayers of St. Josaphat and the grace of God, all of the condemned except one were converted before their death, renounced Schism and with sincere repentance made their confession. With sincere grief for the crime they had committed and with hope of forgiveness from the heavenly father, they gladly laid their heads beneath the sword of the executioner. Were not the fruits of St. Josaphat's martyrdom miraculous, that his greatest enemies and murderers themselves acknowledged his holiness and innocence, condemning themselves voluntarily without hope of mercy and in the end accepted the faith for which they had murdered their pastor?

There was only one among the evil doers who remained a hardened criminal to the very end of his miserable life and this was Peter Wasilevich, a civil official of Polotsk. He had come to Vitebsk especially to help promote the cause of the evil enterprise. As already mentioned, he was the man who Christened children himself and heard the confessions of the dying, just to keep the Catholic priests away from them. He was given the death sentence also for inciting to rebellion and murder and by the will of God his death was very painful.

When the executioners wanted to cut off his head, he began to defend himself with his hands and thus the executioner cut off one hand and then the other and his ears and finally his head. Everyone was convinced of his just punishment by God for the sacrileges he had committed, for with those hands he baptized and touched holy things and with those ears he heard the confessions and in his head had conceived the idea of murder. All who came away from that horrible place acknowledged with the crowned prophet David: (Psalm 118: 137)

"Righteous art thou, O Lord and upright are thy judgments."

Another proof of the blamelessness of St. Josaphat was given by the people of Vitebsk in the year 1628. The Commission appointed by Rome met in the Church of the Blessed Virgin Mary in Vitebsk to gather proofs of the holiness, cause of martyrdom and the favors and graces granted by the intercession of St. Josaphat. The Acts of Beatification testify that more than a thousand persons in Vitebsk admitted taking part in the murder and with tears in their eyes implored the Commission for confessors who would be able to give them absolution for their sins and sacrileges and accept them into the Uniate Church. They unanimously testified to the holiness, gentleness and goodness of St. Josaphat and confessed their own hatred and evil-doing by participation in the murder. No wonder St. Josaphat wanted to die in Vitebsk, because of the hard hearts of those people, it was necessary to make a heroic sacrifice of life in order to convert them to God.

No one can deny the greatest conquest by St. Josaphat was the conversion of Melety Smotritsky, who, as we already know, was St. Josaphat's most powerful enemy and the cause of all the rebellions and persecutions and finally his martyrdom.

It was true that he did not personally incite them to mur-

262

der but with his rebellious pamphlets, writings and books, he aroused the people to hatred of the Union and Josaphat, strengthening this hatred through his agents and in this way brought the people to the point where they undertook to actually commit murder.

When he learned of the death of St. Josaphat and later of the severity of the justice meted out to the murderers, he was frightened lest the hand of justice should touch his part in the crime, therefore, he fled beyond the borders of the country, together with his intimate companions. Not being fully convinced of the truth of his faith, he thought that possibly he might find that conviction in the East, the very center of Schism. That was why he first travelled to Byzantium to see the Patriarch Kirilo Lukarisa, his former teacher. However, he was amazed when he found that the head of the Orthodox Church instead of spreading the teachings of Christ was promoting Lutheranism. From Byzantium he went to Jerusalem in the hope that in that city made holy by the life of the Divine Saviour, he could still his conscience on which weighed the blood of St. Josaphat. But even here, instead of being cheered up, a greater grief encompassed his soul for he saw on every side the falling away of the faith and strict observance of the Rite. He was no better off even after his visit to the patriarch of Alexandria. He found everywhere not only among the people but also the Schismatic priesthood a lack of proper knowledge of the fundamentals of the faith, a falling away of ritual, the desertion and neglect of the Churches, the sale and purchase of holy things and ownership and domination of the Schismatic Church by the Mussulmen Turks. He saw with his own eyes the sad state to which the inept Schism had brought the formerly flourishing Catholic Churches which had given to the world thousands of saints.

He came to the realization of the truth that "Where Peter is not, there is not the true Church." While still on his journey, he became in spirit a Catholic, realizing that the salvation of Ukraine depended on its Union with the See of St. Peter.

Having come to this conclusion, his conscience began to worry him that through his writings he had turned away thousands of souls from the true Church and gave them into the hands of the Schismatics for destruction.

Possessing in his heart a sincere love for Ukraine, he determined to return to his homeland and to work with all the power at his command to right the wrongs he had committed. In order to do this, it was necessary for him to find a place where he could work undisturbed in the accomplishment of his task of making reparation for his crimes. For this purpose there presented itself to him the archimandrate of the Basilian monastery at Derman which post at the time he returned to Ukraine, was vacant. He thereupon went to visit Prince Zaslawsky who was then patron of Derman and applied to him for the position as its archimandrite. Prince Zaslawsky first consulted Metropolitan Rutsky and then promised it to him with the understanding that he must first renounce Schism. Smotritsky gladly agreed to this and came to Derman. Encouraged by Rutsky himself and other good friends on the 23rd day of February 1627, he formally renounced Schism and with true humility and contrition made his confession to Rutsky.

He also wrote to Pope Urban VIII a very humble letter begging his forgiveness for evil doing in the past and requested acceptance into the Catholic Church. Pope Urban VIII with fatherly good grace forgave him his errors and accepted him into Union with the Holy Catholic Church.

For a time his conversion was kept a secret for the reason that Smotritsky hoped in this way to have greater influence over the Schismatics who still considered him as one of themselves.

At Derman, Smotritsky began his work in earnest. He

264

wrote a book entitled, "Epilogue of a Journey to the East," in which he described the sad plight of all the Eastern Churches that had become separated from the Catholic Church, pointing out at the same time all the errors which crept into the Church without a responsible head. Then he made comparison between the truths as taught in the two Churches, pointing out the blunders of the Schismatic preachers. At the same time he criticized his own previous book "Our Afflicted Ukrainian Church," admitting all the lies which he had written into the book and concluded it by making the statement that the salvation of the Ukrainian Church lay only in its Union with Rome. This book he sent to the Schismatic Metropolitan Boretsky for approval.

In the meantime, on the 15th of August, 1628, the Schismatics held their Synod in Kiev. Smotritsky was confident that it would be an easy matter to get the Assembly to agree to the Union and that was the reason he hurried eagerly to the conference. However, it turned out quite differently. The Schismatics, as soon as they had read his "Epilogue" immediately suspected that he had turned Catholic so that upon his arrival at Kiev, he was prevailed upon to return to Schism and to sign a statement that he was renouncing the Catholic faith. At first Smotritsky resisted this demand but finally out of fear of death with which the Schismatics threatened him, the unhappy man renounced the Union he had accepted. As soon as he was able to escape out of the hands of the Schismatics he travelled to Lwiw and there wrote "Protest" renouncing therein any further connection with the Schismatics. Thereafter he began to live the life of penance to make up for his evil doing as St. Peter:

(Matthew 26: 75)

"And Peter remembered the word of Jesus which said unto him, Before the cock crow, thou shalt deny me thrice. And he went out, and wept bitterly."

He returned to Derman and spent his time in prayer, self-mortification, writing of pious Catholic books and observing a strict penance, living the detached life of a monk. He realized after his fall that he was no longer fitted for the Apostolic work and so he did not leave Derman for the rest of his life but devoted himself mostly to attaining the illumination of his own soul. Here he lived until the year 1633. Pope Urban VIII forgave him his second fall and to show his fatherly concern he sent him a document in which he appointed him archbishop of Herapolsk.

Before his death he made a complete confession of the sins of his whole life and received Communion and Extreme Unction standing up. He ordered some of his writings to be burned and bidding farewell to his brethren, he begged that after his death, the letter the Pope of Rome wrote to him forgiving him for his fall and reaccepting him back into the Catholic Church be placed in his hands. Five hours after his death, when his body had already grown stiff, the monks remembered his request before death and one of them having searched and found the Papal brief, put it into the fingers of the dead man. And a miracle happened. As soon as the script touched the fingers they grasped hold of it so tightly that no one could have pulled it out of his hand. Some of them tried to place in his hands the document of the patriach of Byzantium, but the hands moved away and the fingers closed themselves so tightly that it was impossible to put anything into them.

For four weeks the body lay in state and this miracle continued to be repeated. The rumour of the miracle spread throughout the district and many Catholics and Schismatics came to be convinced of it. The town elder, Dubnitsky, who also came to view the body and see the miracle, tried to pull the Pope's document out of the hand of the dead man. He nearly pulled him out of the coffin but the fingers would not let go of the paper.

Finally Joseph Rutsky came to the funeral of Smotritsky.

After praying by the body of Meletius he asked of him in the presence of many others for the paper given to him by the Pope. At this request the hand opened and the writing slipped out of it, as if Smotritsky wanted to show by this act that even after death he was obedient to the rightful followers of the Apostles. Having read the document aloud, Rutsky returned it to Meletius and his fingers grasped it so firmly that it would have been easier to lift the body out of the coffin than to pull the paper out of his hand. They offered him also the papers of the patriarch in the presence of the Metropolitan but the hands moved away. More of the great crowd of Schismatics which followed his remains through the streets were converted by this miracle after the death of Smotritsky than he had been able to convert himself while he lived.

Thus by strict penance and as a faithful member of the Catholic Church, the chief persecutor and enemy of St. Josaphat lived out the remainder of his life, changed by the martyr's blood from the persecutor of God's Church as Saul, to the penitent Paul, as Rev. Kotisky referred to him in his funeral oration.

Metropolitan Joseph Rutsky in reporting the matter to Pope Urban VIII wrote to him saying, "St. Josaphat was to Smotritsky that which Stephen had been to Saul, why should we not attribute his conversion to the prayers of St. Josaphat that grace might heal the stricken soul whose torment he had divined?"

It would be impossible to trace and record all the conversions which took place after St. Josaphat's death, suffice it to state that not only the diocese of Polotsk turned Catholic and remained the longest in the Union despite fierce persecutions by the Schismatics but also all of Ukraine felt a strengthening grace through the blood of the holy martyr. The fact that Ukrainians have continued to remain Catholic despite all the persecutions, persuasions, promises and deceptions practiced by the Schismatics on the one hand and on the other all the slander, depreciation, annoyances and jeering from those who should respect and support the important matter of the Union, we may boldly attribute and be thankful for, the martyrdom of St. Josaphat through which he has become a natural protector and reparation for the sins against Holy Union.

CHAPTER XXV

ST. JOSAPHAT, THE MIRACULOUS

There are very few saints whom God glorifies immediately after death with so many miracles as in the case of St. Josaphat. From the time of his death nearly every day God performed some miracle in St. Josaphat's name, thus demonstrating his glory in heaven.

In order to make a faithful report of all the miracles performed by the intervention of St. Josaphat it would require a complete volume in itself. The Acts of Beatification of the year 1637 list eighty-four miracles witnessed and testified to under oath by the first few persons in the country who recieved the graces. Mention will be made here of only a few of the most important miracles among them to demonstrate how pleasing was the sacrifice of St. Josaphat to God and at the same time to encourage others to seek help in their needs from the Holy Archbishop.

Note: Susha, "Life of St. Josaphat," Chapter V, Page 108-140—

"Of all the miracles recorded and sworn to there are 100, from the year 1623-1660."

If St. Josaphat in his great heartedness had obtained so

many graces for his enemies, as has been mentioned in previous chapters, he could not possibly have forgotten in heaven his friends and servants who remained faithful to him until death and that was why they were able to obtain his aid in both spiritual and material needs. Let the experiences of those who had suffered with him and worked with him in the service of God tell their story:

In the year 1636, the archdeacon of St. Josaphat, Dorotheus Letsikovich became so seriously ill that even the doctors gave up hope for his recovery. Forsaken by his physician, he turned to his archbishop with an appeal for healing and soaking a relic of St. Josaphat in water, he drank the water and immediately afterwards was restored to his former health so that on the next day he was able to celebrate Mass, thanking God and the saint for his miraculous healing.

The four-year-old daughter of the sister of his other companion in martyrdom, Emanuel Kantakuzen, became ill with such a high fever that even a strong man could not have withstood it. Not finding relief from the doctors, he brought his little niece to the tomb of St. Josaphat and in his presence placed her in his care and the child recovered immediately.

The Rev. Hennedy Khmelnitsky, confessor and most intimate friend of St. Josaphat who became archimandrite of the monastery of Polotsk, soon after the death of St. Josaphat became ill and paralyzed so that he was unable to leave his cell for three years. Unable to find relief in medicines, he made the promise that as soon as he became well he would visit the sepulchre of the saint. The very next day he found that he was able to get out of bed and walked to the Church a mile away from the monastery in order to celebrate a mass of thanksgiving at the tomb of the saint.

Michael Tishkevich, a great friend of St. Josaphat, who had offered to accompany St. Josaphat on his last journey to Vitebsk received many graces. His wife, Christina, nearing death and given up by the doctors became immediately healed as soon as he had placed her under the care of his holy archbishop. Also his servant, Sophia, who lay twenty-four hours on the death bed, was restored to health as soon as he had placed her in St. Josaphat's care and suspended around her neck a tiny piece of cloth stained by the blood of the martyr.

Tishkevich himself was seized with an attack of gout so that with the help of his servants he was hardly able to walk on crutches to the tomb of the saint. By the sepulchre of the martyr he was healed and left his crutches there, returning home by himself without requiring anyone's aid.

The Metropolitan Joseph Rutsky, the best friend of St. Josaphat, riding to the city of Zamosta in the year 1627 saw in the city a great fire. He at once hurried to a Church and ordered candles to be lit by the relic of St. Josaphat, requesting at the same time the cooperation of the Chancellor of Zamosta in prayer for help. He knelt in prayer for half an hour, calling upon St. Josaphat. And all at once the fair skies were covered with rain clouds from which a downpour put out the fire in a few moments.

The Metropolitan attested under oath that on several occasions, whenever he had found himself in great need spiritually or materially, he had always received help from St. Josaphat.

Special protection was received from St. Josaphat by another of his confessors the Rev. S. Kosinsky, a Jesuit monk, in the following way: On the 11th day of November 1626, a fire had started at midnight in the monastery of the Jesuit Order in Polotsk which had already destroyed part of the wooden structure of the monastery before it was discovered. Kosinsky was the rector at the time. Seeing that the fire had progressed beyond human aid, he promised to place a silver tablet beside the tomb of the saint and then began with the other monks to pray and call out, "St. Josaphat, save us!"

The fire, as if smothered by a blanket, was put out. At

271

another time when he was driving across the river Dwina he began to sink, together with his wagon and horses but when he appealed to the saint, he was able to make the crossing safely. At another time he was rector in Derman, his eyes began to hurt him, and while praying fervently he placed a particle of the hair shirt of St. Josaphat over his eyes and he was straightway cured. He was, moreover, able to obtain not only graces for himself but also for many others as he testified before the Commission through the intercession of St. Josaphat and by touching his relic many became healed of the most desperate illnesses. One among those healed was the provincial of the Dominican Order Rev. Kelestin. He was so paralyzed that he could not move. In his misfortune he begged Kosinsky to say a Mass for his intention at the tomb of St. Josaphat. Shortly after the celebration of the Mass, he returned to normal health.

Not only the friends of St. Josaphat received graces but whoever appealed to him in sincere faith was not refused by the saint.

It may be well also to mention a few of the most important miracles and graces received through St. Josaphat's intercession. Prince Alexander Zaslawsky from Ostroh was healed of a serious attack of gout.

Agatha Rosowska, a Brazilian nun, was healed of a serious infection of the feet. Sophia, wife of a nobleman, had been chained to her bed for fourteen months. When on the eve of the anniversary of St. Josaphat's martyrdom, she placed herself under his care she was restored to normal health at once. Alexander Asensky and Gregory Korsak on their death beds appealed to St. Josaphat and were healed.

Prince Gregory Chartoriysky was seriously ill for thirteen weeks. Seeing his end approaching he made out his will and awaited the hour of death. When he felt his breath beginning to choke him, he ordered himself turned on his side. It was then he noticed a picture of St. Josaphat hanging on a wall and he was reminded of the many graces others had obtained of this saint and at once placed himself in the care of the martyr promising to visit the tomb. He began to feel a lessening of his suffering at once and in a short time returned to his former health.

Many received very great favors by using with faith and piety a relic of St. Josaphat. A middle-aged woman, Madam Horska, and a young woman from Polotsk, Margarita Soltanovna, and a boy named Atanas suffered from serious eye trouble. When they rubbed a relic of the saint over their eyes they were healed at once. In this same way also the loss of sight was restored to Peter Dankovich, a magistrate of Polotsk who suffered from disease of the head and eyes and lost his sight entirely. In the evening of the same day that the relic of St. Josaphat was brought to Polotsk he ordered himself driven to the Church. Unable to get close enough to the body of St. Josaphat because of the throng, he stood by the hairshirt and the stones which had weighed down St. Josaphat's body under water. Falling upon his knees he implored the help of the saint and rubbed his eyes with the hairshirt and touched his head to the stones. The Schismatics who were present laughed at him, saying that he was worshipping the stones but he did not heed their jeers only continued to wipe his eyes. All at once he regained his sight and saw the crowd of people. He arose in amazement and joy and went home by himself without need of being guided along. Early the next morning he went to Church again and prayed still more fervently, receiving complete healing for head and eyes. This instantaneous miraculous healing took place publicly before the very eyes of the enemies of the Catholic Church and was the first of the miracles which was confirmed by the Congregation of Rites.

The tomb of St. Josaphat became a place of pilgrimage continuously crowded. Many not finding aid from physicians or having lost the hope of recovery here received the grace of healing. It might be well to report at least one from among all the miracles which occurred at the sepulchre:

In the hospital of the Jesuits in Polotsk, there was a woman who for over fourteen years was so crippled that whenever she wanted to go outside of the hospital she had to crawl like a baby or be pushed in a wheel chair. Hearing about all the miracles which took place by the tomb of St. Josaphat, she managed with the help of others to get to the tomb of the Holy Bishop. And when she had prayed fervently she felt power returning to her feet and she stood up and was able to get down the hill on which the Church was built all by herself and to walk back to the hospital to report her cure.

Sometimes St. Josaphat appeared to those who begged his aid and healed the sick himself. Let us relate one such vision. The fortunate woman, Madam Wolowec, a convert of St. Josaphat's, suffered a serious attack of rheumatism in her legs in March 1627. Obtaining from her brother Eustachio, bishop of Vilno, a little of the earth soaked by the blood of the martyr, she applied it to the most painful parts and while praying fervently she fell asleep. St. Josaphat appeared to her as in a dream dressed in his vestments as archbishop with a great wound in his head from which the blood oozed out. The frightened woman asked who he was and receiving reply that he was St. Josaphat, she began to appeal to him again asking for his intercession with God for the grace earned by his martyrdom for her healing. The saint thereupon moistened a finger in the open wound in his head and smearing the painful parts with his blood said, "This blood given for Christ and the ancient true faith of our forefathers and for the Holy Catholic Church will help you according to your faith." The vision vanished and when she awoke the pain was gone.

Only a few of the miracles are being mentioned here which occurred before the process of beatification. All these miracles were confirmed under oath by witnesses.

Besides these greater miracles and graces people reported almost daily other lesser graces which later on were not even recorded.

The result of these staggering and frequent miracles was an increase in reverence and faith in St. Josaphat which in a short time spread among all Ukrainian Catholics throughout Ukraine, Lithuania and Poland. They all tried to get a tiny particle of the relic of St. Josaphat or at least a particle of his clothing or hairshirt, feeling certain that in time of need this would be of help. If they were unable to obtain a holy relic, they tried to obtain a picture of St. Josaphat. From the remotest parts of the country people hurried to the tomb of St. Josaphat with appeals for help for their ills and needs of this life. That they did not hurry in vain to this shrine and treasury of graces is proved by the many rich gifts and holy garments, golden and silver tablets and vessels from the poorest to the highest quality which the people brought to place by the tomb out of gratitude for the graces received even though at the time he had not yet been officially pronounced a saint. All of Ukraine glorified St. Josaphat. From town to town in every house and at every gathering the martyr's praises were sung in songs composed in his honor.

St. Josaphat rewarded this reverence which his lambs and venerators paid him by interceding for graces to all and especially for Ukraine which during his lifetime he had so dearly loved and those for whose salvation he had given his life. The glory that encompassed him could not be concealed.

Some reader might ask why is it now nothing is heard of the miracles performed by the intercession of St. Josaphat in Ukraine? The fault is not with St. Josaphat but the Ukrainians themselves. The saints in heaven do not change, do not grow old, do not lose their power. Miracles are not less conclusive for being less frequent. As St. Josaphat loved Ukraine then, so he still loves her. As he long ago prayed for its conversion and enlightenment so he still prays for it.

If nothing is heard now of new miracles and graces the cause for it must be that Ukraine has neglected to show proper reverence to this miracle performer, that faith and hope in the hearts of the Ukrainians is not as strong as of their forefathers and mostly because the powerful intercession of this saint has been forgotten. Many do not know the feast day of St. Josaphat, have never even seen a picture of St. Josaphat and do not know a single prayer or song in honor of this holy martyr. They have become estranged from their intercessor that is the only reason he does not help them. If they will have recourse to his intercession and return to honoring him as their forefathers had venerated St. Josaphat, he will return to Ukraine and restore the faith to her people. It must be that his influence is still there conferring sanctity both upon the Church where he prayed and the locality where he lived and upon those who come to pray there, for the glory of a saint does not pass away like that of the world. His prayers for Union are as immortal as he is immortal.

Others might ask why were not all the Schismatics who were witnesses of all these miracles converted to the Catholic Church. Why didn't they accept the Union? To this the only possible reply is with another question. Why did not the Jews looking upon the Saviour, seeing his miracles, observing the Apostles and their miracles, become converted to the Christian faith? What was the reason? To both of these questions the Saviour answers with the words of the prophet Isaias:

(St. John 12: 40)

"He hath blinded their eyes and hardened their hearts that they should not see with their eyes, nor understand with their hearts and be converted and I should heal them."

The Jews having committed the crime of killing Christ were punished with the most awful punishment of hard

276

heartedness and this same punishment fell to the lot of the enemies of the martyr for Christ.

If many were converted it was due only to the eternal mercy of God; if many others remained in sin and stone-heartedness, it was not the fault of Almighty God but their own fault and the penalty provided by God for disdaining the period of his visitation and for refusing to listen to the voice of God as He called them to Himself and His Church.

CHAPTER XXVI

THE MIRACULOUS PRESERVATION OF THE RELIC AND PROCLAMATION OF ST. JOSAPHAT AS A SAINT

Because of the numerous miracles which took place after the death of St. Josaphat, on November 12, 1624, King Sigmund, together with his son, Ladislaw and a few Ukrainian and Polish bishops, supported by numerous nobles and gentry, drew up a petition and brought it before Pope Urban VIII, requesting the proclamation of St. Josaphat as a saint.

Although Pope Urban VIII had but recently decreed that no one was to be canonized or the process of canonization carried out until fifty years after the death of the person whom the canonization involves, nonetheless, in consideration of the urgent requests of such important personages and at the same time the spread of the news of the miracles wrought by St. Josaphat, he appointed a Commission for the year 1625 which was to analyze the life of St. Josaphat and his martyrdom to determine the cause for it and to record the miracles manifest by the intercession of the saint.

However, deterred by numerous obstacles, the Commission did not take the matter up until three years later. The archbishop of Polotsk, Silawa, was the chairman of the Commission and Victor Simonese the procurator and as assistant George Tishkevich, the bishop of Miton. The notaries or secretaries were two local Basilian Fathers.

The Commission obtained all of its evidence at the Church of St. Sophia in Polotsk. They listened to one hundred sixteen of the most reliable witnesses and took their depositions although there was a crowd of people pressing forward eager to testify to the miracles. Even the Jews, Heretics and St. Josaphat's greatest enemies all testified to his holiness. Finally they visited the sepulchre, so that according to law they might examine the body of the saint. Upon opening the tomb they found the body incorruptible and pliable, although all the accoutrements, because of the dampness, were mouldy and rotting away. As soon as news had spread throughout the city of the miraculous preservation of his body, thousands of people hurried to the Church to view the body of their shepherd. The Commission desiring to satisfy the pious curiosity of the faithful, dressed the body of the saint in new garments and propped it up on the bishop's throne in the center of the Church. Seeing their pastor's countenance unchanged by the heavenly glory heaped upon him, the people wept and then George Tishkevich, bishop of Miton, raised St. Josaphat's right hand, making the sign of the cross over them, as he pronounced the words of benediction. Deeply moved, the throng fell upon its knees and with tears and sighs accepted the blessing of their holy shepherd.

St. Josaphat also seemed touched by the emotion of the gathered faithful for his face broke out into a sweat and from the eyes there squeezed a few tears. His Excellency George Tishkevich wiped the miraculous sweat and tears off with the aid of several handkerchiefs which were then torn into tiny pieces and passed on to the crowd and these were the means of effecting many other wonderful miracles.

After this public display, the relic was placed in a new

coffin covered inside with good quality plush and sealed with the Commission's stamp and replaced in the sepulchre.

The matter of proclaiming Josaphat a saint proceeded slowly as it is usual for such matters to be thoroughly investigated and analyzed before being decided upon. This was the reason Metropolitan Rutsky sent Bishop Korsak of Halich to Rome in the year 1633 to make a personal request of the Pope to hurry the proclamation along.

Although the first decision after the audience with the Pope complied with the request of Metropolitan Rutsky and his friends, the higher decision rendered by the Congregation of Rites considered the first Commission as inadequate and therefore rejected the request for canonization.

The Metropolitan was disappointed and wrote at that time to Bishop Korsak, saying, "Let Jesus, for whose successor our late holy archbishop gave his life, grant that you may not return without proclamation as a saint of that faithful servant of God and the Holy Father. It would be the only joy of our miserable fate, the hope of the Uniates and a reproach to the Schismatics."

After many earnest pleas by Bishop Korsak, the Pope permitted in 1635 the appointment of a new Commission and placed it under the supervision of his nuncio.

New obstacles presented themselves so that the second Commission did not begin its work of investigation until the 3rd day of June 1637, when the chief pleader for the canonization, Metropolitan Joseph Rutsky, was no longer alive. He was not given the consolation in his lifetime of seeing his friend raised to the altar. He carried the cross of Christ faithfully to his last hour.

Note:

Pope Urban VIII named Rutsky, "The pillar of the Ukrainian Church, upholder of the Union, the Ukrainian Atanas." He indeed deserves these titles. He worked for the Ukrainian Church ceaselessly until death, never deterred by any obstacles despite the fact that misfortune, difficulties and crosses were his daily bread. Such a sacrifice brought forth fruit. When he became a Metropolitan, he found the Union weak and left it strong, so that it could boldly face the future without fear of its enemies. Rutsky led a highly ascetic life; he slept little, never ate any meat and often fasted several days at a time. He died on February 5, 1637 in the monastery of Derman. When in the late spring of that year his body was transported to Vilno and the coffin opened, it was found that the body was entirely unspoiled and gave off no evil odor. He was buried in the Church of the Holy Trinity. When in the year 1655, the Muscovites captured Vilno and opened the coffin, they found Rutsky's body still pliant, white and unspoiled. The Muscovites then took it away but where they transported it or buried it no one knows.

The cause for the martyrdom of St. Josaphat was very carefully investigated by the second Commission, for the post mortem enemies of St. Josaphat had spread the story that he had dealt very strictly and unmercifully with the Schismatics and that was the reason they murdered him. However, the sworn witnesses, Catholic as well as Schismatic, testified unanimously that the sole reason for the martyrdom had been his passionate attachment to the Union and faithful allegiance to the Apostolic See.

On the 21st of August, the Commission repaired to the Church of St. Sophia to officially examine the relic. Of this examination the records of the Commission state: "The piety of the populace had beautified the tomb of St. Josaphat with rich gifts. Over the stone slab that covered the tomb, there hung a large painting showing St. Josaphat in his vestments as archbishop and around it were other pictures depicting the various scenes of the martyrdom of the saint. There were a great number of gold, silver and wax articles, presented as offerings for graces received which decorated the tomb. At the entrance of the tomb there was another painting showing Josaphat dressed in white archbishop's vestments in a reclining position, supported by a green pillow. Directly by the tomb was a great silver lamp burning.

Upon opening the tomb they found the body clothed in the vestments of the archbishop which were completely decomposed so that they fell into fragments at the mere touch. On his head was a silk mitre. The hair of the head and beard fell off and turned to dust at the touch but the body remained whole and unspoiled. The wounds were plainly visible on the head, the great wound from the axe over the forehead, and the face and nose bore traces of blows he had received. In the left hand were found many name cards of individuals and families who had made especially urgent requests for his intercession. The entire body was supple like that of a child, shining pale white with a fine, pliant skin. The hands, shoulders and chest were well preserved, only a little shrunken. The little fingers of the right and left hand and one toe of the left foot were missing having been cut off for use as relics. After the examination the body was clothed in new garments and placed in a new coffin of cypress wood which a wealthy gentleman had ordered made for the saint. The Commission left everything at the tomb as it had found it in order not to offend the pious sensibility of the people.

When the Commission had finished Bishop Korsak journeyed to Rome himself to deliver in person the findings of the Commission in order to see to as speedy a settlement of the matter as possible. Bishop Korsak went to Rome after the death of Metropolitan Joseph Rutsky but even he did not live long enough to see the fulfillment of his greatest desire for the investigation of the facts with its minute attention to detail and conscientiousness took a couple more years while he died in the meantime in Rome while awaiting the matter to be brought to a conclusion.

Finally on the 16th of May 1643, a Papal breviary was

made public in which Urban VIII as the infallible head of the Catholic Church, permitted St. Josaphat to be added to the list of Saints and to celebrate Mass in his honor in the diocese of Polotsk as well as in all of Ukraine on the 12th of November, which is the anniversary of his martyrdom.

After a few more difficulties and hindrances, the ardent desires of the patrons of St. Josaphat were fulfilled. The first actual public service before the picture of St. Josaphat was celebrated as a feast day in Rome in the Church of the Saviour on the 12th of November 1643 in which all Ukrainian Catholics throughout Ukraine participated.

After the official proclamation of Josaphat as Blessed, his greatness as a miracle performer increased with recurring miracles, forcing the public to recognize his greatness and acclaim his power as an intercessor before the throne of God. The following are a few of the miracles:

Kerasim Kulchitsky, a close friend of His Excellency Bishop Krupetsky, was unjustly imprisoned and his life in danger. In his need he appealed to St. Josaphat in whom he had great faith for many years past. Josaphat appeared to him in a dream and the entire matter took a different turn. The judges recognized his innocence and he was subsequently released.

Two priests of the Jesuit Order St. Josaphat cured in a miraculous way and to one of them, the Rev. Tetersky, he prophesied the day of his death and actually on that day the priest died.

When the Polish Princess Cecilia Renata lost consciousness just before her death and for that reason was unable to make proper confession, her confessor appealed to St. Josaphat and placed under her pillow a relic of St. Josaphat. She immediately regained consciousness and was able to receive the Holy Sacrament.

In the city of Lublin, a goldsmith saved his home from destruction by fire by putting it under the protection of St.

Josaphat. In gratitude he made the offering to the saint of his likeness framed in silver.

A Schismatic who did not believe in the miracles of St. Josaphat was floating down the river Dwina with six boatloads of wheat. All at once his canoe was caught into a whirlpool and overturned. He fell into the water and seeing before his eyes inevitable death he called out, "St. Josaphat, if you are a true martyr, save me and I will accept the Union."

Immediately after that he saw the archbishop coming towards him over the water and he gave him his hand. When he took hold of his hand, the vision vanished and he saw that he was already in another canoe and holding in his hand a paddle. The man was converted and placed a silver tablet in the tomb of St. Josphat.

In this same group let us mention one more miracle which took place in that period and brought about the gaining of a new coffin for St. Josaphat. The venerators of St. Josaphat had striven for some time to have his humble coffin changed for one handsomer and more in keeping with his greatness. This desire was fulfilled by Leo Kasimir Sapiha, one of that Sapiha family who had been a friend of St. Josaphat. He was inspired to do this by the following vision:

In the year 1646, Kasimir, together with other senators journeyed to Gdansk to meet and conduct the future wife, Ludwiga Gonzaga, to Prince Wladislaw IV.

One night while in bed in his room, he was pleasantly meditating upon the miracles of St. Josaphat and decided to order a sarcophagus to be made of bronze in which the coffin of the holy relic would repose. All at once he noticed the curtains around his bed parted and he saw before him a person dressed in the Eastern vestments of an archbishop who said to him, "Wouldn't you consider a silver one?" On such and such a street, he gave the name and number, "you will find a capable silversmith." The vision vanished.

Kasimir leaped out of bed, called all the servants and

questioned them, if they had seen an archbishop but they were all amazed and replied that no one had come in or left the house.

Sapiha then realized it must have been St. Josaphat himself. He went to see the workman whom St. Josaphat recommended at the address given and he was further amazed when he learned from the man that an archbishop of the Eastern Rite had been to see him and ordered a silver casket giving him the measurements and describing the type to be made. He was then no longer in doubt but that it had been Josaphat himself and desiring to repay the saint for the many favors his family had received through St. Josaphat's intercession, he ordered the goldsmith to make the sarcophagus of pure silver according to the plan he had received in his vision.

It took almost five years for the completion of this princely gift. On the walls of the casket were depicted in mother-of-pearl the four main scenes of the martyrdom of the saint. On top of the casket was carved a life-size image of St. Josaphat in a reclining position with hands folded on his breast and a battle axe at his head. Six angels of pure silver in a half-kneeling position held the sarcophagus on their shoulders. The silver alone for the coffin cost 35,000 silver dollars without counting the cost of the workmen's wages.

In the year 1650, Sapiha presented this sarcophagus to the Church of St. Sophia in Polotsk. The simple cypress wood coffin was placed within the silver sarcophagus. The sarcophagus itself was placed on a high marble altar enclosed by iron bars. When the coffin with the relic was being placed in the sarcophagus, a new miracle took place at that moment. The wound on the head of St. Josaphat which had been made twenty-seven years before opened and fresh blood seeped out of it.

When the coffin was opened for examination of the body, Metropolitan Silowa noticed that the faithful had taken a number of pieces of flesh and bones for relics. This was why he sought and obtained a decree forbidding the touching of the coffin under threat of the severest punishment possible under canon law.

CHAPTER XXVII

FLIGHT WITH THE RELIC OF ST. JOSAPHAT

In the middle of the 17th century Poland carried on perpetual warfare with her border enemies. Many cities were in ruins. Polotsk only through the intercession of St. Josaphat managed several times to escape annihilation.

Then in the year 1627, the Swedes got through the lines as far as the walls of the city. The frightened townspeople appealed to St. Josaphat for protection in this new emergency.

Suddenly as if frightened off by something, the Swedes retreated from the city.

In the year 1633, the Muscovites captured the city of Polotsk and were preparing to enter the fort in which the Church of St. Sophia containing the relic of St. Josaphat was located.

Suddenly the enemy was frightened off by the sight of a numerous army of soldiers that made its appearance upon the walls of the fortress. This was truly a great miracle for within the fort there were no more than fifty persons who could have defended it.

Wladyslaw, whose father had been related to the Swedish ruling dynasty and had for a time ruled it, decided to make a claim to the Swedish crown and attacked the Swedes at sea with the aid of the Kozaks. He had thirty boats built by Kozak craftsmen on the Niemen River. On the Baltic Sea the Kozaks showed the same skill as on the Black Sea. They attacked a Swedish ship and captured it, striking terror into the enemy who were amazed at the ability of the Kozaks to withstand storm and wind and reforming their fleet when the boats were scattered.

In the war with the Muscovites which took place between the years 1650-1655, when the Muscovites had invaded and conquered nearly all of Lithuania, the venerators of St. Josaphat took the relic enclosed in its silver coffin and other valuable treasures and transported it to a secret hiding place for fear of the invasion and in order to protect it against desecration and robbery. Gabriel Kolenda, the second successor after St. Josaphat to the Seat of the archbishop of Polotsk, for four years kept himself and the holy relic of St. Josaphat under cover in various sections of Lithuania and White Russia. In the year 1655, he was captured by the Swedes together with the relics of St. Josaphat and St. Casimir, but with divine assistance he was delivered safely out of their hands.

This constant seeking for refuge was full of dangers as Lithuania and White Russia were continuously being invaded by hordes of Swedes or Muscovites and only a wise and prudent man such as the Rev. Kolenda could insure the safety of the relics from destruction and robbery of the treasures entrusted to him. Finally he came to Suprasle in 1657 and here the holy relic rested until the conclusion of the peace pact in Andrushev.

After the conclusion of the peace, the Muscovites quit the country and Rev. Kolenda who had attained to the Metropolitanship decided to bring the relic back to Polotsk in state.

The journey was long as it was necessary to return by the same route through White Russia and Lithuania. However, the procession was a triumphant one for the Union and its protector, St. Josaphat. All the surrounding cities, towns and villages he passed turned out en masse to greet St. Josaphat, welcoming him as their protector and helper in repelling the Muscovites who had begun to infiltrate and corrupt the country with their wicked Schism and to kill the Catholic priests forcing them to give their Churches to the Schismatic ministers.

Although the Muscovites ruled the country for almost fourteen years and within that time managed to take over about seventy Ukrainian Uniate Churches and even to convert some of the people to Schism, nonetheless, most of the people remained faithful to the Union and therefore with great rejoicing welcomed the return of St. Josaphat.

The Metropolitan Kolenda made the journey with the relic as far as Trokiw, a suburb of Vilno. In Trokiw was an encampment of the Polish Army and at the news that the procession with the relic of St. Josaphat was approaching, more than 100,000 soldiers hurried to meet it. In Trokiw the relic was placed in a tent which was converted into a Chapel and displayed for public veneration in order that early on the following day the relic could be brought with proper ceremony into the city, which Josaphat loved and where he had so earnestly labored.

The faithful spent the entire night in song, the guns thundered and the bugles sounded taps in honor of the holy martyr.

The triumphal procession was made into the city of Polotsk on the 25th of September 1667.

The Metropolitan, accompanied by the archbishop of Polotsk and five Latin Rite bishops, together with all the local noblemen took part in the celebration. The body was placed in a handsome carriage to which were hitched six of the Metropolitan's handsomest horses which had carried this valuable treasure throughout the period of war. However, a strange thing happened. The horses would not budge a step forward. They were unhitched and six handsome horses of the Polish Army's general replaced them but these also refused to move forward with the hearse. In a moment thousands of hands were upraised indicating that the command of heaven should be obeyed and although the Metropolitan was against it, the coffin with its relic was carried on the shoulders of the noblemen, gentlemen and civil officers, all of whom were conquered by the spirit of respect and reverence for St. Josaphat.

Amidst the songs of praise composed in honor of St. Josaphat, the thunder of guns, the pealing of bells of all the Churches, the holy martyr for the Union was carried in triumphal procession along the gaily decorated streets to the Church of the Holy Trinity. The crowd hung upon him as he passed hoping for a miracle from his mere presence.

Four princes of the Church took the expensive coffin on their shoulders and carried it with proper ceremony inside the Church in which he had as a young boy and later as a humble monk in secrecy prayed fervently for the Holy Union.

For fifteen days the body of St. Josaphat lay in state in his beloved Church and the crowd of people came flocking to make their request for his aid in their distresses.

That his stay in Vilno was pleasing to St. Josaphat was evidenced by the fact that many more miracles were performed here and many Schismatics converted to the Catholic Church in that same holy place where he had begun his monastic life. The presence of the holy relic, the endless services, sermons, all in honor of St. Josaphat, drew thousands of the faithful even from distant places that by the relic of their shepherd they might clear their consciences through confession and strengthen the purity of their faith by the reception of Holy Communion.

However, to cool the fervor of the Catholics, the Schismatics invented a lie which they spread through the city. "That silver casket," they said, "is worth more than that which is in it. There is no body of St. Josaphat. In place of the body the Catholics have placed stones, but if there is any of it left, that has been eaten away by worms and turned into dust."

As an answer to the lie spread by the Schismatics, the Metropolitan ordered the coffin to be opened for public exhibition when there was the greatest throng of people. All of the people saw the body of St. Josaphat dressed in his archbishop's garments untouched and unspoiled by time. The archimandrite of the monastery of the Holy Trinity, turning to the Schismatics said: (St. Luke 24-39).

"Behold my hands and my feet, that it is myself: handle me and see; for a spirit hath no flesh and bones as ye see me have."

He thereupon preached to them so earnestly on this theme that many of the Schismatics that very same day renounced their Schism and joined the Union.

Thereafter, the relic was transported to Polotsk to the Church of St. Sophia which had been rebuilt into a Cathedral to reach it on the day of the anniversary of his martyrdom. It is hardly necessary to mention with what great rejoicing the townspeople welcomed the return of the relic. As if to prove that it was the same and no other holy relic, new miracles were performed so that pilgrims from the farthest points came to visit and venerate the relic and to give thanks for old favors granted and to receive new graces.

The people of Polotsk did not have the opportunity for long to rejoice in the relic of their shepherd. After the death of King John III Sobietsky, new wars began in Poland over the possession of the throne. The candidates for the throne sought the help of local rulers to maintain them in power. They overflowed Poland with their armed forces, impoverishing it mercilessly.

291

The Swedes and Muscovites again occupied all of Lithuania by 1696. The war lasted several years with fluctuations in occupancy of the country. In the early spring of 1705, the Muscovites having conquered Vitebsk, treated the Catholics there with the greatest contempt, destroying everything that pertained to the veneration of St. Josaphat. The Basilian Fathers in Polotsk could not expect any better treatment, therefore they decided to remove the relic of St. Josaphat from the city, especially since news had reached them that King Peter intended to destroy it.

Since they had no really safe place where they might hide it, they gave the relic together with their treasurers into the safe keeping of the Lithuanian King's Chancellor, Carol Radival, who had at his disposal a powerful army of his own, as was the custom of noblemen of the period.

Prince Radival, in accepting the relic, promised that as soon as the war was ended, he would return it together with all the treasures placed in his keeping to the Basilian Brotherhood.

One of the Basilian Fathers was to go along to accompany the relic. Soon thereafter, the Muscovites under the leadership of the fanatical hater of the Union, Peter I, captured Polotsk. It was no wonder that the Schismatic ministers (Popi) before his departure for the Lithuanian wars blessed Peter I, making a novena of prayers for the intention that he might destroy the hateful Union in Lithuania.

Peter was overwhelmed by this blessing of Satanic power in the destruction of God's work for not only did he send his destroyers everywhere to persecute the Uniates but also himself for the "honor" of his "great name" became a persecutor and murderer of the blameless, unarmed, Basilian Fathers.

It can truly be said that in the achievement of ill fame he bested even Nero himself, for the latter had been a heathen ruler but Peter wore on his crown the sign of the cross. No matter how hard Peter strove after the accomplishment of the evil to justify himself and to cover this heathen act, nonetheless, his work remains evil in the sight of all Christian nations.

Of that monstrous visitation to the monastery of Polotsk the annals of the Basilian Order have this to say:

"On July 11, 1705, Peter I entered together with his guards the Church of the archbishop's See at a time when the Basilian monks were conducting vesper services in the choir. Being a fanatical Schismatic with hatred towards the Union, he displayed disrespect for the Church in various ways, finally taking the Holy Eucharist which had been prepared and placed on the altar to St. Josaphat for the Communion of the faithful of the Latin Rite the next morning. He scattered the host over the floor. Seeing this, Rev. Theophanus Kobilchitsky stooped to the floor, gathering all the wafers and ate them. The angry Peter I fell upon him and pierced him with his sword and when he writhed in agony he attacked him again to finish the killing. But his blood was not enough. Three other Basilians, the Rev. Fathers Jacob Kozykowsky, archimandrite, Constantine Zaachknowsky, curate and John Knishevich, ecclesiastic, he ordered to be tortured all night and hung the next day. Other Basilians he beat and maimed and ordered to be locked in the cellar of the monastery. The Church and monastery he thereupon gave over into the hands of his favorite soldiers to do with as they pleased. Then he declared that he would treat all the other Uniates in the same way. He also wanted to burn the relic of St. Josaphat but it was no longer to be found in Polotsk."

This butchery had a powerful effect on the city. Such malevolence was without precedence. The murder was committed in broad daylight on unarmed monks by a king and in a foreign country. It aroused rebellion in all the people. Peter was alarmed himself at what he had done and at least pretended to be sorry for his crime, excusing himself by the statement that he had been drunk and that the monks with their resentful behavior had led him to it. That this was only pretense on his part was proved by the fact that he kept the wounded monks imprisoned and turned the Church into an arsenal and permitted his soldiers to rob the monasteries of the Uniates in the diocese of Polotsk and environs.

Peter I led the way for his successors who were to spread their "holy orthodoxy." That these successors adhered to the example of this redeemer of Russia is proved by thousands of innocent, unarmed villagers and priests who paid with their lives for their faith in the Church and as a rebuke to the bloodthirsty "orthodoxy."

At the close of the war, Prince Radival did not keep his word to the Basilian Fathers. Although he returned to them the treasures and silver coffin given by Leo Kasimir Sapiha, the body of St. Josaphat he retained and placed together with his treasures in a fortress chapel in the city of Bila.

In vain did the Basilian Order demand of Radival the return of the holy relic and after his death of his widow and sons and when this didn't help they brought their appeal before the Apostolic See.

Finally in the year 1743, during the Assembly of the Basilian Order in Dubny, at a suggestion initiated by the Papal legate, Laskar, Bishop of Zenopolsk, an agreement was reached in which the Radival family was to build a Church and monastery in Bila for the Basilians and insure them a subsistence, and to give the Polotsk Basilian Fathers some of the bones from the left hand of the martyr.

This agreement was approved by the Apostolic See. However, the archbishop of Polotsk would not agree to this and the Chartoriy and Sapiha family wanted to resort to the force of arms in demanding the return of the holy relic. In the meantime, in the year 1764, the Muscovites again came to occupy all of the Polisia section. This was the reason the Rev. Lodiewsky, the archimandrite of the monastery at Bila sealed the relic in the fortress in deep secrecy so that no one knew where the relic of St. Josaphat had disappeared. Some thought Radival had taken it with him when he escaped from Poland. Others thought the Muscovites had taken it.

Not until a more peaceful period in 1767 was the relic of St. Josaphat again exposed for public veneration in the monastery's Church at Bila. At present the relic is in safe-keeping in Vienna in the Church of St. Barbara.

CHAPTER XXVIII

PROCLAMATION OF JOSAPHAT AS A
UNIVERSAL SAINT

From the time that the relic was brought to the city of Bila it became the center of inspiration for the religious life of the Uniates and at the same time the most famous and continuous place of pilgrimage in all of Ukraine. Crowds of pilgrims hurried to the shrine of the Holy Martyr.

The Apostolic See, in order to spread devotion to this saint, gave a plenary indulgence to those who in the months of October and November visited the holy relic, made confession and received Holy Communion. This veneration for the martyr of the Union was salt in the eyes of the Muscovites who thought only of how to destroy the Union hated by them. Throughout the other diocese they had nearly completed their devilish work and now were seeking a reason for bringing into Polisia the holy or rather un-"holy orthodoxy." They did not have to wait long for an opportunity. In the year 1862 the Poles were preparing for revolution which was to end disastrously for the Uniates because it was inspired by the Schismatics. In order to arouse the Ukrainians to take part in the stupid uprising the Poles chose for their patron St. Josaphat and having brought themselves a large and handsome picture of the martyr, they set out with it in a body carrying it as their banner to Bila. The Muscovites were awaiting them. Immediately after the suppression of the uprising by massacre in 1863, the Muscovite government razed the four remaining monasteries of the Basilian Brotherhood, including the monastery at Bila, taking from it the abovementioned picture of St. Josaphat and permitting only for a time two monks to remain in servicing the Church.

The Union was in a very precarious situation. The persecutions which had lasted nearly a whole century were doubled. Military force was now used to promote the wicked Schism. The blood of the Uniates flowed over the earth, while over their dead bodies Schismatic archbishops entered and took over the ownership of the Catholic Churches, assisted by armed Muscovite "soldats."

Some of the Catholic priests were exiled to Siberia, the monks murdered in their monasteries and other priests exiled or deported beyond the borders. To take the place of these martyrs were sent either Schismatic ministers or what was worse, Galician traitors who for money and promised honors renounced their Catholic faith and came to help the destroyers of the Union.

The lamentations and tears of the Uniates finally reached the throne of St. Peter. Pope Pius IX, although himself in miserable circumstances, surrounded by enemies who had robbed him of his inherited income, did not forget to comfort the poor Ukrainians. He gave them whatever help he could. He appointed for the canonization of St. Josaphat, the Rev. Dubrowsky, Basilian procurator in Rome and Rev. Michael Contieri, the abbot of the Greek-Italian Rite monastery of the Basilian Fathers in Grotto Ferrata. To their assistance came the Very Rev. Joseph Sembratovich, the archbishop of Nazianzus and Metropolitan of Halich.

On January 8, 1865, the Pope called a conference of the Congregation of Rites on the matter of the canonization of

St. Josaphat and received affirmation from it that St. Josaphat could be officially proclaimed a universal saint since as far back as the year 1642 Pope Urban VIII had given permission for St. Josaphat to be added to the list of saints.

When the Schismatics learned of the efforts made to have St. Josaphat canonized they attacked the holy martyr with their usual weapons.

The head of the Schism, the king himself, wrote to Pope Pius IX that Josaphat was unworthy of this high honor in the Catholic Church, quoting therein from a few false and misinterpreted documents among which was the letter written to St. Josaphat by Leo Sapiha, mentioned in a previous chapter. All the Muscovite newspapers assaulted St. Josaphat unanimously to discredit him and the Catholic Church at the same time accusing it of wanting to make a saint out of a persecutor and tyrant.

All these defamations, lies and falsifications were refuted by a few French and Italian newspapers which made answer and in addition some of the descendants of the old families who venerated St. Josaphat such as Sapiha, Chartoriysky, Rewisky, Zamoysky and others sent their petitions to the Pope to speed up the canonization.

On May 2, 1865, the Holy Father rode to the Greek Church of St. Atanasius and having heard Mass in the Eastern Rite, he commanded the reading of the decree permitting the canonization of St. Josaphat. In the degree in which the life of St. Josaphat and his miraculous intercession was described the Holy Father made also the statement that Divine Providence delayed his canonization as a universal saint until a time when the Catholic Church was most in need of help: "A gang of rebellious people," were the words of the Pope's decree, "have roused nearly the entire civilized world by directing their anger towards the throne of St. Peter. Therefore, this is an opportune time for St. Josaphat to come to our aid. He who so manfully defended the seniority of the Pope until his death with the power of his prayers will destroy the insidious plots of our enemies."

The Holy Father set the official feast day for the canonization to take place on the feast of the Apostles St. Peter and Paul in the year 1867. Pope Pius IX wanted all of the Catholic Church to see the triumph of the Ukrainian archbishop who had backed the Apostolic See all his life. On that day the bishops from all over the world were to arrive for the session of the Vatican Assembly. At the command of the highest Pastor five hundred princes of the Church from all sections of the world hurried to take part in the Assembly and to witness the triumph of the Ukrainian martyr of the Union.

The matter of canonization was brought before the Assembly and once more ratified on the 12th of June 1867. In consideration of the desire of ardent veneraters of St. Josaphat the following is a true description of the first official public consecration of St. Josaphat as a universal saint:

On the morning of the 29th of June 1867, all the cannons of the fort of the Holy Angel and the bells of all the Roman Churches announced to the faithful that the celebration was about to begin. The Rite of Canonization began with a procession which accompanied the Holy Father from the Vatican to the Church of St. Peter. It is the custom to carry at the head of the procession the banners of the saint involved. The banner of St. Josaphat was carried by the arch-brotherhood of the Five Wounds of Jesus Christ and accompanied by Greek Basilian monks from Grotto Ferrata, followed by the bishops of the various Catholic Rites, among whom were the archbishop of Halich and Lwiw, Speredon Litowich and the archbishop of Nazianzus, the Very Rev. Sylvester Sembratovich and administrator of the diocese of Peremysl, accompanied by monks and Ukrainian priests representing the Church for which St. Josaphat had died as a martyr.

The procession entered the Basilica of St. Peter which was decorated in red and gold. There were arcades in the line of march displaying the banners and depicting the various miracles performed by the saints who were to be canonized. On the banner of St. Josaphat, martyr, he was pictured dressed in his archbishop's vestments, breaking the chains of the prisoner lying at his feet. The caption at the bottom explained the miracle of the release through the intercession of St. Josaphat of a nobleman who had been captured by the Tartars.

When the Holy Father sat on his throne seat beside the altar in the Church of the Holy Apostles, the Cardinal procurator for the canonization approached the successor to Christ, with the request that the archbishop of Polotsk, St. Josaphat, be added to the list of twenty-four other candidates for sainthood.

Twice he turned to the Holy Father with this request and twice the Pope replied that he would first seek divine guidance before making such an important decision.

When the choir had sung the prayer to all the saints and the Holy Ghost and the procurator for the third time pleaded for St. Josaphat's canonization, then the Pope, placing the tiara on his head, and as the infallible teacher of the Church, replied to him as follows:

"To the glory of the Holy and Undivided Trinity, the exaltation of the Catholic Church and spread of the Christian faith, after a long and careful consideration in advance, fervent prayer for divine guidance, and after conference with the Reverend Brothers of the Holy Roman Church, the cardinals, patriarchs, archbishops and bishops who are present here in Rome, we in reverence to Jesus Christ, the Holy Apostles Peter and Paul and our deceased venerable Josaphat Kunevich—(here a list of the other saints to be canonized followed. It is noteworthy that St. Josaphat's name was placed and mentioned first on the list of the beatified)

—with the decree that the Universal Catholic Church should honor them on their feast days every year, namely, St. Josaphat on the 12th of November, the anniversary date of his martyrdom."

Thereupon followed announcement of the various names and dates of feast days for each of the other saints canonized that day.

When the Pope had finished speaking the cannons of the fort of Holy Angel gave a salute and all the bells of the city were rung announcing that the long-awaited decree had been proclaimed and one of the cardinal deacons in the name of the Universal Catholic Church uttered the first words of prayer to the new saints:

"St. Josaphat and other saints listed, Pray God for us!"

The Holy Father thereupon read a prayer to the new saints and then celebrated Mass in their honor. During the Great Offering, the cardinals of the Holy Congregation of Rites made an offering to the Holy Father of six ornamental candlesticks, two big loaves of bread on trays, one of which was trimmed with gold and the other silver, two small barrels of wine, one gold and one silver plated, and three beautiful cages with doves and other dainty birds, as a symbol of the purity of the newly made saints.

In the evening the whole city was illumined. The Churches were especially decorated for the occasion and brightly lit up. The Greek Church of St. Atanasius and of St. Claudius of the Fathers of the Resurrection were both decorated in honor of St. Josaphat.

On the same day, that is, the 29th of June 1867, the Holy Father issued a special decree or Apostolic message in which the life of the saint was described in brief, his works, cause of martyrdom, when he was first proclaimed a saint and a brief survey of the canonization proceedings.

In conclusion he stated that everything that he did in the canonization proceedings for St. Josaphat was done with the full knowledge of all the facts involved in his martyrdom and under Apostolic authority. In addition, he reaffirmed the previous canonization of St. Josaphat on November 12, 1643, and made the following closing remark:

"If anyone should attempt to set aside the elevation of St. Josaphat to sainthood as patron of all priests having charge of souls, or to oppose the decree of canonization, he would automatically arouse the wrath of God and of the Holy Apostles Peter and Paul."

After each canonization, Rome is the first to celebrate the feast day of a new saint. The Vicar Cardinal set aside the 12th of November and the Church of St. Atanasius for the first celebration. The services lasted three days.

The Church was decorated according to the Greek Rite and over the Ikonostasis was placed the picture of St. Josaphat for glorification. The feast day services on the first day were celebrated by the Metropolitan of Lwiw, Speredon Litwinowich with the assistance of archbishop Sembratovich and the Bulgarian bishop Popiw, accompanied by fourteen priests and two deacons.

In the evening after vespers the Metropolitan gave a sermon on the life of St. Josaphat in Ukrainian. The second day of the festival Mass was celebrated in the Latin Rite and the sermon was given in Polish by Rev. Ironim Kaysevich, the provincial of the Resurrectionists.

On the third day, the Mass was celebrated by the Greek-Italian Rite patriarch with the assistance of four bishops of his Rite and the eulogy was given by Monseignor Calicstan Giorgi in Italian. The festival services were closed by His Excellency Cardinal Reyzak giving his blessing by displaying the Holy Eucharist. On all three days of the saint's festival, Masses were said in the Church of St. Atanasius by the cardinals, bishops and priests of the various Rites of the Eastern and Western Church.

Note:

To carry on the process of canonization and to meet the expenses of the festival celebration which took place during canonization, funds were collected from the Ukrainians, Poles, Czechs and even Southern Slavs. However, the offerings were meager so that the Metropolitan Joseph Sembratovich gave 6,000 skood (skood—4 kronen) and His Excellency the prelate Isadore Dolnitsky, 1410, sk. 70. In addition, Monseignor Dominic Bartolini secretary of the Congregation of Holy Rites, who later became a cardinal, 12642, sk. 39; miscellaneous 15, sk. 81. The total sum expended for the canonization of St. Josaphat was 8690, sk. 92. The offerings amounted to 6000 sk. more than was needed so that this balance was set aside for future use in the canonization of some Ukrainian saint (Commentarium auctor, omn. canonis St. Josaphat Kuncewicz and the oral confirmation of His Excellency, the Prelate Dolnitsky). Taken from the "Life of St. Josaphat."

A similar celebration took place on November 12, 13, 14 in Lwiw under the direction of the Papal Nuncio Falcinelli Antoniacci, the archbishop of Athens with the assistance of the priesthood and the faithful of all three Rites (Ukrainian, Italian-Greek and Latin).

Only that section of Ukraine which was under Muscovite Rule was unable to take part in this festive celebration in honor of its shepherd but it did not lose hope that the time would come when it would cast off the chains of Muscovite servitude and appropriately honor the good Father, shepherd and teacher of the flock while on earth and intercessor in heaven.

CHAPTER XXIX
THE FATE OF THE RELIC OF ST. JOSAPHAT AFTER CANONIZATION

When the Muscovites, despite their defamations, treacherous lies and fraudulent documentations could not stop the proclamation of Josaphat as a saint because of their impotence, they took a beastly revenge on the adherents of the Union.

Throughout Catholic Ukraine which was under Muscovite rule, terrible persecutions broke loose, pillaging and murders, if not resulting in quite as much bloodshed as in the time of Nero, there was indeed more suffering, tears and misery. When reviewing the history of that period, it is difficult to know at which to be more amazed, the beastly ferocity of the persecutions or the fortitude of the peasant villagers who equalled only the martyrdom of the early Christians.

The destroyers of the Uniates were the Schismatic archbishops and ministers which Schismatic Moscow sent out among the faithful Catholics, and their helpers in spreading the un- "holy orthodoxy" were the Muscovite soldats.

In the true Russians there were present at least some human instincts. Sometimes they were able to understand and sympathize with the unfortunate plight of the persecuted, but the most ferocious persecutors of the Uniates were the Catholic renegades themselves who for paltry sums of money and passing glory or position forsook the holy faith, their people, families and like Judas for a few pieces of silver hired themselves to the Muscovites to become the annihilators of their brothers in the faith, Rite and race.

Such traitors the Muscovites found not only among the common people but even among the priesthood and what was most regrettable is that even from Halich, the most civilized section of Ukraine, insatiable gold-loving blasphemers volunteered to help the Muscovites spread their un-"holy orthodoxy."

There is nothing worse or more contemptible than a renegade who for the sake of fame or money becomes a traitor to his faith, Rite and race. With the loss of his faith, all his finer sensibilities are deadened so that he loses his innate human dignity and sense of shame and humaneness towards fellow man. Having deadened his conscience, it no longer bothers him so that he does whatever pleases him for the moment.

That was how it affected the traitors from Halich. Having come to Russia, they became the most zealous persecutors of the Holy Union. Russia gladly accepted the services of these contemptible slaves as it was unwilling to subject its archbishops and heads of its Churches to the wretched role of persecutors and murderers.

At the beginning it rewarded them with honors and paid them money, but when the evil work had been accomplished, it did what is usually done with traitors. Rejection, suspicion and coldness of the Schismatics as well as Catholics was their recompense and the names of Simashkiw, Popel, Kalinowsky and others the Ukrainian Church will permanently record in the same category as that of Nero, Severo, Dekow and Dioclitian.

The Muscovites had long planned to get rid of the relic of

St. Josaphat from the altar where it was in sepulchre and even from the Church itself. They did not want to do this themselves, even though they had no fear of the judgment of God, they were at least sensitive to the censorship of the Universal Catholic Church. Therefore, they needed some excuse and a heedless and senseless Church official on whose authority they could carry out their wicked intention.

Such an authority was found in the person of the priest Lewchak who, turning against his faith, rite and race, left Halich for the sake of a little money and went to work spreading un-"holy orthodoxy."

Until the year 1873, the relic of St. Josaphat was to be found in the city of Bila displayed on the altar of the Church of the Basilian Fathers for public veneration. The martyrs to the Union came here to find consolation and inspiration in continuing to withstand in the Catholic faith.

In the spring of the year 1873, at the time of the remodeling of the Church, it was necessary to make a scaffold. The pastor of the Church, Rev. Lewchak, decided to take advantage of the opportunity to serve Moscow. He, therefore, called the Church Brotherhood to a meeting and explained to the members that it was necessary to remove the coffin to the sacristy in order that during the remodeling process it would not become injured. But to do this, it was first necessary to obtain the permission of the governor which it was the duty of the Brotherhood to accomplish.

The members, unsuspecting any treachery, agreed and Rev. Lewchak promised to write the letter of request to the governor himself, in the name of the Brotherhood. Thereupon, he wrote to the governor stating that the residents of Bila had agreed to secrete the relic of St. Josaphat in the basement of the Church.

The governor, Hromeko, having come to an understanding with another traitor and Muscovite servant, Popel, who was then administrator of the diocese, commanded the deacon,

Rev. Filevich to notify the priests to be present on the date set for the removal of the relic of St. Josaphat from the Church.

Accordingly, on the date set there also arrived at Bila, a captain, the secretary of the governor, and the chief of police with a company of gendarmes and a battalion of veterans.

They arrived at the Church early on the 23rd day of May. The priests did not know the purpose of their visit. The first priest to arrive at the Church was Rev. Leo Shokolsky and learning of the reason for their presence, he expressed his disapproval stating that the body of St. Josaphat had rested on the altar for hundreds of years and it could not be removed from the altar to the basement without offending God. "Such an act," he said, "will be the cause of ill will towards the Russian government, which should respect the relics of the Catholic Church of the Eastern as well as Latin Rite, especially since Josaphat has been canonized and acknowledged worthy of veneration by the Apostolic Church and Catholic world."

He repeated the same thing to Captain Moskwenim who was in charge of the restoration of the Church and who had probably conspired together with Rev. Lewchak to accomplish this sacrilege. Later this zealous priest was arrested for having spoken his mind.

Fearing an uprising of the people, all the streets of the city were policed by the gendarmes and the battalion of armed veterans encircled the Church. Thus having fortified themselves, they made entry into the Church, first the captain and officials, the deacon Felovich with the bribed priests followed by a few men and women from the Church Brotherhood.

The priests put on their vestments, said some prayers in which the name of St. Josaphat was not mentioned while in the meantime, a locksmith was called in to loosen the screws by which the coffin was fastened to the altar. When the

307

priests had finished with the prayer service, the captain turned to them and commanded, "Now take the coffin out of here!" But these unworthy priests still had sufficient respect for the saint not to obey this command. Two of them, John Kuncewich and Job Zupowsky so boldly resisted that the captain did not dare to try to force them. Then turning to the members of the Brotherhood, he said, "You take the coffin for it was you who requested the removal of the relic."

The members replied, "This is a sacred thing. We cannot touch it and will not do so." The officials, not knowing what to do, held a conference amongst themselves and turning to the mayors of the surrounding villages whose presence they had required, they said, "You take the coffin." But no one would move to obey.

Outside the Church were masons at work, "Call the masons," the flustered officials ordered the gendarmes. The gendarmes hurried out of the Church to obey, but the masons hearing in advance what was wanted, dispersed in all directions so that the gendarmes were hardly able to catch more than two of them but these boldly refused. They said, "If you must, take our pay away from us, but let us in peace for we will not do what you order us."

"It doesn't matter!" said the angry Moskwenim. "There are still the gendarmes who will do the job."

But he did not undertake to do it under his own authority without first obtaining the permission of the governor. Therefore, he ordered everybody to leave the Church, locked it and telegraphed the governor. Shortly thereafter, he received a reply, reading: "Take eight gendarmes and finish the business."

While this commotion was going on, there arrived at the order of the authorities, Nicholas Kalinowsky, a deacon from Constantinov. He was a man without faith or conscience. The Muscovites realized that they could do whatever they pleased with him.

Upon his arrival the officials quickly came to an agreement with him. They ordered the Church once more surrounded and entered it again, together with the priests. Rev. John Kuncewich had escaped. Kalinowsky then approached the altar, pulled out the sarcophagus from its niche and said to the gendarmes, "Take it," and they obeyed his command, carrying the coffin to the basement of the Church. To the right, they found a crypt in the wall and here they placed the coffin with the relic in it and fastened it with a wooden door upon which the deacon Filevich and six police officers attached the official seal and stamp. The officials had previously demanded that the deacon open the coffin and tear off the Church Seal which protected the relic forbidding anyone to touch it, but Filevich opposed it.

A few days later, the authorities ordered a wall to be erected in front of the ledge on which the coffin rested so that no one would be able to get at the relic to remove it.

Thus Moscow when it could not stop the canonization of St. Josaphat took vengeance on his relic. It removed the relic but could not and cannot ever despite its mighty power destroy the ideal for which the holy martyr suffered and laid down his life, and it cannot erase the fame and glory which is and will continue to be accorded to St. Josaphat by the Church which is to last until the end of the world.

It is true that sorrow oppresses the heart of every Catholic and especially of Ukrainian Catholics that this upholder of the Union fell into the hands of the enemy, but it is a certainty that God protects him. "He keepeth all their bones; not one of them is broken." At the same time the hope that this sanctuary of the Union would be "delivered out of the hands of the Philistines," comforted the hearts of the Catholics.

Who is not aware of the secret power of the Precious Blood of Christ? The blood of a martyr must likewise issue in works that endure and all may see. Someday the holy relic will come

309

out of hiding and obscurity to take its place of glory among the warriors in realizing a marvelous renewal of religion and to fulfill the prophecy of the Saviour at the time of His Crucifixion, "You shall all be of one fold."

CHAPTER XXX

ENDING

We are fully aware that the life of St. Josaphat has been written with but an inadequate description. That of which other biographers complain, we complain also; namely, the lack of details concerning his life, works and miracles after death. As it was a chaotic period of wars, revolutions and upheavals, it is not surprising that knowledge of many chapters of his life was lost from which we could have derived a greater understanding of St. Josaphat's holiness, the power of divine providence and the paths along which it led him.

Nonetheless, looking upon this incomplete picture of the life of St. Josaphat, we are forced to say with St. Paul:

(Romans 8: 28)

"And we know that all things work together for good to them that love God, to them who are called to be saints according to His purpose."

From earliest childhood God protected St. Josaphat so that the world should not soil his innocent soul with its blandishments. Divine Providence guided him along the thorny path even to the glory of the Martyr's crown. To this guidance of the Holy Spirit, St. Josaphat was completely obedient, and in this way resembled the likeness of the Son of God, whose spirit lived in him and with which his soul had long consummated its supreme alliance. This is the characteristic disposition of those select beings chosen by God to follow in the footsteps of their Saviour.

His childhood, youth and cloistered life as a monk and his zeal as a member of the Basilian Order, his struggles and sufferings in the moments before his death and of his death, remind us of similar events in the life of our Saviour.

The qualities which distinguished Jesus the Saviour were reflected in St. Josaphat. Gentleness, humility, purity, zeal in glorifying God, love of fellowman and enemies, kindliness, poverty, love of God and unceasing prayer were inseparable companions of St. Josaphat. Among all these qualities the greatest was his attachment for and love of the holy Catholic Church and at the same time love for his own Rite and people.

He offered himself for the salvation of his people. He became a sacrifice of love in order that he might lead them to the path of truth and thereby to the gateway of salvation. Of that love not so much his words as his deeds testify, for good works are the hallmark of heroes of the Church, not mere words.

St. Josaphat's great attachment to his Rite is proved by his mortal life and affirmed by the exemplary Schismatics themselves, who were his mortal enemies. These same detractors and malcontents testified before a court of law that St. Josaphat with the utmost exactitude adhered to the laws and precepts of his Rite so that he emerged unscathed by any transgression in this respect. Above all we find in St. Josaphat a sincere and zealous fidelity to the Holy Catholic Church and its supreme head.

Absorbed with the injunction of the Divine Saviour for unity, he steadfastly defended and spread this ideal until his death, "Ye shall all be of one fold." No obstacles, persecutions or trials could deter him from his love for the holy

Catholic Church. He proved by his life that one could be a true patriot, keep one's own Rite and at the same time be a good Catholic.

We should all imitate St. Josaphat in his virtues and in his faithfulness to the holy Catholic Church. All Ukrainians should remember their great and famous mission which has not been given to other people. To Ukrainians, the Divine Saviour through the medium of his successor, the Pope of Rome, Urban VIII addressed himself when he said:

"Oh my Ukrainians, through you I hope to convert the East." Ukrainians should fulfill the will of Christ and the trust which His successors have placed in them. But in order to fulfill this extraordinary mission, it is first necessary to have the same love which Josaphat so wholeheartedly manifested towards the one, Holy, Catholic, and Apostolic Church. If we are not ourselves fired with love for this Church, then we cannot convince others of it. Because of our hesitation, God could punish us by giving this honor and mission to some other nation which would be more faithful to the will of God!

We Ukrainians have often sprinkled our mission with martyr's blood, then let us not forsake it now or in the future, bearing in mind the words of St. Paul. (Epistle of Paul to the Ephesians: 4: 4-6)

"There is one body and one spirit, even as ye are called in one hope of your calling; one Lord, one faith, one Baptism. One God and Father of all, who is above all and through all, and in you all."

Are the Ukrainians capable of fulfilling this high mission? They have already proved it by the thousands of sacrifices which they have made and will continue to make for the sake of the Union. After the death of St. Josaphat other Ukrainians proved themselves by their martyrdom, their tears and sufferings, how great is the need of Holy Union. Neither banishment, separation from their families, nor exile

313

to the frozen wastes of Siberia have frightened away the powerful warriors from the loyalty and love for the Catholic Church.

The adherents to the Union, defending their Church before the Schismatics called to the Muscovite soldiers, "Shoot, we are ready to lay down our lives for our faith."

All of Ukraine to this day groans and suffers from a brutal tyranny. But as in the past, neither the false promises, rebellion, threats, nor the bayonets of Schism could conquer the faith of the villagers and the Uniate Church has survived and continues in strength with the great sacrifices of new Martyrs to the shame of the beastly power of Moscow and the glory of the Catholic faith.

From many another valiant heart was heard the leonine protest of the aged Pikula, a faithful adherent to the Uniate Catholic Church, who said, "I swear by the grey hairs on my head, that I will never sell my Catholic faith!" It was because of such staunch hearts that the Ukrainian Church emerged victorious.

It is true that there are some who make the claim that there are too few Ukrainians to fulfill this great and difficult mission but the history of the Union invariably proves how wrong their contentions are.

Were there more Ukrainian Uniates under Poty, Josaphat and Rutsky? There were only a few hundred not thousands or millions who adhered to the Catholic faith but nonetheless these weak, poor, uneducated hundreds were able to convert millions to the source of truth. Then why should we lose hope that the Ukrainians would be unable to fulfill their mission, especially since it is not the people but the grace of God which has the power to change men's hearts.

This mission grows more hopeful since there is a worldwide interest in the return to religion (despite the prevalence of Communism).

False and godless sects are undermining the Schismatic

314

Church. Only the Ukrainian Eastern Rite Catholic Church, in which the Ukrainians were brought up, which raised a Volodimir, Yaroslav, Josaphat, Alexis, Anthony and Theodosius Pechersky and hundreds of other saints, can remove the errors in faith and reveal the truth, as it was said by the Divine Saviour:

(St. Matthew 16: 18)

"And I say also unto thee, that thou art Peter, and upon this rock I will build my Church; and the gates of hell shall not prevail against it."

When the Vicar of Christ expressed a warm wish that all Ukrainians should adhere to the Ukrainian Rite and even under fear of censure as prescribed by canon law, which forbids the arbitrary change to the Latin Rite, then it must be the will of God as well as of the Apostolic Church for all Ukrainians to cultivate and develop their faith in their own Rite.

Since the Holy Father has constantly expressed his faith and hope in the Ukrainians to convert the East, then they must be ready to fulfill this trust in converting the lost sheep of the Church, by reason of their firm devotion to the Catholic faith, their Rite and their race.

The Ukrainians are not and will not be afraid of this stupendous task for the ideal of a United Catholic Church is not a product of human imagination but is God's plan. Let us quote the compelling words of St. Josaphat:

"We can be certain that almighty God will continue to bless and watch over this work until the end."

That these words are prophetic has been proved by time. There were times when even the priesthood and gentry not only did not support this work but at times were even violently opposed. It has passed through fire and water and fierce persecutions of the Schismatics similar to the persecutions of the first Christians, yet this work was not neglected but outlasted the centuries and will continue until the end.

315

God blessed this work and with His help it will overcome even the power of hell itself.

All farsighted individuals must realize that Ukraine's only salvation is in its Union with the Holy See. The Catholic Church has the right to say, "I am the light, the truth and the way." From it as from an everlasting spring flows the living water that strengthens all who come to draw. There is no stagnation, none of the rot that is present in a stagnant body. There are no calamitous after-effects which might befall those who would drink from a stagnant pool. It is enough to take for example those nations who uphold the Catholic Church and conduct their affairs in conformity with its living, creative teachings.

The Catholic Church leaves room for freedom to her children and does not force upon them unnecessary guardians, does not demand from them exorbitant fees and taxes. Can Ukraine complain that Rome sent to her strangers and usurpers of her people and Rite? Did Rome ever place a monetary yoke upon her Metropolitans and Church leaders? Since Ukraine accepted the Holy Union all the positions of power in her Church and all the Sees were placed under the direction of Ukraine's own sons. In addition, the Roman Catholic Church honors the princes of the Ukrainian Church with the utmost respect, thus indicating that she loves all her children equally. Rome does not sheer its sheep to the skin until they bleed as did ancient Byzantium but is a good shepherd who ceaselessly defends the freedom of its sheep from wary wolves.

Evidence of this may be found in a whole series of letters and writings with which the successors of Christ defended the freedom of the Ukrainian Church from the kings, tsars, Diets, gentry and Latin priesthood.

The Catholic Church respects nationalities. It does not force its members to renounce their allegiance as did the Schismatics, but on the contrary, in Churches and schools

316

and in the home it encourages and supports nationality consciousness, defends and upholds it, as it does not meddle in politics and government except where immorality intrudes itself. It respects and values national freedom because it is mindful of its mission: (Matthew 28: 19-20)

"Go ye therefore and teach all nations, Baptizing them in the name of the Father and of the Son and of the Holy Ghost: Teaching them to observe all things whatsoever I have commanded you; and lo, I am with you alway, even unto the end of the world. Amen."

Therefore, according to the example set by its first Apostles it teaches the one faith to all peoples of all nations.

Volodimir, Yaroslav and Daniel realized that the future progress of Ukraine depended upon its Union with the Roman Catholic Church and so they had contacts with and sent representatives to Rome.

Had Ukraine not fallen into fatal Schism it would have preserved its independence until now. Its greatest misfortune was in abandoning the Catholic Church and falling into the clutches of the Greek Orthodox Church and later into the Muscovite Schism. And so Ukraine lost its political independence and was divided up by foreign powers which sought their own ends. As they tried in the past so they still continue the same ruthless policy of destroying her language, literature and nationality and in that way to annihilate the Ukrainian race.

For Ukrainians the faith of Volodimir should be upheld if in their humble homes the light of freedom and truth is to be preserved, whether they live in Ukraine or have been mercilessly dispersed throughout the world.

Let us all be sincere and zealous Catholics and we will have a powerful guardian and protector in the Catholic Church. Let us keep the old and reliable friend and she will surely not forsake us. If she did not forget us when we were humble, disdained, miserable and in servitude, then she will

317

not leave us when a better future smiles upon us. Let us take for example the indomitable ideal of the hero of Ukraine and upholder of the Union, St. Josaphat. Absorb deeply this love for the Catholic Church and we will become fearful to our bold enemies and false friends and will courageously cry out, "God is with us, with Him is power and glory for ever and ever. Amen."

(Isaiah 12: 2)

"Behold God is my salvation; I will trust, and not be afraid for the Lord Jehovah is my strength and my song; he also is become my salvation."

Metropolitan Joseph William Rutsky

The Great Organizer of the Union—1573—February 5, 1637

Most extraordinary was the life of this great Church Dignitary. When his predecessor to the Metropolitan See, Ipaty Poty, who was strong as steel, shed bitter tears in his old age, continuously persecuted, it is said of his successor, Joseph Rutsky, that he cried but once in his grown-up years and this was while he was still a very young man, when the Pope of Rome, Clementine VIII asked him then a young theological student to accept the Greek Rite. Rutsky, who was aware of the deplorable state of the Ukrainian Church, and as if sensing what fate awaited him, left the Papal audience chamber in tears and would not consent to make his vows to join the Ukrainian Church and cleave to it until death.

Divine Providence rules the lives of nations as well as individuals. The strongest proof is that during the most trying times God sends powerful, spiritually enlightened persons who become leaders and saviors of nations. Such leaders were sent in the times of the Old Testament to the Jews His chosen people, for instance, Moses, Samuel, David, Elijah, etc.

Since the coming of Christ, every nation can boast of such leaders who like Moses guided their people through all kinds of dangers and calamities to a better future. Even the Ukrainian nation cannot complain on this account. Divine Providence also gave it great leaders who played a powerful part in the history of the nation, for instance St. Volodimir, Yaroslav, Anthony and Theodosius Pechersky, Metropolitan Ipaty Poty and St. Josaphat.

It was during the most difficult period in the history of the Ukrainian Church that Metropolitan Rutsky assumed its leadership and like Moses who led his people from Egyptian slavery to the promised land, this great Metropolitan, together with Josaphat his closest friend, freed the Ukrainian nation from the dreadful slavery of spiritual darkness to which the Eastern Schism had led it by its separation from the life-giving center of the holy Catholic Church.

William Rutsky is a fine example of one foreign born and probably of a different race who once he had given his word before God that he would serve the Ukrainian people and the Ukrainian Church, kept it faithfully as a native son.

For overcoming many great difficulties and overwhelming obstacles in the work, Pope Urban VIII called Rutsky the pillar of the Ukrainian Catholic Church, the Ukrainian Athanasius.

In the midst of that period of spiritual darkness in the life of the Ukrainian nation, Metropolitan Rutsky appeared like a burning pillar of fire rending the gathered darkness and opened the way for its spiritual rebirth. It is true that not all of the Ukrainians followed him, but this does not detract from his greatness.

He made the supreme sacrifice of his life for the Ukrainian people in order to free them from spiritual slavery. His whole life was devoted in a ceaseless struggle for the spiritual regeneration and renewal of Catholic life of his people. For his holy life and heroic struggles, self-sacrifice and sufferings for God and the Catholic Church, Joseph William Rutsky has earned a right and deserves to be canonized as a saint, the Saint Joseph of the Ukrainian Catholic Church, so that he should as in life, stand beside his friend Josaphat on the altars of the Ukrainian Eastern Rite Uniate Church and the Universal Catholic Church.

II

The Ukrainian nation accepted the Catholic faith in the year 988 during the reign of the great King Volodimir. The Christening of the Ukrainian nation was in the Eastern or Greek Rite. That is why Ukraine came under the religious influence of the East; and as the center of religious life was found in Greece, then from Greece came the first priesthood. Greece sent its bishops and priests to Ukraine and the Ukrainian Church owed allegiance to Greece.

In the period when the Ukrainian nation accepted the Christian faith, the Greeks were then united with Rome and recognized the Pope of Rome as the head of their Church. Therefore, the Ukrainians in accepting the Catholic faith were united with the See of Rome.

Subsequently, the Greek Byzantine Patriarch Cerularius broke off with Rome and announced himself as the Eastern Pope. The Greek priesthood and people accepted him and here began the Greek Schism or separation. It can be understood that the Eastern See wanted to convert all the churches of its influence under the new rule, especially the Ukrainian Church. For sometime the Ukrainian Church rebuffed these advances, recognizing Rome as its authority in religious matters.

During that period a Holy Day or feast day was accepted by the Uniates, pronounced by the Roman Apostolic See and this was the removal of the relic of St. Michael which the Greek Church did not accept. This is an important proof that the Ukrainian Church did not immediately follow the Greeks in separating from the Catholic Church. Nonetheless, being under the influence of the Greeks, dependent upon their culture and higher priesthood, it could not continue the rebuff and eventually also fell into Schism.

From then on all kinds of misfortunes befell the Ukrainian people. Misunderstandings, quarrels, wars among the Ukrainian princes, were followed by division and loss of central government, which opened Ukraine for invasion by the Tartar hordes and so depleted the powers of the nation that in the second half of the 14th century, it lost its independence entirely and the Ukrainian nation stopped being a free nation.

Then it fell into religious slavery. Christianity brought to Ukraine by Volodimir had just begun to dig its roots into the national soil. Volodimir and his sons did everything they could to spread the faith to all ranks of the Ukrainian people. Their work was not in vain. Christianity grew in power to disperse the pagan practices. But immediately following it came the separation and the Ukrainian Church gradually fell away from the Catholic foundation. The words of the Saviour were fulfilled: (St. John 15:4-6)

"As the branch cannot bear fruit of itself, except it abide in the vine, no more can ye, except ye abide in me. I am the vine, ye are the branches: He that abideth in me and I in him, the same bringeth much fruit, for without me ye can do nothing. If a man abide not in me, he is cast forth as a branch and is withered and men gather them and cast them into the fire and they are burned."

The Ukrainian branch of the Catholic Church, separated from the living vine of Christ's Church, began to wither and die.

The Greek-Byzantine Church separated from the Catholic Church at the end of the 11th Century, and having lost its life could not give it to its daughter the Ukrainian Church. The Byzantine patriarchs who were the head of the Ukrainian Church gave it very little attention and took hardly any interest in its activities. They were chiefly concerned with the offerings they could collect from it. They were forced by circumstances to be of profit to the Turkish sultans and officials and their main interest naturally was the amount of money they could collect from it.

For this reason the Ukrainian Metropolitans were forced to pay high prices for their positions to the Greek patriarchs. Whoever was able to pay the price became the Metropolitan, regardless of his qualifications for the post. Then again those became the bishops who could pay the Metropolitans and priests who could pay the bishops; finally these moneys had to be collected from the faithful. Therefore, it was not surprising that in the highest Church offices were often found persons not entirely devoted to the spiritual betterment of their flocks, but persons of pride, stupid, immoral, caring only to enrich themselves and their families.

Religious life is dependent mostly upon the priesthood. What then could be said for the priesthood of that period? The community chose any man, collected money to pay the bishops to ordain him, although many times he did not even know how to read and write. Most often the priesthood passed from father to son. The father taught his son prayers and Church services by word of mouth, from memory, a little Catechism and he showed him how to incense. Then he collected the money from the congregation to pay the bishops for ordination and that was all there was to entering the priesthood. There was no thought even of organizing schools to teach candidates for the priesthood. The priest was hardly any different from any other villager. He had to work just as hard on the land, to plow and serve as a slave.

It is understandable how miserable was the religious life of the people of that period. They practically never heard a sermon or Catechism for there was no one to teach them. The priests simply celebrated Mass and the people followed the customs of their forefathers. They prayed, fasted and went to Church. This comprised all of their religious life. For that reason superstition flourished. Without religious enlightenment, deprived of personal freedom, enslaved, the people lived in almost total darkness.

Divine Providence finally turned its attention upon the fate of the Ukrainian nation. When its religious life had fallen to the lowest ebb, Divine Providence provided as heads of the various dioceses, persons who had their eyes fully opened to the dreadful state to which their Church had fallen. They determined to come to its rescue. For this purpose the bishops called a Synod in 1594 at Brest and there under the leadership of Michael Rohoza, they determined to rejoin the Roman Catholic See and to recognize the Pope as the supreme authority in all religious matters. They thereupon elected from among themselves as delegates Ipaty Poty and Kirilo Terlecky. Pope Clementine VIII received them graciously and accepted them and the Ukrainian nation under the protection of the Roman See. After the return of the delegates, they again called a Synod at Brest and on the 8th of October 1596, they publicly announced the Union of the Ukrainian Catholic Church with Rome.

However, this important action by the bishops created a tremendous opposition among the Ukrainian people. The opposition was begun by Prince Constantine Ostrowsky who had at first favored the Union. Feeling insulted that the bishops had undertaken the matter without first obtaining his permission or consulting him about it, he began to oppose all who had joined the Union. On his side he had a few bishops such as those of Lwiw and Peremysl and the Church Brotherhoods who controlled the Churches and were, therefore, independent of the bishops. The opposition to the Union was also backed by the Zaporozian Kozaks who were fanatically Orthodox.

Of course this opposition was encouraged and promoted by the Byzantine patriarch through his representatives, as he

324

was not anxious to lose a considerable portion of his income which came from the Ukrainian Churches.

In other words, the union of the Ukrainian Church with the Roman Catholic was opposed by nearly everyone, the gentry, army, higher priesthood and rebellious citizens. Backing the Union were only a few Church dignitaries and a small number of the laity. But through their earnest efforts and self-sacrifice and especially the martyrdom of the great upholder of the Union, St. Josaphat, the sacred work of the Union not only did not become lost but was strengthened and spread throughout Ukrainian lands. The Union took root and would surely have continued its existence if it had not been for the fierce persecutions of the Muscovite rulers. That the great work of the Union was not neglected despite all these obstacles so that finally nearly all the people joined it, is due in large measure, in addition to St. Josaphat's work and martyrdom, to Joseph Rutsky. He was a man sent by Divine Providence to help the Ukrainian nation during a period of direst need. By his great wisdom, learning and especially his earnestness and religious zeal, he upheld and strengthened the Holy Union. Therefore, he has earned the right to be known and honored by every Ukrainian as the guardian of the Ukrainian Catholic Church and universally as the "Pillar of the Union."

III

Metropolitan Rutsky took the name of Joseph upon his entry into the monastic life. He came of a resolute and influential Calvinist family which had come to Ukraine from foreign parts. He was born in the village of Ruta from which the family derived their surname of Rutsky, near Novhorodok. It's possible that they were not very fanatic Calvinists since they Christened their first-born son, John, in an Orthodox Church of the Eastern Rite. However, his upbringing was exclusively Calvinist and he attended various Calvinist schools in Vilno.

When the infant grew into boyhood, his father asked him one day what he would like to be and little John promptly replied, "I want to be a servant of God."

It would have been impossible for the older William not to observe the unusual intellectual gifts of his son and being wealthy, he determined to give him the best education which was then available by sending him for many years to the greatest centers of learning. Endowed with the highest gifts of mind and body, William made great advances in eloquence and literature. Yet to him eloquence was but a secondary consideration to his earnestness to be with God, earning the things above by earnest effort below and acquiring all that was great in conduct or pure in thought, drawing lessons in virtue and holiness from the sermons of prominent Jesuit monks, through whom he became acquainted with Catholic morals, teachings and discipline at Vilno. He displayed great stability of character. His fame spread rapidly winning glory for himself while he remained insensible to the deep impression he was making on everyone with his remarkable eloquence and purity.

John's school companions did not prove themselves to be exactly shining examples of morality and it would have been very easy to become infected with their disease. Nonetheless, Divine Providence protected its chosen one. John not only did not fall into temptation but with his own good example in virtue and humility upheld his companions. Just his appearance in their company put a stop to unclean talk.

He had a most remarkable memory and was very diligent in his studies. He read and studied days and whole nights through. Sometimes when he had no light at night in his room, he read and studied by moonlight. Once he had memorized something, he never forgot it. He was especially interested in religious subjects. The Gospel was his best loved teacher, nearly all of which he committed to memory. Through it he tried to come to a knowledge and love of Christ. But this same Gospel gradually proved to him the errors of the faith of Calvinism. After a time he began to have doubts concerning his own religious beliefs and not knowing how to straighten out these doubts he began to visit Catholic Churches, especially the Church of the Jesuits and listened to their sermons. Gradually he lost interest in Calvinism and became convinced that the true faith is to be found only in the Catholic Church.

It was the custom during that period for the fathers of genteel families to send their sons to serve as pages at the courts of noblemen in order to gain social polish. The father of John Rutsky did likewise. Upon the completion of his son's studies in Vilno he sent him to the court of Prince Zaslawsky and then to the court of Prince Ostrowsky. Although the prince was himself Orthodox, he was sympathetic to the Catholic Church while his wife was a Roman Catholic. He was also a great Ukrainian patriot. Therefore, at this prince's court, John learned to love the Ukrainian people and the Catholic faith, although he did not formally accept it.

At the time that Rutsky was at his court, Prince Ostrowsky made an effort to have the Ukrainian Church united with Rome. Here the young Rutsky was fascinated by Catholicism. Deeply stirred by the grace of God, he would have then renounced Calvinism if his parents had not upon learning of the change in their son taken him away from the court and asked the Calvinist bishop to give him his confirmation. When John found out about this, he prayed fervently for divine help and his faith in Divine Goodness was not mistaken. The bishop was unable to meet the appointment for his visit to Ruta and the matter was postponed indefinitely.

In the year 1590, Rutsky's father died. His mother, noting

his insatiable thirst for learning, sent him to Prague to continue his studies in Czechoslovakia. Prague was at that time mostly heretic, Hussite. John had to fall in with their company. He was encompassed by evil influences and example. As in Vilno so in Prague, the Hussite youth was spoiled and immoral. Nonetheless, the young Rutsky did not permit himself to be swerved from the true path and resisted all temptations. It is said that when his friends, jealous of his chastity, brought him a harlot and tried to force him into sin, John grabbed a knife and thus defended his purity.

Thereafter Rutsky determined to forsake Calvinism and accept the Catholic faith. He made known his intention to the rector of the Jesuits in Prague. He was eagerly accepted by the monastic Order with which he underwent a retreat for a few days and was taught personally all the essentials for being accepted into the Catholic Church in the Latin Rite. Having become a Catholic, Rutsky left Prague and went to Germany and entered a university to take up the study of philosophy where in due time he obtained the degree of Doctor of Philosophy. Here his powers were still more brilliantly developed where he made the acquaintance of eminent monks and priests. His features and bearing, his keen eyes and grave demeanor, marked him as of aristocratic origin. Frank, generous and patient, he invariably made a profound impression by his conduct and character upon his contemporaries and charmed his friends.

In the meantime, his mother found out that her son had become a Catholic and ordered his immediate return home, threatening to shut him off from all support, if he did not obey.

Rutsky was in a difficult situation. If he disobeyed his mother, he would have no assurance of subsistence. If he obeyed, his faith would be in danger, as he had determined to enter the religious life and to continue his studies in this direction. He was not the man to do anything by halves.

When he gave himself to God he would do it wholly. There-fore, it didn't take long to make up his mind not to return home but to remain beyond the border and to study for the religious life, even if he had to starve to do it. And Divine Providence came to his aid. A Jesuit missionary Rev. Boksa came to the German city where he studied and Rutsky be-came acquainted with him. Seeing Rutsky's difficult position and his unusual ability and talents he advised him to apply for entry into the Greek Seminary of St. Athanasius in Rome, where he would be assured of a subsistence provided by Papal funds to continue his studies. Rev. Boksa also wrote a few letters of introduction to important persons in Rome who would help Rutsky to enter the Seminary.

Rutsky was so pleased he started out for Rome at once. How kind-hearted he was is proved by the fact that he gave all of his remaining cash to his friend who came with him to Rome. The journey to Rome of some two hundred miles Rutsky made on foot, but none of the inconveniences and humiliations to which poor travelers are subject served to discourage him.

At Rome he was accepted without any difficulty by the Brotherhood of St. Athanasius. The purpose of the Seminary which Pope Gregory XIII had founded was to train mission-aries to work for the return of the Uniates to the Catholic Church. The novices were obliged to accept the Eastern Rite and had to make their vows to adhere to this Rite until death. When Rutsky had read this in the regulations of the seminary, he was alarmed. He didn't want to change from the Latin to the Greek Rite, as he was fully aware of the state of the Ukrainian Church rent by internal dissensions. He finally sought the advice of his father confessor who after considering the matter said, "Maybe God has chosen you to be a leader of these people and in your homeland."

Rutsky thereupon submitted himself to the will of God and stayed in the Seminary, but he did not make this vow until after he had finished his studies. He spent four years studying for the priesthood, concentrating especially on the study of the writings of the Church Fathers. He was so diligent in his studies that the seminary authorities postponed the vows required.

His four-year stay in the Holy City in which each unit of ground has been soaked with martyr's blood, grounded him thoroughly in the Catholic faith and strengthened his soul with an unbeatable power of endurance in the fight for the truth, which task he was soon called upon to undertake.

Everything that he gained at Rome he was soon to bring to the Ukrainian nation. He studied and deepened his knowledge, preparing ammunition for his difficult task and yearned for the time when the Eastern Church would be united with the Catholic Church.

In the meantime, the four-year term studies were drawing to a close, while Rutsky still delayed taking the required vows, unable to make up his mind. He thought of leaving the seminary in order not to make the necessary vow and to become instead a priest in the Latin Rite.

Just at this time his sponsor, Rev. Boksa came to Rome. Rutsky confided to him that he was not anxious to take the vow in the Eastern Rite but to remain in the Latin Church.

Rev. Boksa, who was convinced that Rutsky could do a whole lot more good in service to God in the Eastern Church than in the Latin, began to persuade him to obey the will of the Church. But without result. Rutsky held fast to his decision. Then it was Rev. Boksa decided to accomplish this with the aid of the Pope of Rome. One day he took Rutsky to an audience with Pope Clementine VIII who had recently accepted the Ukrainian Church into union with Rome. Rev. Boksa first made his report to the Pope on the sad state of the Church in Ukraine and Bilorus and indicated Rutsky as a capable man who could do a great deal for the Church in those lands if he would accept the Greek Rite.

However, Rutsky here also resisted acceptance of the Eastern Rite with the excuse that he knew nothing about it and was not drawn to it. But the Pope would not accept his self-justification. Exercising his authority, the Pope ordered Rutsky to accept the Eastern Rite and to make his vows in it and to adhere to it all his life. This great Pope, anticipating the great difficulties the Ukrainian Church would have to overcome in its union with Rome, realized that Rutsky with his deep learning and organizational genius could accomplish the most for it. That was why he said to Rutsky, "John, we want you to take your vows in the Eastern Rite and promise to adhere to it until death."

Such an open and powerful order Rutsky could not ignore and finally took the necessary vows. And he kept to the Eastern Rite faithfully until death. He sacrificed his whole life for the good of the Ukrainian Church. The behavior of Pope Clementine VIII towards Rutsky proves how highly this successor to St. Peter valued the Eastern Rite and defended it. "The Apostolic See," as said later Pope Benedict XIV, "wants everybody to be Catholic but not Latin Rite!" The promise given to the archbishops at the signing of the Union with the Apostolic See that the Eastern Rite would not be changed, has been kept to this day by the Apostolic See.

IV

After finishing his theological studies, John Rutsky returned to his homeland in the year 1603 at the age of thirty. He settled in Vilno and applied to Metropolitan Ipaty Poty for acceptance into the Eastern Rite priesthood. But the Metropolitan's attitude towards his new helper was not at all cordial or trusting. Plainly he didn't want to accept him. He advised him instead to accompany the sons of Prince Radival as their teacher and guide abroad. It is understandable how this attitude on the part of the Metropolitan hurt Rutsky's feelings and he began to again consider return to the Latin Rite and even to seek from Rome the release from his vows. Why was it the Metropolitan Poty treated with indifference and even coldness, this man who could render the Ukrainian Church such a great service? The Metropolitan was worried about the fate of the union of the Ukrainian Church with Rome and was afraid of anything that might interfere with it. It was of greatest importance to him that there should be no cause to accuse him and the Union of trying to Latinize the Ukrainian Church. This was why he was afraid that Rutsky, schooled in Rome and attached to the Latin Rite himself would disdain the Greek Rite or try to Latinize it. The enemies of the Union were seeking new excuses by which to oppose the Union. For this reason the Metropolitan first awaited proof of his genuine attachment to the Eastern Rite.

In the meantime Rutsky continued to live at Vilno and took note how weak was the structure of the Union. There was only a small number of people who admitted membership in it. The general public and most of the priesthood ignored it, considering it as traitorous to the nation, lacking complete understanding of the will of God in the matter. Especially opposed to the Union was the gentry organized in the brotherhoods. There was no one outstanding for piety or learning among the priesthood. The only monastery of the Holy Trinity, which was nearly empty, had joined the Union. In it lived more laymen than monks.

This sad plight of the Union seemed to discourage him completely from any hope of improvement. He did not feel an urge to join this small and weak group of fighters for this holy work and began to waver wondering if it were not better to leave the Eastern Rite and return to the Latin. But he continued to lead a strictly ascetic life. He wore black clothing similar to that of the priesthood, and went to Mass every day to the Church by the monastery. There he became acquainted with a young merchant's apprentice who often served the priests at the altar and who distinguished himself by his great piety. This was John Kuncevich who was later to become St. Josaphat. Rutsky got acquainted with him and they became friends. He never gave up his ambition to become a priest either in the Eastern or Latin Rite. At this time, there came to Vilno the monk Carmel Paul Simeon whom the Pope had sent to Moscow and Persia on a special mission. Rutsky speedily became acquainted with the Papal legate and determined to accompany him on the long journey. He served him as a guide, interpreter and even driver.

However, the Muscovite Grand Prince ordered them driven out of the country. Then the Papal legate to whom Rutsky had confided all his troubles thought everything over and said that it seemed to him that Rutsky was like the prophet Jonah who ran away from the fulfillment of God's will. Therefore, he parted with Rutsky, advising him to return to the work in the Ukrainian Church and thus obey God's will in accomplishing the mission upon which he had been sent by the Apostolic See.

Rutsky returned and again suffered in his soul, repelled by the chaos which reigned among the Ukrainian people. Only the personal acquaintance with St. Josaphat who had already entered the monastery of the Holy Trinity, encouraged Rutsky to remain. His piety and strict penances were the talk of the town. Rutsky realized that under his leadership and example there could begin a new monastic life and that from the monastery of the Holy Trinity there could come new, earnest workers for the Ukrainian Catholic Church. Nonetheless, he did not at once follow the example of St. Josaphat. Disinclination towards the Eastern Rite was still very great in him. He was anxious to do as much as possible for the Union, especially to renew and increase membership in the Basilian Order but not as a monk of the

Eastern Rite. He thought of joining one of the Latin Rite Orders, the Jesuit or Carmelite and as a Latin monk to interest himself in the revival of the Basilian Order. He thereupon applied to the Apostolic See for permission to enter a Latin Order, promising at the same time to spend his life working for the Union. And this time the Apostolic See, persuaded by Rutsky's fervent pleas gave him permission to enter either of the Orders he mentioned. But Divine Providence had other plans.

V

Just at the time that Rutsky was deciding to enter the Latin Order, he suddenly changed his decision and entered the Eastern Rite Order of St. Basil the Great. How did this come about? The biographers of Rutsky such as Korsak and Susha and others relate a supernatural occurrence in connection with Rutsky's entry into the Basilian Order.

On Sunday, August 30, 1607 Rutsky was attending Mass at a Church of the Jesuits in Vilno. The sermon that day was given by Rev. Fabrician, an unusually pious and learned monk. After the sermon as he was about to leave the pulpit, he suddenly turned to the people and said, "Dear Brethren! I invite you all to an important ceremony. William Rutsky, well-known to you all, will enter the Basilian Order in the monastery of the Holy Trinity a week from today." These words struck Rutsky like a thunderbolt from heaven, as he had made up his mind to enter a Latin Order and to forsake the Eastern Rite. He had even stopped going to the Ukrainian Church and here without his permission an announcement was made that he was to enter an Eastern Order. Angered by Rev. Fabrician's action, he immediately complained to his superior. The prior of the monastery called the Rev. Fabrician to explain why he had publicly insulted Rutsky, whereas Father Fabrician disclaimed any remembrance of having said any such thing. The matter could not be cleared up. It was difficult to suspect Rev. Fabrician of ulterior motives. Although he liked the Basilians and would have been glad to see Rutsky as a member of that Order, he would not dare to use the pulpit in furthering this end by forcing Rutsky to enter the Basilian Order. Rev. Fabrician who was an exemplary holy monk and died in sanctity could not have done such a thing and it is certain if he had done it purposely, he would not have denied it. It is also difficult to imagine that Rev. Fabrician would be so naive as to imagine that he would thus force Rutsky to enter the Basilian Order. Also Rutsky was not under obligation to heed Rev. Fabrician and do as he said.

After he had made so many efforts to be permitted to enter the Latin Order, he could have completely ignored the words of Rev. Fabrician if he had not seen in them the will of Divine Providence, for within a week, on the 7th of September 1607, he entered the monastery of the Holy Trinity in Vilno. On the 8th of November, on the feast day of St. Michael, he accepted the robes of the Order from Metropolitan Ipaty Poty at which time he changed his name to the monastic Joseph. After a brief period as a novice he made his monastic vows on the feast day of St. Basil the Great on January 1, 1608 and shortly thereafter was ordained into the priesthood. Once Rutsky had entered the Basilian Order he gave up all thought of ever returning to the Latin Rite. The Greek Rite and Ukrainian Church he adopted as his own and from henceforth devoted all his energies to promoting the work of the Union. He never regretted having accepted the Eastern Rite and defended it and made every effort to obtain for it the same rights as the Latin Church had under the Polish government. Above all things he tried hardest to get the law passed forbidding the change from the Eastern to the Latin Rite.

In the monastery Rutsky followed a strictly ascetic life.

He found his friend, Josaphat Kuncevich, who had preceded him into the monastery, already far advanced on the path of Christian virtue in his monastic life. Two great and holy souls were united in friendship and mutual help. Josaphat respected Rutsky who was older and more learned than himself. On the other hand, Rutsky revered and loved Josaphat for his saintliness and austerities in penance. They applied themselves together to the renewal of the Basilian Order in the monastery of the Holy Trinity.

The monastery was occupied by worldly people and the few old monks who lived there did so according to their own ideas, completely disregarding monastic rules. When following Josaphat and Rutsky's example, a few young men joined the Order, there was no room to place them. They were forced to live, eat and work in one room. It required work and diplomatic effort to bring the monastery into proper order.

This work was in two phases. First, Rutsky and Kuncevich taught and prepared the novices for the monastic life. Rutsky taught the young novices the principles of the Catholic faith, dogma, and monastic virtues, also he taught them the Latin and Ukrainian languages, while Josaphat, who was well versed in the Church services and his Rite, taught these things to the young monks and at the same time inspired them to lead a pious and holy life of which he was himself a living model.

In addition to the renewal of spiritual life, it was also necessary to improve the monastery in a material way by rebuilding it to provide more living space for the new monks.

For this purpose Rutsky sacrificed all of his personal inheritance. He was also fortunate in finding other generous donors. In a short time the monastery was rebuilt and properly furnished for the acceptance of a number of new monks.

The archimandrite of the monastery of the Holy Trinity
and prior of the monks was Samuel Sinchilo. Previously he
had lived in the monastery at Suprasel but he was dismissed
for secretly plotting against the archimandrite of the
monastery.

At the outset Sinchilo pretended to be a fervent Catholic.
He was strict in his obedience to all the monastic laws thus
indicating his submission to the Metropolitan. However, in
his heart, he remained a fanatical Schismatic awaiting only
the death of the Metropolitan, expecting that the Holy
Union would then collapse. But this hope began to die out
when Rutsky entered the monastery and started to train
young monks in the real Catholic spirit and attachment to
the Apostolic See. Sinchilo sensed that Rutsky and his Basilians were prospective warriors for the Union of the Ukrainian
Church with the Roman Catholic Church. This was why he
sought a plan whereby he could be rid of the new influx of
novices to the monastery and turn it over to the non-uniates.
Of course he could not do this openly because the Metropolitan was in the way. Therefore, he devised a crafty plan
by which to accomplish this end.

In the spring of 1608, Metropolitan Poty left for Warsaw
on Church business. Sinchilo had waited for just such an
opportunity. The first thing he decided to do was to separate
the two close friends, Rutsky and Josaphat and then to rid
the monastery of the young monks. Therefore, he ordered
Rutsky to leave Vilno on some pretended important business
for a city about twelve miles distant.

As soon as Rutsky left the city, Sinchilo called Josaphat to
him and with the help of other outstanding citizens, members of the brotherhood, began to persuade Josaphat to forsake the Union and return to the Orthodox Church. But
Josaphat was entirely deaf to these persuasions. He would

not even listen to them. All their efforts in this direction were futile. However, Sinchilo thought of a new method. Josaphat in Rutsky's absence was in charge of the novices. Sinchilo with the purpose in mind of taking over the monastery for the use of the Orthodox, ordered him to leave, together with the novices to be with Rutsky.

Josaphat was in a precarious situation. He was fully aware of Sinchilo's aim, yet he was under obligation to obey the archimandrite as his superior. What should he do? Unable to make a decision himself, he appealed for guidance to Rev. Fabrician, the monk who had predicted Rutsky's entry into the Basilian Order. Rev. Fabrician advised him to send a messenger with a letter to Rutsky as soon as possible, requesting his immediate return to Vilno.

Rutsky lay ill at the time the messenger from Josaphat arrived. When he read the letter he got out of the sickbed and departed for Vilno without delay. On the way he was overcome several times by the illness so that he was barely alive when he returned to the monastery.

It just happened that day Sinchilo was out of the city and did not return until evening, feeling certain that his order had been obeyed. Imagine his surprise when he saw the monks occupied at their usual tasks. He burst into St. Josaphat's cell angrily accusing him of disobedience.

Josaphat replied quietly, "It was not necessary to send the monks away, because Rev. Rutsky has returned."

Sinchilo then realized his trick had failed. He calmed down and awaited a more opportune moment.

VII

Rutsky having learned from Josaphat that Sinchilo had been trying to persuade him to leave the Catholic Church and convinced that the archimandrite wanted to obtain control of the monastery of the Holy Trinity by trickery and turn it over to the Orthodox, he informed the Metropolitan who was then in Warsaw. The Metropolitan was unable to come to Vilno at once, nor to remove Sinchilo without due recourse to Canon Law, therefore, on November 27, 1608, he sent Rutsky his appointment by mail as his Vicar General of the diocese in Lithuania giving him full power of authority in his absence. In addition, he placed the monastery and all properties connected with it under his management. The Metropolitan could not have found a better successor. He was the ablest, most eloquent and most learned candidate. The best of the people and the clergy together with the monks were in his favor, but many were bitterly opposed to him. An immense compassion and ardent love for the Ukrainian Church overpowered him with the desire to reform it. Remaining the obedient son of the Church he had bent all his efforts to develop the inner life in himself under St. Josaphat's direction while at the Basilian monastery. He preached and wrote and managed the affairs of the diocese, lending a helping hand wherever it was needed.

St. Josaphat had revived and renewed seven of the Basilian monasteries. But there was no unity among them until Joseph Rutsky's genius succeeded in organizing them into a united body.

While he was yet a student, Rutsky had realized the need of a reform in the Basilian Order to enlighten the ignorance of the faithful by preaching and that of the clergy through the bishops who are taken from the monasteries. From the records of the Papal nuncios it is evident that Rutsky had formed his plan for the reform of the Order while still a student in Rome. The object most prominent in his mind was to secure the unity of the Church. He attracted all by his nobility and goodness and so effective were Rutsky's efforts that when he was thirty-eight years old, Metropolitan Poty requested Rome to appoint him as his assistant with a full right to succeed him. Two years later, when the Metropolitan Poty closed his eyes forever, he left in his place as successor, the still young but eminently powerful Rutsky as head of the Church.

Sinchilo continued as archimandrite but he no longer held the place of authority over it. In a short time, however, he demonstrated his aims very plainly.

It was in the early part of winter in 1608. Sinchilo was celebrating a Feast Day Mass in the Church of the Holy Trinity with the assistance of several young Basilians. Everything went smoothly until the Great Entrance. Here Sinchilo failed to mention the name of the Metropolitan in his prayer, as it was the custom to do at this part of the service. Everyone was surprised but they thought it was just a mistake. But after the blessing of the Holy Gifts, when the archimandrite repeated the prayer, "First of all, remember God—" here he again omitted the name of the Metropolitan in the recitation of the prayer. Now the attendant Basilian monks had no further doubt but that the archimandrite had forsaken the Catholic Church. They all left the altar and took off their vestments as an indication of their disapproval of his action and refused to further participate in a Mass by a non-Catholic. This Sinchilo had not expected. He had thought that at least a few of the monks would remain with him.

Rutsky thereafter forbade him to celebrate Mass in the Church of the monastery. He also had the full authority now to train a new generation of monks without any hindrance. The monastery which had been nearly empty only a short time before was rapidly being filled to capacity with young applicants. Under Rutsky's direction, they learned to become earnest and pious workers in Christ's vineyard.

Rutsky was gratified to see his work bearing such satisfying fruit. But Sinchilo did not want to admit defeat. Since he had been unable to take possession of the monastery by trickery, then he wanted to do it by force. He had to destroy the nest where new warriors for the Union were being nurtured. He began to arouse the Vilno laybrothers, members of the Church Brotherhood against Rutsky, representing him as a Jesuit who planned on turning over the monastery of the Holy Trinity to the Latin Order. Obviously, this was deliberate calumny, but it was very easy to frighten members fanatically attached to their Rite. The aroused citizens determined to take the monastery by force and turn out Rutsky and his young monks. With this purpose in mind, they gathered on December 10, 1608 and under Sinchilo's leadership determined to break off with the Metropolitan and place themselves under the authority of the Greek patriach and on the 15th of December to attack the monastery in force.

Their plan was as follows: On Sunday at the Matin Services when the monks, in long array, come out with Rutsky to sing in the center of the Church, to fall upon them and cast them out of the Church and monastery and then occupy the monastery and Church. Everything was thought out in detail, but the plan failed because a citizen, having learned of it, reported it immediately to the assistant voyevod (sheriff) Demeter Karpo. He informed his superior, Voyevod Radival at once of the intended attack who on the day planned placed a guard of soldiers about the Church and sharply rebuked Sinchilo and his companions for their attempt upon the Church. Provoked by the failure of his plan, Sinchilo together with his company publicly renounced the Union and Membership in the Church of the Holy Ghost. There began an open battle against those who remained loyal to the Catholic Church especially against Rutsky and his novices.

VIII

The Vilno laybrothers, who under Sinchilo's direction renounced the Union, did not content themselves with this simple act but began an open agitation against the Union and the Metropolitan. They went about organizing the people and whenever they could they inspired rebellion against the Union, calumniating the Metropolitan and the bishops. Under the influence of this agitation, it came to the point where nearly all of Bilorus forsook the Union and broke off all relations with the Metropolitan. Only the Cathedral Churches and the monastery of the Holy Trinity remained loyal to the Union. In the interim, the Metropolitan having learned of Sinchilo's underhanded activity sent papers in Rutsky's care in which he excommunicated him and discharged him from his post as archimandrite. The Metropolitan also requested the government officials of the city of Vilno to turn over to Rutsky's care the churches whose pastors had left the Union. But no one heeded the command of the Metropolitan. It seemed as if the Union were at an end.

An Assembly was to be held in Warsaw in the early part of 1609. For this session the non-uniates prepared themselves well in advance. They tried to influence the delegates by word of mouth and bribery or any means available just to win from the Assembly the vote to cancel the Union. It is true the Assembly treated the matter of the Union unsympathetically. It rendered the decision that each side, the Uniates and Orthodox should retain the Churches which they held at the time of the Session of the Assembly. This was a great blow to the Uniates for at that time the Uniates held but a few churches. However, Metropolitan Poty objected to this decision and, moved by his rousing speech, King Sigmund III added to the Assembly the following clause: "If either side should feel itself unjustly treated then by the year 1607, the side feeling itself slighted has the right to appeal to the Religious Tribunal or the Crown."

After the session of the Assembly, Metropolitan Poty felt his power waning in continuing the fight for the Church and that he needed a helper. Therefore, he appointed Rutsky as the archimandrite of the monastery of the Holy Trinity and obtained affirmation of the appointment from the king. The Metropolitan called Rutsky to Warsaw and presented him with his appointment as archimandrite. When Rutsky returned from Warsaw, he was taken seriously ill so that he did not think he would ever recover. But the earnest prayers of his monks won for him the grace of healing. Although the illness left its mark until death, it did not interfere with Rutsky's capacity for work.

Not long after Rutsky took over the post as archimandrite, Sinchilo returned to Vilno, although the Metropolitan had excommunicated him and the king had forbidden him to live in the city. Sinchilo began to celebrate Mass and announced that the recent session of the Assembly had given him the right to the archimandrite in the monastery of the Holy Trinity. Having obtained the backing of the citizens and after awhile also that of the city officials, he planned to take the monastery of the Holy Trinity by force. He gathered a company of sympathizers from among the citizens and planned to carry out his plan on the 9th of October on the feast day of the Holy Martyrs when there would be a festive celebration in the Church of the Holy Trinity.

When the monks after the services were coming out of the Church they saw in front of it a large group of people commanded by Sinchilo. Rutsky, having heard the commotion, came out together with Josaphat and asked Sinchilo to explain the meaning of the attack. But no sooner had the words come out of his mouth than the group dispersed before his eyes as if approached by an army. A strange fear gripped the mob. What was the cause of it?

The biographer, Korsak, Susha and others report that at the exact moment when the non-uniates under Sinchilo's command gathered in front of the Church and prepared for attack, the holy Mother Superior of the Basilian nuns in

Vilno, Basilicia Sapiha, had a vision and saw how the forty martyrs under the leadership of St. Basil appeared before the Church and frightened off the attackers. This miracle was later made the subject of a painting hung over the entrance door of the Church.

But even after that Sinchilo did not cease his efforts to destroy the Union and by new plans, intrigues and law suits to repossess the monastery of the Holy Trinity. Despite this all his efforts proved useless against Metropolitan Rutsky's solid and patient resistance. In the end he was forced to give up.

IX

The Metropolitan, Ipaty Poty, disabled by old age and his many years of hard work, sensed his approaching end. The fate of the Union was very close to his heart, for this reason he sought a helper who could effectively take his place. A better assistant and successor than Rutsky could not be found. Accordingly, in June 1611, he appointed Rutsky as bishop and his assistant, giving him the title of Bishop of Halich. A year later, in 1612, he resigned the Metropolitanship to him.

The appointment of Rutsky as bishop with the right to succeed to the Metropolitanship, raised the spirit of the Uniates. After the death of the original warrior for the Union, the Uniates would be assured of another powerful defender in Rutsky. Joseph Rutsky was a personality, a phenomenon. His fine breadth of shoulders and powerful voice marked him out as one destined to command. The fact that Rutsky would naturally succeed Metropolitan Poty, prevented any possibility of confusion that might arise after the death of the Metropolitan.

Halich at that time was entirely Orthodox except for a small group of Uniates in the city of Lwiw, so that his title,

"Bishop of Halich" had no practical value. The Metropolitan merely wanted to demonstrate that he did not wish to forsake his faithful even in so small a number as were in that diocese.

He was well occupied with the business of the diocese as assistant to the Metropolitan, but he did not use this as a reason to neglect his interest in the monastery. As its archimandrite, he guided the novices in acquiring a competent spiritual development. He was concerned with more than just the spiritual and ascetic side of their lives. To carry on the battle, the non-uniates began to issue a constant stream of publications. This polemic battle was under the direction of Meletius Smotritsky, a clever and talented author. It was necessary to train also good authors from among the Uniates to counteract the propaganda.

Of course the Metropolitan Poty and Rutsky had published works in defense of the Union but it was not enough. It was a matter of absolute necessity to train a few authors who would produce polemic literature in defense of the Union. For good authorship, it is necessary to have a wide education. There were no very learned persons in Ukraine as there were neither schools nor teachers.

To overcome this lack, Rutsky decided to place some of the young Basilian monks into other schools. He begged the Latin Rite bishops to admit a few students in their seminaries. Also the Jesuit schools, which were very highly rated at that time did not refuse admittance to a few theological students.

The monastery of the Holy Trinity began to be filled to overflowing. Young men came from all sections to the monastery to offer themselves in service to God and their Church. The monastery could not hold them all and it was necessary to find a new one. And Divine Providence provided one. A Bilorus nobleman, Gregory Tresna, had built a monastery in the city of Baetan for his daughter who had gathered about her a few young ladies with the same ideal to devote themselves to the service of God in leading the monastic life. Because Baetan was some distance removed from Vilno its spiritual leadership could not be wholly satisfactory, therefore, she had placed her monastery under the authority of the one at Vilno and Rutsky moved the nuns from Baetan to Vilno where it was easier for the Basilian Fathers to provide proper guidance for their spiritual development, enlightenment and progress. The monastery at Baetan, Tresna transferred to the ownership of the Basilian Fathers. The first prior appointed by Rutsky to this monastery was St. Josaphat. In a short time thereafter in 1616, St. Josaphat appropriated a new monastery containing the marvelous image of the miraculous ikon of the Mother of God from Zirowetz. This was the third Uniate monastery.

X

On July 13, 1613, the distinguished Metropolitan Ipaty Poty, who was known as the Father of the Union, died. Joseph Rutsky was naturally to succeed him. The Apostolic See and the king approved the appointment and on June 28, 1614, he became the Metropolitan of Kiev and Halich.

Since the beginning of the 15th Century it was the custom of the Metropolitan to make his residence in Bilorus, Vilno or Novhorodok, as there was very little communication with Kiev. When Joseph Rutsky took office as Metropolitan he determined to change this tradition and visit Kiev and especially to take over the Cathedral Church of St. Sophia and thus secure more firmly the rights of the Uniates to this diocese. This was not an easy task. The city of Kiev and the entire diocese were stubbornly Orthodox. There were no Uniates. Rutsky realized that the non-uniates would not release the Cathedral of St. Sophia without resistance, that he might be disrespected and even put to death. But this did not deter him from carrying out this plan. He took St. Josaphat with him on his journey to Kiev.

They had to drive through the forests, bogs and hills. There were very few good roads. They had to stop overnight at Inns or cottages in the villages. However, they made the journey safely and arrived at the Ukrainian diocese. Here also good fortune met them. The Metropolitan was able to take over the Church of St. Sophia without obstacles and in addition he succeeded in converting to the Union the mayor of Kiev, Batalia, and two priests. St. Josaphat had the courage to go to the hornet's nest of the non-uniates, the famous Pechersky monasteries and there by quotations from their own Church books proved to them that only the Catholic is the true faith of Christ. The Orthodox monks listened to him patiently and did him no harm. Rutsky was likewise able to take possession of the Vidubutsky monastery in Kiev where he placed a few of his Basilian monks from Vilno to begin their mission work in the very heart of Ukraine. He also brought four Basilian Fathers from Vilno to take charge of the Cathedral of St. Sophia. When he had accomplished this, Metropolitan Rutsky applied himself to strengthening the Union in those places where it had taken root, in order that he might have the additional backing to spread it further afield.

His work was divided in the following way: (1) The reform and reorganization of the Basilian Order (2) To raise the profession of the priesthood to a higher spiritual and moral standard (3) Defense of the Union (4) Defense of the Ukrainian Church and the Eastern Rite from the soul snatching activities of Latin-Polish priesthood.

XI

Who is not aware of the importance of the monastic brotherhoods and Orders? The monastic state represents the highest flower of Christian manhood. The monks and nuns devote their lives to the service of God. Not tied down to earth by any obligations they can devote themselves to the service of fellowman and to prayer. It is the missionaries who convert millions of people to the Catholic faith. The nation which possesses numerous monasteries full of pious and earnest monks and nuns is assured of vigorous religious life, for the monasteries are bulwarks against the forces of darkness.

Metropolitan Rutsky was fully aware of this. While he had lived in the West, he recognized the importance of well-organized monastic brotherhoods for the preservation of the religious life and progress of the nation. He also realized of what great help numerous, enlightened monks would be to him in his Apostolic labors of bringing about the Union of the Ukrainian Church with Rome. The monastic life in Ukraine during the period of interrupted Union with Rome was nearly non-existent. There were, of course, monasteries and a few monks in them, but they did not obey monastic rules.

While Rutsky had yet been a student in Rome he had thought about reorganizing the Basilian Brotherhood. He understood fully the importance of this brotherhood to the Eastern Rite Ukrainian Church, especially since bishops were selected from members of the Order. He realized that if the Order were reformed, then the bishops would automatically be reformed and through them the entire Church.

While still in Rome he had planned how he might carry out this reform and this ambition he revealed to the highest Church authorities, probably also to the Holy Father. The idea of the reform was still in his mind when he returned to Vilno until he entered the Basilian Order himself and together with St. Josaphat began to put this plan to work in renewing the Order.

At the time Rutsky became Metropolitan, the monastery

of the Holy Trinity under St. Josaphat, as its archimandrite, shone with earnest zeal in the monastic life. Under the leadership of this monastery, other monasteries such as in Minsk and Novhorodok were revived and new ones organized in Baetan and Zirowetz. The disadvantage was that each monastery lived according to its own set of rules and fended for itself. There was no unity of action among them and for this reason they could not progress very rapidly.

In the year 1616, Metropolitan Rutsky founded a common novitiate for the reformed monks. But he was short of teachers and begged the general of the Jesuits to send him two members of their Order to manage the Basilian novitiate. To do this needed real courage as it can be understood that opposition to Western Orders was very great under the existing inclination to Schism in the Ukrainian Church. The invited Jesuits worked in the Ukrainian Novitiate with real self-sacrifice and it thrived.

Metropolitan Rutsky called an Assembly of the reformed Order to his home town of Ruta. It sat in session for a whole week July 20-26, 1617. At this Assembly the Metropolitan presented a new set of rules for the centralization of the Order. Under this plan, the pro-archimandrite was to be elected for life, subject to ratification by the Metropolitan, while the archimandrites were to be appointed for a definite period of time. The general Assembly of the Order was to be held every four years. At the first Assembly only eight monasteries agreed to accept this rule, but by the year 1624, there were twenty of them.

Out of these monasteries came a number of extraordinarily capable workers. By their efforts the Union was upheld and made further progress.

By the following Assembly in 1621, Rutsky had prepared the rules for the Order which it voted upon and ratified. These rules applied to the directors of the monasteries as well as the monks, their method of life and occupation. These monastic rules were ratified by the Apostolic See on February 4, 1624.

He placed education and training of the young ahead of all. In order that this educational program might bear the greatest fruit, the Metropolitan obtained permission to organize the "Children of Mary" which was so highly regarded by the Western monasteries. Thus he became the initial organizer of the "Children of Mary" in Ukraine in the Eastern Rite.

It can readily be seen how Rutsky's reform of the Order opened new avenues of activity for the Basilian Brotherhood. Up till then the Ukrainian monks did not even call themselves Basilian Fathers but only monks or hermits. Not until the reform came into effect did they become generally known as, in the centuries when there was but one Catholic Church and faith, the Basilian monks or Basilian Fathers. In the Order piety flourished, adherence to the monastic vows, Apostolic-mission spirit and attachment to the Catholic Church. Metropolitan Rutsky made no mistake, the reformed Order produced fine assistants to help carry out the work of the Union.

XII

As soon as Metropolitan Rutsky had provided for the efficient reorganization of the monastic life of the Basilian Order, he turned his attention to the needs of the secular priesthood. It was in a worse state of decadence than had been the monastic life. The educational and moral life of the secular priesthood was of a very low order. This was not amazing as no one had bothered to educate and train the priesthood for there were no schools. Therefore, Rutsky's first act in this direction was the organization of schools. By the year 1616, he had provided two schools for candidates to the priesthood, connected with the monasteries in Minsk and Novhorodok, where he resided. Soon thereafter he organized schools under the direction of the monasteries at Zirowetz, Volodimir and Borin.

There were no funds for even a single seminary. Rutsky barely managed to sustain himself on the income from the Church properties, most of which had been confiscated by Prince Ostrowsky while the last Metropolitan was in power. But he did not become discouraged.

The expense of building and maintaining these schools was met mostly from his own private income. Nonetheless, these schools could not supply entirely the educational lack of the future priests. The Metropolitan made plans of organizing a higher school for the future priesthood, a seminary.

To obtain the necessary funds, the Metropolitan began negotiations through the Apostolic See and nuncio in Poland for return of some of the inheritance of Prince Ostrowsky in the Lutz diocese which had been taken from the Ukrainian Church illegally. But these efforts proved fruitless. The illegally obtained properties of Prince Ostrowsky had been turned over to the Latin Rite Polish Church and monasteries. Therefore, Rutsky was forced to appeal to Pope Urban VIII stating his absolute need of a seminary.

Thereupon the Pope donated 5,000 franks or 1000 skud from his personal funds and at the same time called all the Ukrainian bishops to help Rutsky with his worthy plan. The Metropolitan sacrificed all of his personal fortune of 10,000 for the purpose and induced other bishops to make like sacrifices and to take up collections. All the reformed monasteries promised to donate over a period of four years an eighth part of their income. In a short time thereafter, this seminary was opened in Minsk.

Besides the matter of the opening and upkeep of the seminary, the bishops who were assembled in Korbryn also considered further progress in the Church. Enlightenment among the priesthood had fallen to a very low level indeed. It was not surprising since there was no one to watch over it, the bishops before the Union being entirely unconcerned about their priesthood. They were anxious only about the material and monetary needs of their own immediate families. They considered their positions as bishops merely as a good source of revenue and gave the spiritual side of their responsibilities very little thought. It often happened that the bishops were not even ordained priests. It was not surprising under such circumstances that enlightenment was very rare among the priesthood. The Metropolitan was fully aware of this situation and tried to improve conditions. However, it was not easy to change the custom of centuries. He determined first of all to eliminate the worst element which was responsible for neglect and inefficiency in the priesthood and that was the purchase of a living. Church trustees or whoever was in charge could retain only the priest who had paid for the privilege. For this reason the parish and other Church authorities were placed in the hands of the undeserving. Under the zealous leadership of the Metropolitan, the Church Synod in Korbryn passed a strict rule against parsimony, or buying of a living with threat of dire punishment to those who would try to obtain positions of Church authority under false pretenses. In addition to this new law, the Synod took up various other business under consideration in connection with a more efficient management of the Church.

Without the slightest assistance from the state and with only voluntary offerings, Metropolitan Rutsky established seminaries and schools in all sections of his diocese. Is it any wonder that the enemies of the Union determined to destroy such an organizer?

A reform very seldom brings immediate results. Often it is the reverse, the better the reform, the less likely it is to be accepted until the first seeds ripen into fruit. Thus it was with the Basilian Order. The Schismatics omitted no opportunity of calumniating the members of the Order and fomenting cabals against them.

The exodus of the best people from the Ukrainian Church caused Rutsky the greatest amount of pain because he had worked so hard and sacrificed so much for the sake of a Church torn with dissension to achieve the reform of the Order. However, no ungratitude drove him to relax his efforts amid the calamities which came over him during all this troubled time, even when it seemed the Apostolic See would also lose hope that it was possible to create a disciplined Church and would discontinue interest in the Union especially since the Latin Rite Polish bishops represented the results of the Union in the worst possible light. The majority of even the country bishops were unfavorable to his claims because they knew his unflinching adhesion to the Union while many of them were inclined to Schism and other heresies.

Who knows what the result might have been if it had not been for Rutsky's earnest and powerful appeal to Rome when through the exodus of the monks the Basilian Order was tottering on the verge of doom.

Year after year he wrote and struggled despite open and secret opposition doing his utmost to secure the unity of the Church, explaining to the Holy Father how it grew in popularity among the people, being forsaken only by the top-rank workers. As a preacher he was indefatigable, touching the hearts of men by his earnestness. Finally, Rutsky obtained the decree from the Apostolic See forbidding the change from the Eastern to the Latin Rite, but Poland weakened his position endeavoring to discredit him by refusing to enforce the decree.

In the Polish diet, in the Assemblies of the Schismatics and

Protestants, there was powerful opposition to Rutsky and the greater was his work, the more they harassed him and attacked his faithful helpers.

Meanwhile fresh dangers threatened the Church. The Union was in danger of ceasing to exist because of the fierceness of the persecutors. The Polish government did nothing to protect the Uniate Church against these attacks.

XIII

The hardest task undertaken by Metropolitan Joseph Rutsky was the defense of the threatened Union. At the time when Rutsky assumed his office as Metropolitan there was comparative peace on the religious front. Only from time to time there occurred differences between the Orthodox and Uniates. This was how the Metropolitan was enabled to devote the first few years of his Metropolitanship to the revival of religious life, especially among the priesthood. He also made the effort to see that the unoccupied Cathedral Churches were held by bishops who favored the Union. They all followed the example of the Metropolitan in spreading the work of the Union. It seemed as if all the Orthodox would soon join the Union and Ukraine would be united as one flock under one shepherd. But the enemy was awake.

The enemies of the Union who had lost their leader and protector Prince Ostrowsky by death, began to seek new protectors and helpers in their hateful fight against the Union. They succeeded in winning the Kozaks over to their side. This was a very big help to the non-uniates. The Zaporozian Sitch (guard) comprised the greatest military power in Ukraine. Even the Polish kings were friendly to the Kozaks because they needed their help in the wars with the Turks.

The Kozaks were strongly attached to their Orthodox faith. But they were for the most part uninformed about religious matters valuing the outward form higher than the spirit. Therefore, they were easily persuaded against the Union by being told that it would mean the annihilation of their Rite. Influenced by a false understanding of the meaning of the Union, the Kozaks often attacked the Uniates, especially the priests and monks and these attacks sometimes resulted in bloodshed.

It was salt in the eyes of the non-uniates that in Kiev, the very center of Orthodoxy, the Cathedral of St. Sophia and the monastery of Vidubutsky were in the hands of the Uniates.

The archimandrite of this monastery Anton Greekovich, openly and courageously defended the Holy Union and thus brought upon himself the greatest hatred of the Orthodox. But neither the Orthodox nor the Kozaks roused to rebellion by them, had yet the courage to fall upon the monastery and soil their hands with human blood.

Before long, however, there came a stranger to Kiev, the Greek patriarch of Jerusalem, Theophanes, who influenced the Orthodox, especially the Kozaks to bloody persecution and rebellion against the Union. He came to Moscow in 1619 at the invitation of the Russian Prince and ordained the father of the Prince Philareta as patriarch of Russia. On his return from Moscow he stopped at Kiev and began at once to rouse the citizens and Kozaks against the Union and Uniates. But the greatest confusion he created was by ordaining on the 15th of August 1620, new bishops for all the dioceses held by the Uniates, including a Metropolitan, Jonah Boretsky.

This action on the part of Theophanes was even from the Orthodox point of view, illegal, because as patriarch of Jerusalem he had no authority over the Ukrainian Orthodox Church and in addition, did it without permission of the Polish king who alone had the right to appoint Orthodox bishops. He did it, of course, at the request of the Kozaks whom he expected to shield him if necessary from the Polish authorities while the Polish government on the other hand depended upon the backing of the Kozaks in the threat of a new war with Turkey.

It can be easily understood what a disturbance and confusion was created in Ukraine when in each diocese held by the Uniates, a bishop ordained by Theophanes made his appearance to take over the See by rousing the people not yet accustomed to the Union against their Uniate bishops and the Union.

Especially active in this work was Meletius Smotritsky whom Theophanes appointed as archbishop of Polotsk of which the rightful archbishop was Josaphat. In addition, Theophanes conspired against the life of Metropolitan Rutsky and assigned seventy of the conspirators to the killing.

It is true the king would not recognize the illegally ordained bishops and ordered them to be cast out and the Metropolitan excommunicated them but it didn't affect them. The political situation saved them.

Poland had but recently experienced great losses in its war with Turkey and was preparing for another war in an effort to regain them. In that war forty thousand Kozak troops had a powerful influence, which under the leadership of Hetman Peter Konashevich made a stipulation that it would back Poland if the king would ratify the Orthodox appointments. Every one awaited the outcome of the session of the Diet which was to take this matter up for consideration. The non-uniates sent a numerous delegation to this Assembly under the leadership of Hetman Konashevich and bishop Kurtsevich ordained by Theophanes. In order to have a greater backing they joined forces with the Protestants.

When Metropolitan Rutsky learned of the plan of the Orthodox, he also hurried to Warsaw in the company of St. Josaphat who was then archbishop of Polotsk in order to protect the interests of the Union. The Assembly was held in the early part of the year 1621. It seemed as if the existence of the Union were doomed for not only the Orthodox and Protestant delegates opposed it but also many of the Latin Rite Catholics including some of the bishops. And this is what would have happened if Rutsky had not come to its defense. His enlightening speech made on the floor of the Assembly saved the holy work of the Union.

Because the opposers of the Union claimed that the Union had brought dissension into the country, Metropolitan Rutsky proved that neither he nor any Uniate bishop had caused any disturbance. There was perfect accord until Theophanes appeared on the scene and against all existing laws ordained Orthodox bishops to destroy the authority of the Uniate. He further revealed what wonderful benefits the Union had brought and how deeply it took root and spread widely despite the fact that the government gave it no support whatever. "All better class Ukrainians have become Uniates," he said. "There is not a place where they are not in power. Entire provinces have joined the Union. All bishops except that of Lwiw are in Union with the Apostolic See. The membership and sanctity of its members is increasing and through the efforts of the Basilian Brotherhood the work of the Union is being disseminated. We are accused of being bloodthirsty. It is not we who are bloodthirsty but the non-Uniates who have murdered several of our monks."

He reminded them that seventy assassins were awaiting an opportunity to murder him and the bishops under his authority. "But God is my witness," he finished, "that it will be easier to kill us off than to make us give up our dioceses into their hands. In a Catholic country and under a Catholic king our lives are threatened just because we are Catholics. Even the Jewish Rabbis and Mahometan Mule are better respected in Poland than our Catholic bishops!" But the enemies of Ukraine then as now still claim that Poland "protected" the Union!

Influenced by the speech and the efforts of the Papal nuncio, the king would not agree to the cancellation of the Union as its opposers demanded but because he did not forbid the enemy bishops they continued to spread dissension. The result was a continued chaos, and from it arose a new threat, that the government officials who had been sympathetic towards the Union would become prejudiced against it.

Rutsky fought as best he could to overcome this menace. Then seeing that he was unable by his own powers alone to cope with the situation, he turned to Rome and received support. To the following Assembly in 1623, Pope Gregory XV sent his personal legate who was instructed to help the Papal Nuncio defend the Union.

The Assembly in 1623 was more turbulent than the previous one. The non-Uniates made every effort to destroy the Union. The illegally appointed Metropolitan Jonah Boretsky and archbishop Smotritsky came personally to Warsaw to lodge complaints against Metropolitan Rutsky and to prove the falsity of their claims. However, he not only proved their complaints had no ground whatever, but also listed the evils committed against the Uniates. Nonetheless, the committee would not admit the justification of the Uniates but recommended a Synod be called of both Uniate and non-Uniate bishops. This discouraged Boretsky and Smotritsky for they left Warsaw secretly and thus the matter remained unsettled. Nearly the entire membership of the Diet turned against the Union, only the king defended it staunchly. But because of the strength of the opposition, he could do very little to promote its cause. The only real defender and hope Rutsky had was in the Apostolic See. The Metropolitan continued to make detailed reports of all his problems and difficulties to the Pope of Rome and wrote to the Cardinals and various friends begging their continued interest in and support of the Union.

A large part of this correspondence has been preserved and bears witness to Rutsky's great zeal in working for the glory of God and salvation of the faithful, of his learning and extraordinary genius.

Right in the midst of all these worries concerning the fate of the Church and defense of the Union against attack by the non-Uniates, he received the most saddening news towards the end of the year.

On the 12th of November, long-aroused by the illegally ordained archbishop of Polotsk Meletius Smotritsky, they murdered St. Josaphat Kuncevich, in the city of Vitebsk during his visitation. This news spread rapidly throughout Ukraine, but it brought the greatest pain to the heart of Metropolitan Rutsky as Josaphat had been his dearest friend and most reliable co-worker. On account of his personal zeal and sanctity, his diocese had become almost wholly Catholic. The religious life flourished. But Smotritsky had interfered with the work by his polemic writings and sermons, rousing the people to such a state of rebellion that a group of hatred-blinded citizens had the courage to stain their hands with the blood of the holy archbishop. Later on, Smotritsky recognized his error and sincerely repented, becoming converted to the Catholic faith. The Orthodox, driven by fear, hid themselves after the death of St. Josaphat.

Nearly all persons of influence or authority who had looked upon the Union with indifference or animosity now held a different atttiude so that Divine Providence in this way came to Rutsky's aid.

The martyrdom of St. Josaphat inspired the Ukrainian bishops with new zeal. At a gathering after his funeral, they made a solemn declaration, "We are ready to give our lives for the Catholic faith!"

As in the first centuries of the Christian era, the blood of the martyrs was the seed of new Christians, so St. Josaphat's blood promoted the growth of the Uniate cause. This was most in evidence in his own diocese in Bilorus. When in the year 1624, his successor, Anton Silawa, took over his See, he met no opposition from the non-Uniates. He stated that he found in the diocese more Uniates than his predecessor non-Uniates when he first took office. From henceforth Polotsk and Vitebsk became the strongholds of the Union.

In the meantime, in Kiev, the Metropolitan Jonah Boretsky, illegally appointed by Theophanes, decided to destroy the only center of the Uniates, the Basilian monastery of Vidubutsky.

On June 15, 1622, he called a meeting of the Kozaks and exhorted them to defend Orthodoxy and destroy the Uniates. Roused to rebellious action, some insurgent Kozaks fell upon the monastery and murdered the archimandrite, Anton Greekovich and the other monks they took with them to Trechtimerov and imprisoned them. After a time Rutsky's personal efforts succeeded in freeing them, but they were forbidden to ever return to Kiev. The Orthodox also took over the Cathedral of St. Sophia.

For sometime after the death of St. Josaphat, the non-Uniates ceased their attacks upon the Churches of the Uniates. Nonetheless, from time to time, such attacks did occur. But the Union had as its staunch backer King Sigmund III, whom the opposers of the Union could not remove. But this outward peace did not last long. King Sigmund died in 1632 and he was succeeded by King Wladislaw IV who was not so sympathetic to the Union and the Orthodox benefitted by this succession. They immediately brought their complaints before the new king.

The king who was not particularly interested in religious matters but was more ambitious politically considered peace and order in the country to be of prime importance. For this reason he issued a decree stating that the non-Uniates were free to retain their Orthodox faith, to build and renew their churches, seminaries, hospitals, etc. The diocese of Lutsk,

Peremysl and Mstyslav, were to be placed under the authority of the Orthodox. A part of the last diocese had formerly been controlled by the Archdiocese of Polotsk.

It seemed the Union of the Ukrainian church with Rome for which St. Josaphat died was to be wiped out right in his own diocese. The king also appointed a committee which was to portion out the churches and monasteries to the Uniate and Orthodox. To this committee were assigned two Orthodox and two unsympathetic Latin Rite men so that it could be expected that the side of the Orthodox would be upheld. Whereupon Metropolitan Rutsky issued a statement signed by his Uniate bishops that he would not release a single church or monastery except under force of arms.

When Radival, the leader of the Lithuanian Protestants, under the authority of the committee and the backing of a few hundred armed Protestants and Orthodox wanted to take the three churches in Vilno by force, Rutsky stood on the doorstep in his festive vestments, together with the priesthood and barred the path to the sanctuary. At Radival's command to remove himself, he replied, "We are here to guard our churches and only over our dead bodies will we permit you to desecrate the sanctity of this place. We are ready to sacrifice our lives in defense of the souls the Catholic Church placed in our keeping." The churches continued to be held by the Uniates.

The king's plan had failed. Instead of bringing about peace which he desired, it was the cause of rebellion and dissension. Finally the king realized his mistake and although he did not recall his decree he didn't insist on its being carried out. He even tried to bring about religious unity among the Ukrainians and it was with this idea in mind that he desired to create a patriarchate in Kiev which would be under the jurisdiction of Rome. This is what Rutsky desired and had made some effort in this direction, but the plan was never carried out.

That the Union despite the enmity of all the highest government authorities and the Polish Church, did not dissolve, but on the contrary was considerably strengthened is due entirely to Metropolitan Rutsky's efforts.

Despite his age and illness he was indefatigable and fearless in his defense of the rights of his Church. The Papal nuncio Visconti gives an excellent account of Rutsky's character in this letter to Cardinal Barberini in Rome. This is what he said:

"The reliability and zeal of Metropolitan Joseph William Rutsky are known to your Excellency and that his work for the Union is worthy of being remembered by posterity. He tried as hard as Elias not only to defend from the enemy but also to uphold the spirit in others less dauntless than himself against the attacks of the enemy. It required greatness of character to withstand all the persecutions. It needed also such persecutions to come to an understanding of the virtues and the great faith of a righteous man. His patience upheld me and it was with joy I joined my efforts to his in the solution of our mutual problem."

Metropolitan Rutsky ruled the Ukrainian Church for nearly a quarter of a century with an ability and energy without rival. All those years were filled with hard work, worries and struggles against calumnies, persecutions and heartaches innumerable. No wonder this leader in his youth shed bitter tears when Pope Clementine VIII asked him to accept the vows of the Eastern Rite and adhere to them until death. No wonder he fled from the Audience Chamber in tears!

It was the Saviour immolated as an unresisting lamb who was his model. He suffered all without complaint and even surpassed his predecessor Ipaty Poty in his concern for the Church. He was a man of good faith with whom every honest man was delighted to be able to associate. He judged no one, reserving all his disapproval for his own faults, honoring the least of his fellows with respect and spoke to all with gentleness and courtesy.

God who saw the sacrifice of his life to the Ukrainian Church rewarded him in an extraordinary way. At a crucial moment during his life when it seemed all his work was in vain, God granted a martyr's death to the friend of his youth, St. Josaphat, who desired such a death for the good of the Church.

When on the 12th of November 1623, the enemies of the Union killed St. Josaphat and trampled his body, weighted it down with stones and threw it into the river Dwina, the news flew with lightning speed all over the land. Then it was the exodus from the Church stopped. The Church was revived by the bloodshed of the saint and martyr archbishop.

Metropolitan Rutsky was able with his own eyes to see the blossoming forth of his beloved Order of St. Basil and the excellent episcopate which even admitted by the Poles exceeded in greatness the Polish episcopate.

Divine Providence thus rewarded unexpectedly one who was a stranger in upbringing and birth, for sacrificing his life for the welfare of the Ukrainian Church and the Ukrainian people. He labored all his life earnestly and valiantly to restore the Ukrainian Church to her old love and her old power and to unite the bishops in an imposing body of one great general council whose decision should be sufficiently unanimous to check the persecutions of the Schismatics and secure the peace of the Church.

XIV

In the midst of the war Metropolitan Rutsky was forced to wage with the non-Uniates and their partisans, his greatest sorrow was that he had to defend his churches and his faithful from those who should naturally have been their friends and backers, the Latin priesthood and bishops. The battle with the Orthodox sharpened his wits and increased his courage but with those who were of the same faith, it was very painful to him.

Nonetheless, as a good shepherd of his flock, he had to carry on the fight. His letters to Rome concerning this matter are very doleful as if written in grief.

It has often been mentioned that the Latin Rite bishops with only a few exceptions did not back the Union at the Assemblies and often came out openly against it. They were disrespectful and hateful towards the bishops and even the Metropolitan. The auxiliary bishop of Vilna refused to recognize Metropolitan Rutsky as above himself at church gatherings. Even the Latin curates considered themselves higher in rank that the Ukrainian bishops and at the funeral of King Sigmund III wanted to precede them in the procession.

If they behaved thus towards the bishops then what could be expected was their attitude towards the common priesthood? It all depended upon their patrons, who despite the fact that Rome considered them on an equality with the Latin priesthood, nonetheless, forced them into slavery along with the villagers and to pay taxes for services rendered. Concerning this Rutsky wrote to Rome in 1624:

"Our hearts are filled with anguish because of the superciliousness and disrespect of the Latin priesthood towards us, as we are human beings like themselves. Thank God this attitude on their part has not turned us away from the Union and by the grace of God shall never turn us away even if they treat us like dirt. There is no lack even among the higher rank priesthood such as the bishop and monks who tell us to our faces that they would rather destroy than back the Union."

However, this was not the greatest disappointment to Rutsky. What hurt him most and filled his heart with discouragement as to the fate of the Union, was when he saw the most intelligent element of his fold, the Ukrainian gentry, joining the Polish Latin Rite Church, and thus becoming lost to the Ukrainian Church and race. Before the Union of the Ukrainian Church with Rome, a large number of the gentry left the Rite mainly because of the unenlightenment of the priesthood and lack of harmony in the Church. Others were disgusted with all the dissensions between the Uniates and Orthodox, especially after the Polish Assembly in 1623 when it seemed the Union would pass out of existence and not wishing to remain Orthodox, they joined the Latin Church. There were a few who held positions of authority or jobs in the government and in order to retain them more securely, joined the Latin Rite.

There was also strong agitation on the part of the Latin Rite priesthood in the schools which was responsible for this. As has already been stated, there were no Ukrainian schools except a very few primary ones sponsored by the Church brotherhoods. Therefore, most of the youth of the gentry was sent to Polish schools which were owned and taught by the Latin priesthood of the monastic orders. The Ukrainian students in these schools as a result of constant association with Latin Rite fellow students and disrespect for the Orthodox faith by their companions and insinuations of the teachers plus forcible attendance at Latin Rite services became separated from and unaccustomed to their Rite and thus automatically adopted the Latin Rite.

Metropolitan Rutsky reported to Rome in 1624 that since the signing of the Union two hundred students of the Ukrainian gentry changed their Rite and every year at least one hundred persons of the gentry left their church to join the Polish Latin Rite.

Worried and grieved as to the fate of his Church, sacrificing his health and his life, Rutsky saw no other solution to the problem except in action by the Apostolic See.

From the year 1621-1627, he often described in his letters to the Apostolic See all the injuries which the

Ukrainian Church and individual souls suffered through the change of Rite of the gentry and begged the Pope to issue a decree forbidding the change from Eastern to Latin Rite. He wrote in his letters that if Rome did not stop the change of Rite by the gentry, the Union would soon be made a laughing stock to the non-Uniates who were already spreading abroad the accusation that the Ukrainian Eastern Rite was losing through the Union its finest element and had become but a bridge over to the Latin Rite and annihilation of the Eastern Rite Ukrainian Church.

However, the Apostolic See did not obey the Metropolitan's request for several years. The reason was that the Latin bishops also sent their reports to Rome in which they stated that the Union had no prospect of survival whatever, so it was necessary to save what they could by converting whom they could to the Latin Rite.

They also assured the Apostolic See that the difference in Rite in the country was the cause for a lot of misunderstanding, dissensions and arguments, thereby creating chaos. In addition, in the Eastern Rite Church there remained a great number of untrained and uneducated priesthood who could not inspire and affirm the spirit of the faith to promote religious piety in the people.

Finally, however, Rutsky obtained what he desired. His pleas and especially the news of St. Josaphat's death as a martyr to the Cause of the Union persuaded the Pope to back Rutsky and the Ukrainian bishops.

In his message to the king the Pope placed the Union and the Ukrainian bishops under his direct protection. At the same time, he reminded the Latin bishops and priesthood that the Ukrainians are their equals and have exactly the same rights.

A decree was issued by Pope Urban VII on February 7, 1624, stating that:

"IT IS FORBIDDEN ON THE PART OF EITHER THE

PRIESTHOOD OR LAITY TO CHANGE FROM THE EASTERN TO THE LATIN RITE WITHOUT PERMISSION OF THE APOSTOLIC SEE."

Thus Metropolitan Rutsky was given the satisfaction and hope that the change of Rite would not be as frequent as in the past. Nonetheless, the change continued secretly so that finally the Ukrainian Church lost nearly all its membership of the gentry. This careless change from the Rite into which they were born with grievous results to the health of their souls troubled Rutsky greatly in his old age as he had a sincere interest in each human soul entrusted in his care and considered only the highest good.

XV

As throughout his life so in his old age Rutsky passed in unceasing struggle with the problem of the Union. His only remaining bright hope was to see his best friend, Josaphat, raised to the altar as a universal saint. The process of beatification was being taken up by Rome. But this process was continuously postponed so that Rutsky did not live long enough to see Josaphat proclaimed Blessed.

Despite his age and illness he did not change his manner of living. He never ate meat, slept little on a hard bed; often he fasted for several days at a time. His unbreakable will power kept his weak flesh under subjection. He seldom stayed home, journeying constantly over the diocese, lending a helping hand where it was most needed, inspiring all by the warmth of his zeal with the ideal of the Union, faith and love of God and the Catholic Church. When they wanted to stop him from forcing himself beyond his powers, warning him to take care for his health, he said, "Is that how much you love me that you want to lengthen my exile here on earth? I will live as long as God wills, but I will not change my manner of living." Then he would add quietly to himself, "Almighty God, Thou knowest I have no desire to live any longer!"

Back in 1627, during Rutsky's serious illness, when the news spread that he had died and it was inadvertently learned by him that the non-Uniates were pleased, he said, "Tell them that I won't die before at least ten years have passed."

Before his death he wanted to gather his spiritual family about him and for this reason called an Assembly of the Basilian Monks. As a general who is passing on his rank into other hands, he wanted to strengthen the position of his army which he had led for thirty years to the wars. He chose for the Assembly the monastery of the Holy Trinity where in the company of St. Josaphat he had begun his monastic life.

To the saddened Basilians he said, "I will die like an ox in harness."

After the close of the Assembly he left Vilno to occupy himself further with work among the faithful stating that he would die on the road.

At the beginning of the year 1637 he stopped at Derman in the Province of Volyn and there wrote his testament. This was on the 28th of January and on February 5, he passed into eternity. His life was holy and his death came easily.

The body of the Metropolitan remained in the monastery of Derman until spring when it was brought to Vilno. On the way the funeral procession was detained in various places, being detained the longest in Pinsk. There at the request of relatives, the coffin was opened and it was attested that despite the fact that several months had elapsed since his death, his body was absolutely unspoiled. The holy relic was exposed for veneration for a period of fifteen days. The people thronged the Church. The Uniates and non-Uniates both kissed the hands of the great man.

When the procession with the bier approached the city all the citizens turned out to greet it, regardless of religious beliefs as well as the priesthood of both Rites. His body was entombed in the Church of the Holy Trinity.

The body of Metropolitan Rutsky remained there until the year 1655. At that time the Muscovites came to occupy the city of Vilno and falling upon the Church of the Holy Trinity they took away the coffin containing his body. And to this day no one knows what happened to this relic so precious to the memory of every Ukrainian Catholic. The Muscovites thus took their revenge on Rutsky for his work in bringing about the Union. When he first entered the monastery of the Holy Trinity, there were but a handful of those who admitted being Uniates. When he died there were nearly three million faithful Catholics. This was the fruitful result of a lifetime of self-sacrifice, zealous effort and suffering.

An effort has been made to give as clear a picture as possible of the great shepherd and Ukraine's Metropolitan Joseph Rutsky, but this picture is not complete without the famous last testament he wrote just before his death. It is like a program or example for the behaviour of all the workers of the Church. The Metropolitan emphasizes above all, the importance of faith and discipline and obedience to the Apostolic See. "I was always obedient to the Pope of Rome and die in this obedience," he said. The Archbishop and priesthood he urges to unite themselves with the Metropolitan and under stress of circumstances not to quarrel but have recourse to their spiritual authorities. He further urges the monks to love and respect the secular priesthood as brothers and that the secular priesthood should not resent being criticized by the monks and bishops. He begs the priesthood to look after their flocks and uplift their morals and the rebellious gentry and townspeople to respect the authority of the priesthood in spiritual matters. He urges his successor to add to the material and spiritual wealth of the diocese. He finishes his testament by declaring that "all of you will follow me—I only bid you adieu!"

It was rumored that he was poisoned to death, possibly because he wrote such a fine testament on January 28 and died on February 5, which means that he was in full possession of all his faculties until death. Whether it is true or not that he was put out of the way no one will ever know.

The chief lesson to be learned from the life of this great churchman was that we should not distrust "strangers" who show by their deeds and self-sacrifice that they want to help us. For many times a stranger will do more than a native.

What a wonderful service the Apostolic See rendered the Ukrainian people when it obliged this great worker to vow obedience of a lifetime in continuing his work despite the most chaotic conditions in the Church! Let us pay tribute then to those strangers who by continual immolation of self for truth prove their strength in sacrificing their lives for the good of the Church and the nation.

The following is the testament written January 28, 1637 by the hero of the Church before his death on February 5, 1637:

"I, Joseph William Rutsky, unprofitable servant of God as Metropolitan of Kiev, Halich and Ukraine, called before the council of God to give account of all the words, thoughts and deeds of the sixty-three years of my life and to hear the sentence which awaits me, tremble in fear that I am soon to appear before God for judgment. Nonetheless, I place my hope in His infinite compassion and although I am a sinner that he will not cast away my soul from His Presence.

"I offer to Him, in atonement, His Holy Passion of the Cross, whose value is immeasurable. I put my trust in the help of the Holy Mother of my Judge, whom I venerated all my life, although an unworthy servant. I also call upon the help of the Holy Angels of God, especially my guardian angels and those saints whom I chose to be my protectors and to whom I prayed each day. With my heart and soul I beg of them to help me in this last struggle.

"I confess before the world that I believe in all that the Catholic Church teaches and that only in that faith is there salvation. I believe in the Holy Apostolic Church and I am ready and willing to die for it at any time necessary.

"I was always obedient to the Pope of Rome and to his representatives and I die pledged to this obedience.

"I beg all whom I have offended in word or deed or example for the love of God to forgive me. In the future let them not follow my example or way of life but the life and actions of good servants of God who will live after me.

"On my part I forgive everyone who offended me from the bottom of my heart, even those who persecuted me, my family and brethren and I ask the merciful God that their sins should be not accounted to them but they should be converted and live.

"I beg my brother and fellow worker, the auxiliary bishop of Pinsk to go to the great king at the first opportunity and bring him this last farewell which his faithful servant sends to him. Offer him my prayers and I will offer them before the throne of the King of Kings, if I am permitted to see the face of God.

"Let the bishop of Pinsk place the Union under the king's protection, requesting him to dispose of the Ukrainian Church properties according to the direction of my successor. For who, other than the bishop, knows the people who are best fitted to take charge of the Ukrainian Church, especially since according to the most ancient custom of the Eastern Church it was the monks and not bishops who were chosen to rule the Church. All who seek an opportunity for obtaining such positions through the backing of their noble retainers should be removed as unworthy and if by any chance the unworthy should attain to it, the responsibility should fall upon the conscience of the Metropolitan and his guilt shared equally by the king.

"There is only one thing I ask of their Excellencies, the Holy Fathers, Ukrainian bishops and noblemen that for the love of Christ to join their work with that of the Metropolitan. Let them with deeds as well as words testify that they respect him as their superior and if he should offend them, let them so inform him, having determined first in brotherly love if that offense was actual or imaginary. If the Metropolitan refuses to apologize then there is a higher authority to which the bishops can make their direct appeal.

"I urge the monastic priesthood to love and respect the secular priesthood as fellow-workers and brothers. Let the monks who are assigned by the Metropolitan to visit and criticize the secular priesthood proceed in that in the spirit of love and compassion forsaking superciliousness and depreciation. I also remind the secular priesthood and strongly urge them to heed the duty of their high position as guardians of the souls entrusted to them. Let them teach their flocks the faith and what it means to lose it and let them not be resentful whenever the bishop sets monks in authority over them.

"Those of the gentry and nobility who hold positions of authority in government I request to obey the decision of the priesthood in all religious matters as this is the law of God. Let them not interfere with the government of the priesthood or interfere with their ways of living but leave it all up to their spiritual directors whom God has chosen and placed in authority over them.

"Finally, I beg the gentry and Church officers not to annoy the priesthood by judging them according to their own ideas as to their aims for God has retained their judgment to himself.

"My successor in Christ I beg to see to the increase of the priesthood and material possessions in my diocese and

Metropolitan area, for he will have to answer to God for it.

"In a separate communication, I leave my will as to the disposition of my inheritance and my house.

"Finally, I bid good-by to all who outlive me. Eventually you will all join me, until then, adieu!"

IPATY POTY

Protector of the Legal Existence
of the Union
(1541-1613; died June 13)

The Union of the Ukrainian Church with the Apostolic
See was brought about during the subjugation of Ukraine by
Poland. Although under the domination of Poland, it was
illegal despite all promises. The legal existence of the Union
had yet to be effected. This accomplishment was attained by
the Ukrainian Metropolitan Ipaty Poty in consecrating his
life under very difficult personal and national circumstances.

Who was Ipaty Poty? He was a descendant of an ancient
aristocratic family which had somehow managed to survive
the devastating Mongol invasion which destroyed the
castles, burned villages and reduced men to slavery and
serfdom, causing the dismemberment of Ukraine by her
border enemies. He was an orator and attorney, member of
the Diet, who had gained the highest reputation for intellectual eminence and exemplary life. His first assignment
was as parish priest and eventually he rose to the exalted
position of Metropolitan. As if to make up for the great loss
suffered by the Ukrainian Church and the Ukrainian nation
through the defection of its aristocracy who joined the Polish
Church and thus were assimilated into the Polish nation,

374

Ipaty Poty sacrificed his life and his personal ambitions for the sake of attaining a legal existence for the Ukrainian Uniate Church under Polish rule.

In order to become a Ukrainian bishop he had to give up his high position as a senator and willingly enter into a life of poverty and struggle against suspicion and malice, and in his old age to live in want. Many of the bishops at that time were ignorant and deeply tainted with Schism. Even the best of them had compromised the teachings of the Catholic faith in those trying times. He bitterly lamented the hasty ordinations by which so many were elevated to the priesthood, without proper training in the minor offices and who had no preparation worthy of their status as servants of Christ.

Attacked by his own people as well as strangers, calumniated and persecuted, physically maimed by his enemies in the last years of his life, he was forced to move to a village because in the city he had nothing to live on. Thus had his enemies robbed him of the properties and subsistence of his Metropolitan See.

Nonetheless, "Even if I have to beg, I will continue to serve the Church," wrote the man of noble birth, whose learning, lofty genius and exemplary virtue complemented a powerful will and truly heroic courage. This was a real native prince in the bishop's See of the Ukrainian Church.

Immediately after the assembly at Brest, when he was still a bishop in Volodimir, of the province of Volyn, Ipaty began his work in earnest to make the Union a reality. This was no easy task. Not only was the Union illegal under Poland but it had to face the opposition of the powerful Prince Ostrowsky and the brotherhoods incited by the Greek patriarchs and also the priesthood prompted by the brotherhoods resisted it.

A great traveler, handsome, eloquent, robust, this statesman and man of God possessed an ability and energy without rival. The enemies of the Ukrainian Church realized what a tremendous power such an individual would exercise. This is the reason why after the death of Metropolitan Rohoza in August 1599, when Ipaty Poty was made Metropolitan to replace him, a protest was raised in the Diet in 1600 by the Orthodox and Protestants of various sects. Although they did not belong to the Ukrainian Church, they made a protest against his nomination demanding his resignation, just as the present agitators who despite the fact that they do not belong to the Catholic Church try to interfere with its administration.

Metropolitan Poty appeared at the Diet and made such a persuasive appeal in defense of the Uniate Church that it effected a most favorable impression on the Diet and obtained its legal stature.

"Who without just cause can deprive another of his position?" said His Eminence in the Diet. "As a reason they state, 'separation from the Byzantine patriarch.' The patriarchs gave us neither teachings nor administration. They visited us not as shepherds but as wolves, who instead of bringing peace brought dissension, loss of the Holy Spirit at our altars through separation and consequent corruption. To the common people in the brotherhoods they gave the unheard of rights conferred only upon the bishops and ecclesiastical administrators who are instructed in the administration of the Catholic Church which has led to confusion and bloodshed. We started nothing new. My predecessor, the Metropolitan Isidore, one hundred and fifty years ago accepted the Union at the Florentine Assembly and accepted the Roman Pope as the head of the Ukrainian Church. Now the Byzantine patriarchs are appointed to their Sees by the heathen Sultan. Must we then accept such a patriarch who is himself a slave and, therefore, cannot help us with our salvation?" No one could resist his courteous nature and charm. His speech was zealous and penetrating dissolving all doubts.

376

Upon its conclusion, the chairman of the Diet made a motion which was carried that the bishops who had accepted the Union had not violated the law of the State and, therefore, could retain their positions.

It seemed that the Metropolitan Poty saved the Union at the Diet in 1609. But the complaints of his enemies did not cease. Uselessly the Metropolitan demanded justice. He was put off by the statement that there was no time for a hearing.

Thereupon the Metropolitan issued a public declaration that: "We asked the Pope and the government to give us a hearing and thus determine whether or not there was any valid cause for the charges brought against us. It happened that more than once a complaint was brought against us at the Diet.

"Nonetheless, when we offered to justify ourselves before them, without court action, they would not permit us to do it, which is not denied even to the worst evil doer. They humiliate us and pass judgment against us unlawfully without proper resort to courts of justice. We do not ask for any charity, we are willing to bear our sentence or pay a fine but first give us a chance to be heard and then pass judgment. How can such important matters as ours be set aside thoughtlessly without a hearing, without justice or legal action just because of the voice raised against us by our enemies? How can there be justice without trial?"

The arguments presented in the declaration are terrible in their meaning. From them we can understand what oppression and injustice the Union suffered under Poland.

The Metropolitan Poty despite his difficult task was indefatigable in his zeal and found time from his worries to look over the archives and gather proofs for the defense of the Church. He wrote a book about his work for the Church.

Ipaty Poty ever a gentleman in manner and appearance as he was by birth, drew upon himself the undeserved suspicion and even open accusations of the religious world despite his great works of moral reformation and charity. He truly imitated Christ in his life of poverty and suffering, insulted and repelled by heretics, he forced himself to face the humiliation which his ceaseless struggles for the Church brought upon him. But the more he worked for the Church the worse grew the rebellion and persecutions. Of these he writes thus: "What is clear is the futility of argument which results in rivalry and blasphemy as is proved by those arrogant scribes who by their reasoning fall into heresy. If it concerned only my honor and my aristocratic birth, I would keep silent about the persecution of evil persons for such people are no different than dogs who bark behind the fence. People know of my noble birth, and as to my position, I have from my youth held executive positions and finally attained senatorship. God sees that I do not speak of these things out of pride but only to prove that if I had been all those things of which they accuse me, I could not have attained the dignities of a man in the government and ultimately as head of the Church. I have a duty to fulfill to the Christian peoples over whom I am the pastor.

"I have learned that in the brotherhood's Church in Lwiw, there is a priest who whether himself, or inspired by others, had the temerity to say that I was a heretic, then a Christian and then a Jew who denied the cross. Then others say that I had myself circumcised and that the patriarch Jeremiah converted me. Now my dear Christians aren't these deliberate lies?

"I can prove from letters in my possession that I was urged against my will to accept the bishop's See because they considered me the best Christian and praised me to the very heavens and now that I follow in the footsteps of my predecessors by honoring the successor to Christ on earth, the Pope of Rome, they throw me into hell.

"They say, 'In Poty's residence everything is silver and gold, plates, trays, etc., but the priest, his brother in Christ doesn't have any bread! Poty has golden vessels but the altars and walls of our churches are bare! That is why we must break with the Union as soon as possible!' "

Thus wrote the demagogues and traitors of humanity, at a time when he had nothing to live on and suffered great poverty and persecutions, forever engaged in lawsuits, in a harassing struggle with the implacable fanatics and with some of the bishops of the province who were too ready to aid the foreign princes in their revolt by seizing revenues which properly belonged to the Ukrainian Church.

Who was responsible for this demagoguery among the people against this powerful worker who lived in extremely humble circumstances and declared that nothing drew him nearer to God than his poverty and suffering? In the forefront of the secret plots against this great Metropolitan, organized in the spring of 1608, were his own disloyal priests whom he had himself ordained and trusted. It is no wonder that the Metropolitan, although by nature very patient, at one time gave way to his feelings and wrote in desperation to his friend Leo Sapiha, "There is so much stubbornness in them that one can truly call them not priests but illiterates, common folk, like an infectious disease among God's creatures, rascals, undisciplined derelicts, traitors and bandits. It is fearful to relate what a rebellion has arisen among them. When the patriarchs want to punish them for their misdeeds, they say, 'You have no right, it is not your diocese.' And when the bishops would reprimand them, they seek refuge behind the patriarchs. There is no help even from the Roman Catholics who prefer to help the non-uniates. Such is Catholicism!" He writes further to Sapiha, "Is there anything else I need to add? God take vengeance on the injustice for I can do nothing! I only wash myself in my tears. In the end there is no other solution except to notify the Holy Father, the Pope."

Such was the martyr's life led by the great prince of the

Church. Is it any wonder that the punishment of God eventually came upon those who had so hounded their bishop? The Muscovites chained them to plows and plowed with them and many of them died in absolute faithlessness.

In spite of disappointments and defeats, Ipaty Poty bore his troubles bravely and continued laboring for the revival of the Church with as much vigor as ever. There are more than one hundred notebooks full of sermons which he wrote by hand before they had cut off the fingers of his hand. He set down briefly the doctrinal principles of his work with a view to building an edifice of mortality as a basis for Church truth. His teachings scattered here and there by enthusiastic disciples were germinating silently in many hearts giving back hope of salvation.

Ivan Tupeka was prevailed upon by the Schismatics with promises of great reward to attempt the murder in broad daylight as the sixty-eight-year-old Metropolitan walked along the street in the center of the city accompanied by friends. Ipaty would have been instantly cut down by the sword if he had not protected himself with a stout walking stick. As it was his assailant cut off the fingers of his hand, otherwise wounding him slightly.

The old man collapsed and William Rutsky, one of the friends accompanying him, shielded him from further attack.

When they brought the wounded bishop to a neighboring house, Rutsky took his fingers to the altar of the Church of the Holy Trinity to be used as a martyr's relic. This occurred on August 12, 1609 in Vilno and caused many to forsake the Schismatic iconoclasts and return to the Uniate Church.

The Metropolitan spent the last four years of his life in comparative peace as his enemies refrained from annoying him further.

When he felt that his death was approaching, he begged William Rutsky to accept the appointment as his assistant with the right to succeed him as Metropolitan.

The hard-working and self-sacrificing life of the Metropolitan who entertained for himself the severest views of obedience to duty, came to an end at the age of seventy-two.

What a great power for good the Ukrainian Church might have become under such leaders as the protector of its cultural and permanent political existence if the people had not permitted themselves to be used as mediums for rebellion by the factions, the Schismatics and foreign politicians against their own Church dignitaries!

The oldest educational institutions were those established by the Church. That is why the Church has the right and the duty to evaluate what is true culture and what is ruinous under the false guise of culture. Perhaps at this juncture it might be well to define culture. It is an advance in all phases of human endeavor so long as it does not interfere with moral law which is the foundation of all communal human effort.

The destruction of the Ukrainian nation was only the evil fruit or after effect of centuries of demagoguery spread by agitators who would give recognition to no one and nothing superior to themselves but only destroyed everything. These malefactors contributed to the dissolution of the Ukrainian nation which was revived at the sacrifice of such heroic lives as that of Ipaty Poty but the revival did not last long because of the interference of the demagogues who did nothing to promote the cultural interest of the nation. It was the malicious unbelievers in God who destroyed without compunction and then delivered the country into the hands of foreign occupants and exploiters.